RED'S STORY

Charles Simpson
1005-8 Fead St
Orangeville ON
L9W 3X4

BY RED STOREY

WITH BRODIE SNYDER

Macmillan Canada
Toronto

Canadian Cataloguing in Publication Data

Storey, Red, 1918-
   Red's story

Includes index.
ISBN 0-7715-9090-3

1. Storey, Red, 1918- .   2. Athletes—Canada—Biography.
3. Sports officiating—Biography.   I. Snyder, Brodie.   II. Title.

GV697.S76A3 1994   796'092   C94-931504-4

Macmillan Canada wishes to thank the Canada Council, the Ontario Ministry of Culture and Communications and the Ontario Arts Council for supporting its publishing program.

Macmillan Canada
A Division of Canada Publishing Corporation
Toronto, Canada

  2 3 4 5   FP   98 97 96 95 94

Printed in Canada

To my mother and my sister Irene

for their encouragement

and their inspiration

Contents

Foreword

Explanations And Acknowledgements

When I was inducted into Canada's Sports Hall of Fame in 1986, it was in the category of "All-round." I was proud to be in good company. Among the others listed the same way were such giants from our sporting past as Lionel Conacher, Frank Shaughnessy and Harold Wright, names I had known as a youngster. There have been only some two dozen people honored in that way among the almost 400 members of the Hall, and that includes several members of the media.

At the reception, someone asked me what the "All-round" designation meant. I explained that I had played most sports at a senior level or higher when I was young, and had officiated for a number of years in both the National Hockey League and the predecessor of the Canadian Football League.

"You should write a book," the fellow said. I've thought about that, on and off, ever since. It's taken a while, but here it is.

Red's Story is, by and large, a happy one. When most people go to work, it feels like work. When I went to work, I always felt it was going to be fun—and it almost always was. What made it so enjoyable was being involved with one great bunch of people after another. I've had a lot of help along the way.

In Barrie, Ontario, where I was born, there was my mother, Beatrice Storey, and my sisters Irene and Helen and brother George, as well as the kids I played with and the men who coached me in school and on the playgrounds. In Toronto, there were my Argonaut teammates with whom I won the Grey Cup, the national football championship, twice in six years. There were lacrosse buddies in Orillia and Hamilton, baseball pals in Barrie, and hockey friends in places from Camp Borden to Atlantic City to Montreal.

There were almost all of the men I've officiated with over the years in all those sports, from pee wee and high school up through junior, intermediate, senior and professional. In particular, I should mention Kenny Mullins in the early years in Montreal and George Hayes throughout my NHL career.

Players and coaches were usually kind to me, and I understood when they weren't. As the late Frank Selke Sr. said, "Sometime a losing team is going to accept defeat graciously and half the referees in hockey will die of shock." That applied to the other sports, too.

Writers and broadcasters all across Canada and in the United States have been good friends—even Don Cherry, who once posed the riddle: "On the highway, what's the difference between a dead dog and a dead referee?" ANSWER: "Skid marks for the dog."

Incidentally, criticism never bothered me—and I heard enough of it to last a lifetime, as they say. The lifetime continues, and so does the blasting of officials in every sport.

Seagram's was good to me during the quarter-century I worked there, giving me the freedom to travel the country and beyond and thus meet new groups of fine people through speaking dates and old-timers' games and tournaments.

I thank the people who encouraged me in this book project. Denise Schon of Macmillan Canada was enthusiastic and supportive from the start. Her colleague Kirsten Hanson, the editor, fine-tuned it after Brodie Snyder, the veteran Montreal writer, helped me with the words.

Of course, I owe debts I can never pay to my wives Helen and Bunny, my sons Bob and Doug, and my grandsons Bob Jr. and Michael. My family has always been there when I needed love and support.

Finally, there are the sports fans. I loved them all, although sometimes there were places I'd rather have been than standing at centre ice or midfield with 20,000 of them screaming and spitting and throwing things at me. But I knew that if they ever stopped, it would mean I wasn't doing my work the right way.

People still ask me how I could have stuck with sports, especially the NHL, for so long when there was so much abuse night after night. My answer was that it was part of the job, and I liked the job.

This was the life I chose, and *Red's Story* talks about it. This was also the life I'd choose again and *Red's Story* explains why.

Red Storey
Montreal
July, 1994

1

Crunch Time In Chicago

I was at the very top of my profession in the early spring of 1959. I was completing my ninth year as an official in the National Hockey League, doing something I really loved. As the senior referee in the NHL, I was given some of the biggest games to handle and one of those was on the night of Saturday, April 4, of that year in Chicago Stadium.

Let me set the scene: the Blackhawks were in serious contention for the Stanley Cup for the first time in many years. After being doormats through much of the 1950s, they had assembled an exciting mix of youngsters from the farm system and veterans from trades. This included future Hall-of-Famers like Glenn Hall in goal, Pierre Pilote on defence, and Bobby Hull, Stan Mikita and Ted Lindsay up front, along with a pretty good supporting cast.

The Montreal Canadiens were Chicago's first playoff obstacle, and the Canadiens were heavily favored. They had finished first in the six-team league through the 70-game schedule, 22 points ahead of the Hawks, who had made the playoffs for the first time in six years despite being one game below .500. The Canadiens had won the Cup the three previous seasons and had eight future members of the Hall themselves. They led the best-of-seven series 3-2 after a 4-2 win in Montreal in the fifth game, so the Hawks faced elimination this night.

But they were confident, and they had an incentive. They had won both previous games in the series played before their home fans and Jim Norris, the team owner, had issued unsigned cheques to all his players for $3,350 each. "Win the Stanley Cup and I'll sign them," he told the Hawks.

I knew this was probably the biggest game I'd ever done in Chicago. I'd been there when there were only 3,500 fans, a time when they'd move home games to Indianapolis, Omaha and Minneapolis, hoping for bigger crowds. It looked for a while like Chicago might go right out of hockey. But what had happened over a couple of years was that the other teams decided to contribute something to help the Hawks become more competitive and thus strengthen the whole league. They wound up with some fine talent being practically donated—Eddie Litzenberger, Murray Balfour and Dollard St. Laurent by Frank Selke Sr. in Montreal; Eric Nesterenko and Tod Sloan by Conn Smythe in Toronto; Hall, Lindsay and Al Arbour by the Detroit Red Wings, a team also owned by the Norrises; and Jack Evans, Danny Lewicki and Ron Murphy by the New York Rangers, in whose arena, Madison Square Garden, the Norrises had an interest. It must be said that some of these guys were involved in the new players' association and were dumped by their former teams for that reason.

There were going to be 20,000 people in the building for this game—never mind about the official figure of 16,666; that was the count for the fire marshal—and half of them had started drinking right after work.

I remember they used to turn out all the lights in the stadium for the national anthem, and put a spotlight on the flag and the guy at the organ. I'd learned to go and stand in the corner where the screen above the boards gave me some protection, and in the darkness I'd hear plop . . . plop . . . plop. The lights would come on and I'd be surrounded by garbage. There'd always be a delay of the game before it even started, to clean up the ice. Red Dutton, the former NHL president, told me that once, after littering had held up an opening faceoff for 20 minutes, they got 24 extra policemen for the next game and searched many of the fans as they came in. They took 1,700 pounds of garbage away from them. They also slapped them on the sides and thighs, breaking eggs and squashing tomatoes in their pockets.

There's always tension in the NHL, from the first game of the season on. But for a playoff game, the pressure is 10 times heavier. But I did exactly what I always did to get ready. I never ate much the day of a game; I wasn't a big eater anyway. My heaviest food on the day of a game would be eggs. I'd eat big meals on off days on the road, to replenish my body.

I didn't have any superstitions, like some people who, if they were going good, wouldn't change their hat or suit or even their underwear until it could walk down the street by itself. However, I never wanted to have too much time to pace or think about things. I didn't want anyone getting nervous, so I wouldn't ever let myself or the linesmen I'd be working with—this night George Hayes and Roger Strong—arrive at the rink too early or start to get dressed more than a half-hour before we were to appear. I was free and easy. I didn't want to hype anybody up. The idea was to just go out and do your work and keep as cool as you could.

In the light of what happened later, it's ironic that Rudy Pilous, the Chicago coach, asked for me specifically to referee this one. He had ripped Frank Udvari for his work earlier in the series, particularly in the previous game. Pilous, like the rest of the people in the NHL, knew that I would be prepared physically and mentally for every game. Now, I'm not going to deny that I enjoyed life. I wouldn't try to tell anyone I didn't take a drink. In fact, I was probably the first guy to find a bar and have a few beers after a game. I enjoyed the relaxing, and I had to replace the fluid I'd lose during a game, when I'd drop anywhere between five and 10 pounds and become dehydrated. But when the time came to blow the whistle again, I was always 100 percent for any job I was given.

When we went out there exactly five minutes before game time, we couldn't believe the noise. As soon as the gate opened for us at the end of the rink, the players on both teams, who had been on the ice for 10 or 15 minutes by then, stopped warming up to see who was refereeing. They wanted to find out what kind of a game they had to play that night, because the three regular referees all worked differently. My style of refereeing was always to let more go than some others. Let them play hockey, that's why they were there. When there's body contact in a game, you can give a penalty any time two players come together, but I don't think hockey should be refereed that way.

They say that the Stadium's Barton pipe organ could equal the sound of 25 brass bands. That night, I believed it. The fans in Chicago always started cheering during the anthem, building to a peak for the opening faceoff, and then levelling off. This night, they just kept going. It was a madhouse, but I thought it was wonderful—a great atmosphere. But I didn't let it interfere with the way I handled the game. A referee only feels right if he's doing a job that's fair to both teams. I don't say good or bad, but fair. I know I did that this time, too.

The first two periods were tough hockey, and the game was close. Except for a couple of minor arguments over offsides and penalties, when the fans littered the ice, no real incidents occurred. During one of the stoppages, George and I were leaning on the boards. In those days, there was a screen around the corners and behind the net, but none along the sides. You were wide open there. For some reason, I took a look at this guy sitting with his wife or girlfriend in the promenade seats and he pulled open his coat. He had a gun in a holster and he said, "I'm gonna blow your guts out." I said, "Well, I hope you have a good aim. I don't want to be wounded or a cripple." That's exactly what I meant.

Just as I finished saying that, a couple of cops rushed down and wanted to know what was going on. I said, "This guy's going to shoot me." They grabbed his gun and hustled him out of the seat. I figured that was the end of that. I watched them go. They took him up 10 rows, walked him in to another aisle, sat him down and handed him his gun back. I guess the cops didn't like me either and they were getting him up where it was an easier shot. I had him in the back of my mind for a while, but then things started to happen and I forgot all about it. The longer the game went on, the more the crowd was getting into it, becoming more and more convinced the Hawks could beat the Canadiens and stay alive. With seven minutes to play and the score tied 3-3, the trouble started.

Litzenberger, who had scored a couple of goals, was coming out of his own end. He stepped on the blade of Marcel Bonin's stick, which was on the ice at the time, and fell on his behind. All the Blackhawks were looking for a penalty. I wasn't going to call anything on the play, and while they were waiting for me to blow the whistle, Dickie Moore picked up the puck and scored, giving the Canadiens the lead.

Now there were a lot of very angry people—the Hawk players and the fans. Somebody was going to catch hell, and the obvious target was the big guy out on the ice with the red hair. They were throwing things and yelling, but there was no real harm done. And not long after the game started again, Lindsay scored; it was 4-4, and everybody was happy . . . for the time being.

With just under two minutes left, Bobby Hull was flying down left wing and, as he got to the blue line and made his cut, Junior Langlois nailed him with a great bodycheck. Bobby might have been the first guy in outer space. Since he was going to go down anyway, he decided he might as well make it look good. Once again the Hawks were looking at me for the penalty call. They didn't get it because Langlois simply hit him with a helluva hip. But they were waiting again for me to blow the whistle and this time while they were waiting, Claude Provost went down and scored, giving the Canadiens the lead.

The game was over for Chicago. The season was over. Oh, there was still about a minute and a half left but it was over, and the people didn't like it, to say the least. Now, I never worried about the fans in any rink I was ever in. People screaming at me didn't scare me. You might say that when you had 20,000 people on their feet threatening you at the tops of their voices, anybody with a brain in his head had to be scared. I guess the answer is that I didn't have a brain in my head. I wasn't scared. Let them yell. But when they start to throw stuff, you have to be careful.

And these Chicago fans started to throw stuff—18 bottles by one estimate, as well as papers, cans, programs, decks of cards, rubbers, cushions, a chair, parts of seats and anything else that wasn't nailed down. I skated to the centre ice circle so that anyone who hoped to hit me was going to need a good arm. Then, suddenly, I heard somebody yell, "Look out!" I turned around and a fan was coming across the ice at me. He threw one of those plastic cups full of beer right in my face. I grabbed him. I was so teed off, I was really going to clean his clock.

I'll never forget Doug Harvey, the great Canadiens' defenceman, for what he did next. I had got hold of the guy on one side and Doug yelled: "Red, Red, you can't hit a fan. Don't hit a fan!" I let go, and Doug grabbed the guy from the other side and piled him one right in the kisser. I was still mad as hell, Doug could see that, and he yelled again: "Don't hit a fan!" And then he hauled off and hit him another one before he let go. The guy staggered away.

By this time, Pilous, the coach who had wanted me to referee this game, was giving me the choke sign from behind the bench, in full view of the TV cameras, and egging the crowd on. Doug was facing me now, about three feet away, and, in the noise, I couldn't hear what he was yelling, but I could read his lips: "Watch it!" I turned my head and there was another guy coming at me. He was in mid-air, about to jump on me from behind. I ducked down a little, he slid off my back onto the ice, and Doug stabbed him with his stick and cut him. Oh, he cut him bad, a 15-stitch job. The guy went off bleeding like a stuck pig. I never figured I needed any protection. I always thought that, one-on-one, I could take anybody. But I was happy Doug was there that night. He no doubt headed off what could have been a terrible riot by putting an end to any more civilians coming out. There were a dozen or more guys with one leg over the boards ready to jump onto the ice, and a lineup behind each of them, but they all changed their minds when they saw the blood.

By now, the players were so scared for their own safety, they were sitting on the ice huddled up against the boards so they wouldn't be hit by the stuff coming down. I was still out at centre ice, and there was really nothing that George and Roger and I could do while this was going on, except to make sure we didn't get hurt.

After the delay reached about 30 minutes, I was saying to myself: "What the hell am I going to do? Should we call off the game?" Even as I was thinking it, I knew we couldn't. Stopping the game wasn't my decision to make. I could see Clarence Campbell, the president of the NHL, sitting just up from ice level. When the trouble started, he had moved down from his box seat to sit near Jim Norris, right behind the Chicago bench. I requested that Campbell come to the penalty box to discuss the rules for a forfeited game. He didn't budge and wouldn't even look in my direction. When the debris continued to pile up, I asked once more that he come down and talk to me. He just sat there, his face ashen.

Anyway, we finally did get the game started again, but not until Jacques Plante, the slightly eccentric Canadiens' goalie, was satisfied that every scrap of debris had been cleared away.

He absolutely had the right to insist on that. I wouldn't start any game unless everybody on the ice was happy. You can't start until both teams are prepared to play. I guess the fans had run out of ammunition. We lined up for the faceoff at centre ice. The tension was still as thick as could be. Tod Sloan was ready to take the draw for the Hawks and before I dropped the puck, he looked up at me, and said: "Tell me something, Red. If you'd known that first guy had beer in the cup, would you have opened your mouth before he threw it?" That eased the pressure. I started to laugh. So did he, and we finished the game.

That wasn't the only funny thing said to me that night. After the first case when I didn't call a penalty, Litzenberger charged at me and screamed: "You're nothing but a bleep-bleeping homer." That was usually the one word that would get my dander up, that would be guaranteed to get a guy tossed out. This time, I looked at him in amazement and asked him, "What rink do you think we're playing in, Litz?" I could have been a hero that night by being a homer; all I had to do was call two penalties against the visiting team. But they weren't warranted. Incidentally, I handed out 22 penalties in the game—12 of them to the Canadiens and only 10 to the Blackhawks. That was unusual because the home team normally gets a few more penalties than the visitors. That's because there have been very few players in hockey history who haven't played it tougher at home or backed up a little on the road.

With the game over, I now had to get to the officials' dressing room, one level down a flight of stairs. Before we left the ice, Danny Lewicki of the Blackhawks gave me a stick and said, "Red, you might need this more than I do now." He was my friend; they were all my friends when it counted. As you went to go down the steps, there was a row of seats. In those seats were some pretty tough guys who were in a really ugly mood. They were spitting and throwing things and trying to get at me. I combed about six of them, opened a few heads. I literally made sure I stayed alive. But I wasn't out of trouble yet.

Did I say all the players were my friends? Not quite. I got down to the foot of the stairs and Lindsay was waiting there for me with a stick. He yelled, "I'm gonna cut your goddamn head off." I said, "Make your first one the best one you've ever had, kid, because now I've got a stick, too, and I'm going to carve you in half." I meant it; I was ready to kill him. If he'd moved that stick, I was going to let him have it. Just then Jim Norris came along and grabbed Lindsay and literally threw him into the Chicago dressing room. "Get in there, you little bugger, and leave Red alone." Then he turned to me: "Don't take any shit from any of my players. You don't have to take that in my building, or in any building. You go to your room and have a shower. Forget about this."

In the officials' room, I had a couple of beers and relaxed. When a game's over, it's over. That's the end of the nonsense. This had been one of the hardest games I'd ever handled. But it had been a terrific game and we had kept the play flowing. I felt it was one of the best games I'd ever done. That also applied to George Hayes and Roger Strong, who had done a great job on the lines.

I was tired. Usually I lost about 10 pounds during a game; this time I'm sure it was more. Mentally, I was in good shape, which is more than I can say for Campbell when he came into the room. He was very pale, didn't say anything at first, seemed to be almost in a state of shock. "Why didn't you come to the bench when I called for you?" I asked him. "I feared for my safety," he said. "I was afraid I wouldn't get out of there alive." Fair enough, I guess. It was an honest answer and I couldn't ask for more than that, although I wasn't sure what he was worried about. "It was me they wanted to kill," I told him. "You weren't wearing one of these striped sweaters." He did ask me about the two plays that caused the trouble. I told him they were judgment calls, that the Chicago players had done swan dives. He didn't offer any criticism at all at that point. He didn't seem disturbed about anything. We asked him if he wanted to ride downtown with us, but he said no.

We had our showers and started to head out for our hotel. As you left the officials' room in Chicago Stadium, you always turned right. We did, and ran right into a wall. In less than a half-hour, they'd brought in cement blocks and built a wall. "Hey, what's this?" I asked a policeman. He told me: "There's a big crowd, maybe 5,000 people, waiting for you guys upstairs. We can't get you out that way." Then he pointed us downstairs. I didn't even know they had a sub-basement, but down we went. There was the chief of police himself, and a big station wagon was waiting to take us away.

The chief said to get in the car and we did, asking no more questions. The driver yelled to somebody upstairs, "All clear?" and a guy yelled back, "All clear." We were all set to go when the driver thought of something. "Oh, just a minute, Chief. What happens when I get up there and they maybe know we're comin' this way and some guy gets in front of the car." And the chief said: "Run over the bastard. It's as simple as that." I thought, "Oh, oh, we're in for some fun now." And we were. It was a spiral exit ramp and we went up burning rubber. There was nobody in front of us as we went through the parking garage, but then we saw a crowd of angry fans running for their cars, and the chase was on.

Hollywood never filmed anything better than this. We just tore away down the street, tires screaming and the car sliding. Finally, we had about a 100-yard lead, rocketed around another corner and slammed to a stop. The driver yelled, "Get in that other car." They had it all planned. We jumped out with our club bags, got into the new car and slammed the door. Our original car took off. The mob chased it and we just sat at the side of the road watching them go by before driving on in our own time.

We hung up our stuff when we got back to the Chicagoan Hotel and went out for a few beers. At the first place, the bartender told me: "Red, there was a man in here with a gun, who said he was looking for you and was going to kill you." I asked him which way the man went when he left, and he told me. So I had a couple of beers there and then I headed in the same direction. At the next bar, they told me, "Red, there was a man in here with a gun," and so on. I asked which way he'd gone, and again I went the same way. The same thing happened a couple more times. I figured I was safer chasing him than having him chasing me. Anyway, we never caught up with each other.

I heard later that a few dozen of the most lamebrained fans had turned up, after closing time, at another hotel they thought was mine and tried to start a riot in the lobby. But by then I was sleeping the sleep of the innocent and untroubled, having realized again the truth of something a former NHL official named Mickey Ion used to say: "The only sane person in the building during a game is the referee."

2

A Breaking Point In Boston

George Hayes and I arrived in Boston about five o'clock Monday afternoon. We'd flown in from Chicago after a lazy Sunday off day. I was feeling great and eager to referee the seventh and deciding game of the other Stanley Cup semi-final playoff series between the Bruins and Toronto the next night. But when I checked into the Hotel Manger, right in the Boston Garden complex, there was a message to call my wife at home in Montreal, and that bothered me. Helen and I had an arrangement. Long-distance phone calls upset both of us, so we never called each other unless it was really serious. That meant this was urgent.

"Have you seen Mr. Campbell?" she asked. I told her I hadn't and she explained: "He phoned here and said there are going to be some things coming out in the paper. He said not to pay any attention to them. What did he mean?" I didn't know because I hadn't seen any papers that day, and told her so. I sent my love to our two boys, Bob and Doug, and hung up.

Almost immediately, the phone rang. It was Carl Voss, the NHL's referee-in-chief. He was my boss, Campbell's errand boy, and perhaps the weakest man I've ever known. He told me to come up to Campbell's room. When I got there, Campbell appeared upset. First, although he hadn't said anything about it right after the game, he criticized me severely for my

work in it, particularly the non-penalty calls on Eddie Litzenberger and Bobby Hull. I repeated to him that I thought both
Chicago players had taken dives. Then he asked me if I'd seen
any papers. I said I hadn't, and he told me: "Well, there were
some things said, and they weren't meant the way they
came out."

"Mr. Campbell," I told him, "there have been an awful lot
of things written about me in my lifetime. I've been called a
lot of names. I'm sure you couldn't say anything that would
hurt me." He seemed relieved and said: "Fine, fine. I just
wanted you to know before you read about it."

I went downstairs and found George and Bill Morrison,
who would be my other linesman the next night, and Eddie
Powers, an old friend who would be the stand-by referee. By
now it was evening and we went over to Jack Sharkey's bar. It
was a day off and we were entitled to a few beers like everyone
else, right? We were sitting there when a kid came in with the
latest papers. I bought one of everything.

The headlines shocked me. CAMPBELL SAYS STOREY
CHOKED and NHL PREXY SAYS STOREY CHICKEN and
STOREY FROZE: CAMPBELL. I read the stories and Campbell
was quoted as saying, "I've never felt so rotten about a game
in my life." But the statements he made were not about my
refereeing, they were about my character. Hell, if he had said I
was a bad official, I would have agreed: "Yeah, at times I've
stunk out the joint. I've had bad nights." But don't call me
chicken. Don't say I choked. Don't say things that aren't true.
If you're going to run me down, say things that may be right. I
read those papers and going through my mind was a picture
of my boys going down the street and other kids telling them
their old man was gutless.

Now I was boiling mad. I couldn't believe that Campbell,
the man who should be defending his referees and should be
the last to publicly condemn them, would subject me to such
ridicule. It was his privilege to criticize me if he wanted to, of

course—but in private. We were used to being blasted by the fans, players, coaches and team executives and couldn't have cared less. But this was different.

"Don't drink too much tonight," I told Eddie Powers. "You're refereeing tomorrow night. I've done my last game. I won't be there." Eddie slapped me on the shoulder. "C'mon," he said, "don't talk stupid." I told him I'd never been more serious about anything in my life. He said, "Have a night's sleep. Think it over." I had a fistful of papers quoting the league president, my boss, as saying I choked, and Eddie wanted me to sleep on it! "You get a good night's sleep," I said. "You're refereeing."

I could tell they weren't convinced I meant it, but we called it a night because I wanted to make sure the others got to bed early. But there was no way I could sleep, and I walked the streets of Boston all night. I saw every statue and monument and historic site you could name. I had a lot to think through. I went over the entire situation in my mind again and again.

First, there was the question of Campbell's criticism. He had told Bill Westwick, the sports editor of *The Ottawa Journal*, that I had called a good game for 55 minutes but then I froze. He said I had missed the tripping penalties on Litzenberger and Hull that he thought were obvious calls. He said I was to blame for the wild demonstration because I didn't drop the puck soon enough to get the game started again after Montreal's last and winning goal. In fairness, though, he also said Canadiens' goalie Jacques Plante was partly responsible because he was so finicky.

In my opinion, Campbell was in no position to have seen the penalties. He was in a box seat behind the boards and I was no more than 20 feet from the play. Both players looked to me as if they deliberately tried to draw penalties by taking the best dives seen since the Olympic Games in Melbourne three years earlier. Any referee who can't tell the difference between a dive and a trip hasn't been around very long. As it happened, both plays backfired and resulted in Montreal goals; otherwise, no one would have paid any attention. In addition, both were judgment calls. If a referee gave a penalty on every judgment call, the goalkeepers would play most of every game by themselves and the third period would usually start at dawn.

The charge that I encouraged a near riot by not putting the puck into play immediately was ridiculous. Parts of the rink were ankle-deep in garbage. Anybody who knows the difference between hockey and hopscotch knows that the first thing you need to play hockey without breaking a leg is a clean sheet of ice. Plante was absolutely right in wanting everything removed from the area of his crease. Even a tiny piece of paper could have caused injury to one of the players and made Plante himself slip and miss a shot. Campbell also told an out-and-out lie when he said he wouldn't come down to talk to me because I wanted permission to appeal for order over the P.A. system and that would have made the situation even worse.

What about the fact that Campbell was saying he was misquoted and his words had been taken out of context? To me, that was like shooting a guy and then saying you thought the gun wasn't loaded. Should I really have been surprised at Campbell's statements? Perhaps not. A headline from a few years ago flashed through my mind: MEHLENBACHER GOOFED—CAMPBELL. Jack Mehlenbacher was a good referee who retired after being involved in an incident similar to mine, with eerily similar results. And what if Campbell apologized? I decided that, even if he did, it wouldn't matter because he couldn't remove his accusations from the minds of the fans. The story by now had been picked up in every hockey city in Canada and the United States.

Then, too, I thought about whether I ever wanted to work again for Campbell and Voss. Campbell officiated in a total of only 155 regular season and 12 playoff games in the NHL before getting the president's job when he came back from World War II. The Patrick brothers, Lynn and Muzz, who played for the Rangers, used to say he was the worst referee that ever put on skates. About Campbell as president, Stafford Smythe of the Toronto Maple Leafs once asked this question: "Where else could we find another Rhodes scholar, graduate lawyer, decorated war hero, and former prosecutor at the Nuremberg trials who would do what he was told?" That about summed it up.

Voss had been a player with eight different NHL teams in 12 seasons, which indicates something, and then a substitute linesman in the American Hockey League. George Hayes worked with him there. Hayes told me that when they were in Buffalo, where Voss lived, he'd let plays go for the home team that were 10 or 15 feet offside. I called him the bloodhound because he was always snooping around; George called him the weasel. One time Voss came into the dressing room and, after washing down a couple of pills, said, "It's no wonder I have to take these things with all the worry you two guys cause me." I looked at him and said, "I don't know why you worry about us because we don't worry about you." That's exactly how I felt about him. Anything he told me went in one ear and out the other.

Then there was the whole question of the way the NHL was being run. I still had a vivid memory of a meeting a couple of years before at which I was the referees' spokesman. Any thought that I'd have any real input into how to make the game more appealing disappeared when one of the governors stood up, slammed his fist on the table, and said: "We own this league and by God you'll run it the way we tell you to."

Finally, I considered that night's Leafs-Bruins game. It was another important one since the winner would go on to play the Canadiens for the Stanley Cup and the losers would go home. I knew I was in no shape mentally to handle it. The way

I felt, I couldn't be honest to either team. I would be cheating them both.

I came to the conclusion that when you weren't backed up by your superiors, it was time to quit. It was time somebody in the league showed some guts, and apparently it had to be me. Somebody had to set an example. The NHL was becoming a circus, I decided, and it was casting the referees as the clowns. It was too late for anybody to do that to me. I knew I could never work for Campbell again, and maybe what I was doing might make things better for the younger officials coming along.

With my mind made up by about eight o'clock in the morning, I felt I had to talk to somebody, so I put in calls to a few sportswriters I knew and trusted. I figured if Campbell wanted to criticize me publicly in print, then I'd tell the newspapers about my quitting and not him. "I want to talk to you," I told them. "Can you be in my room at one o'clock? I don't know if it's important to you, but I've got something to say." I also asked Powers, Hayes and Morrison to be there. When everyone had arrived, I told them I was through and why I couldn't work in the NHL any more. Then I went to Voss's room and told him I was finished. He didn't say anything at all—no encouragement, no disapproval, just a question: "Are you going to tell Mr. Campbell?" I told him I wasn't. If I'd gone to Campbell's room right then, there would have been one less president in pro sports. In fact, I didn't see or speak to Campbell for five years after that; I never saw Voss again.

When I got back to my room, there was a message to call an operator in Toronto. That worried me because I thought something might have happened to my mother, who was living alone in our hometown of Barrie, Ontario, and getting along in years. But it was my brother, George, who told me, "I hope you're going to tell Campbell what he can do with that refereeing job." I laughed. "George, you're a half-hour too late."

I decided I might as well head home to Montreal, and I went down to the lobby to check out. By now, the word had spread and everyone knew I'd quit. The first guy I saw was Kenny Reardon, the former defenceman who was there to scout the Boston-Toronto game for the Canadiens. He looked me up and down, and finally said, "Red, you're making a big mistake." I looked at Kenny and just walked away from him. I didn't trust myself to speak. But I remember thinking: "How's he supposed to know how I feel? How's he supposed to know if I'm making a mistake? Was he the one being hammered by the president of the league?"

In my mind, I knew I hadn't made a mistake, even though I was in my 40s at the time and I had a family to support. All I had was a part-time job selling with Seagram's, the liquor people, and I didn't know if they'd want me on a permanent basis. I could have stayed in the NHL, I guess, but I don't think I could have lived with myself if I had. I was angry and I felt humiliated. Thirty-five years later, as I look back, I'm sure I did the only thing I could. I took the only course to keep my self-respect. But I loved that job.

I went out to the airport and caught the 6 p.m. Northeast Airlines flight to Montreal. The papers the next day said I got a hero's welcome. I'm not sure about that, but Helen was there, along with Bob and Doug, and several reporters and photographers. I mumbled something like, "It's nice to see I still have some friends." And it was, especially at that moment.

I've had a lot of sad and fearful days in sports because I've had many injuries and other disappointments, but that day in Boston had to be the lowest. I can't remember a sadder time in my life that didn't involve death, even though a lot of people were on my side. In the days that followed, I was cheered by hundreds of messages, phone calls, telegrams and letters. Some were from friends and acquaintances, others from total strangers. One that I still treasure was a telegram from one of the great men in hockey:

DEAR RED: YOU BEING ONE OF THE MEN WHO HELPED BRING THE NATIONAL LEAGUE BACK AND PUT IT ON ITS FEET, I HOPE YOU ARE NOT GOING TO RESIGN NOW. DON'T FORGET EVERYBODY QUITS A THOUSAND TIMES IN THE PLAYOFFS AND AMONGST THE OWNERS YOU ARE VERY HIGHLY RESPECTED. YOU HAVE DONE A GREAT DEAL FOR THE GAME AND CAN DO A LOT MORE.

REGARDS, CONN SMYTHE

Red Dutton declared he couldn't understand what his successor as NHL president was doing and that it was "a terrible thing." I had great support from coaches and players, like the Canadiens' Toe Blake, who said: "Red shouldn't resign because of any criticism. He's a capable referee and has real courage." The other officials were with me strongly, including Eddie Powers, who told the press: "Red is 100 percent right in this deal. The front office has not backed up the officials this year."

It was ironic that during the Toronto-Bruins game for which Eddie replaced me as referee and which the Maple Leafs won, the unhappy Boston Garden crowd began to chant: "We want Storey. We want Storey. We want Storey." It was ironic too that Eddie would quit the NHL four years later, in February of 1963, citing "insufficient support" from Campbell. That came after Eddie worked a Canadiens' loss to Toronto and Blake was fined only $200 for saying that the officials did their jobs "as if they'd bet on the game."

There was a flood of mail to the newspapers, almost all of it in my favor. A *Toronto Star* editorial declared: "Red Storey is part of hockey, and an important part. He should not be allowed to depart the game he loves in this fashion." Arthur Daley in *The New York Times* said Campbell had been "seriously stricken the other day with foot-in-mouth disease . . .

Storey did the right thing while Campbell acted with inexcusable impropriety." Red Fisher in *The Montreal Star* wrote: "It makes me ill to see this lack of support for an official from people who should know better." Other top columnists like Dan Parker in New York, Milt Dunnell in Toronto and Harold Kaese in Boston also backed me. Perhaps the most amusing letter came from New York to Baz O'Meara, sports editor of *The Montreal Star*. A Rangers' fan wrote: "I have been booing Red Storey for so many years, I now consider him a personal friend. Please tell him to come back so I can boo him some more."

As you can see, Campbell came out as the villain. That was natural. He was the big guy who forced the little guy to quit his job. In fairness, I have to say that I'm convinced to this day that Campbell never meant for the story to come out. Bystanders in the hotel where Campbell and Westwick talked told me both had been drinking. Campbell thought he was speaking off the record. Westwick always denied that he broke a confidence, but it didn't really matter whether he did or not. What counted was that this was really what Campbell thought of me. I couldn't keep working for a man who felt that way, no matter what pressures he was under towards the end of another season of fighting with the six awfully tough guys who owned or ran the NHL clubs. I didn't care if his nerves were frayed, or if he just thought he was getting things off his chest that would not be repeated.

Besides, whatever happened to the so-called "gag rule"? It was a league regulation to preserve the authority and respect a referee needed to do his job. It stated that nobody employed by the NHL could publicly smear a referee. Being drunk was no excuse for breaking it. With all of that, I couldn't stay. I hated to leave. As I said, I loved that job and physically I could have done it for another 10 years. I think I was skating faster in 1959 than I did when I was playing hockey.

Campbell wasn't finished with me. Offers of jobs started to

come in, and he blocked all the ones he could. An example was the Canadian Football League, in whose Eastern division, then called the Big Four, I had officiated for 12 years until 1957. Ted Workman, owner of the Montreal Alouettes, said hiring me back "would be our gain because I've always considered him one of the finest officials in professional sports." There never was an offer, however, and I didn't find out why until years later when I ran into Hap Shouldice, a good friend and great football referee. He told me: "Your friend Campbell put the kibosh on you. He phoned Halter [the CFL commissioner, Sidney] and told him not to hire you because they were going to force you back into the NHL." Campbell also kept me from doing analysis on *Hockey Night In Canada* for 10 years.

A few weeks after I quit, a top administrator with one of the NHL teams asked me what it would take to get me back. "Just have Campbell apologize to me," I told him, "and make sure it appears in every paper in the world that carried the original story." He said he didn't think that would be a problem, and they'd take care of it at the league meeting in June. He called me back after that and said, "I'm afraid I have bad news. We really tried, but Campbell absolutely refuses to apologize to you. Are you sure we can't do this some other way?" I told him I wouldn't change my mind, and that was that. Quite frankly, I was just as happy. I really didn't want anything more to do with Campbell. I learned later that he had said at the meeting: "Red's so dumb he won't find a way to feed his family. He'll be back in my office in September, begging for his job back." At least Campbell was consistent; he was wrong as usual.

In the meantime, I had been offered jobs to referee playoff games in both the American and Western Hockey Leagues at far more money than I was making in the NHL, but turned them down. Mentally, I just couldn't do it. After thinking it all over, I decided that there was a lot more to life than lacing on a pair of skates. At my age, the time had come for me to spend more time with my family. I couldn't do that if I continued to referee. In 1959, I managed to have my first Christmas at home in 10 years.

It wasn't too long before I was vindicated. Right after the 1959 season, I went overseas to referee a series of exhibition games between Boston and the Rangers. Campbell tried to keep me from doing that, too, but the Patrick brothers, Lynn and Muzz, who were running those teams then, said they'd made a commitment to me and were going to keep it. If Lester Patrick—one of the game's greatest men as player, coach and general manager—had had six sons, one for each NHL club, the officials wouldn't have had any trouble at all. Several of the Rangers were hurt and Bobby Hull was one of the players picked to fill out the roster. He was the first guy I saw in the hotel bar when we all assembled in New York before the flight to Europe. He came over and shook hands with a big smile. "Red," he said, "you only made one mistake that night." I asked him, "What was that?" He said, "You were too close to the play and you saw what really happened."

Years later, Bobby said the same thing much more publicly. It was the night the Winnipeg Jets retired his sweater. On a national television interview the first question he was asked was, "What about that big night in Chicago, the night of the riot when . . . ?" Bobby jumped right in and said, "Before you start, I want to tell you something. Red Storey was right on every call he made that night."

3

Starting Out

I was born in Allandale, Ontario, now part of Barrie, in 1918 to Robert Roy and Beatrice Storey. They were from English-Scottish-Irish stock. I guess the family's closest brush with fame was a grandmother who had been in household service for Queen Victoria at Buckingham Palace. I was christened Roy Alvin, but never used those names. I have no idea why Dr. William Little, who brought me into the world, nicknamed me Buster, but it stuck right through my early teenage years.

I grew up on a heavily mortgaged 2¾-acre property at 130 Tiffin Street that my father had bought in the district of Ferndale, which then was well out of town. It was a great place for a kid. A trout stream ran right through our land. At the far end of it was the Dyment farm, where they raised horses and had a full-sized race track, the site of the Queen's Plate at one time. Best of all, they also had a pond, where we skated in the winter.

Though that may make it sound idyllic, my childhood was far from perfect. I think the happiest day our family ever had was the day my father left, when I was about 11 years old. I can't ever remember not living in fear of him, and I don't think anyone in our family lived any other way. He was a railroader and apparently well-liked by his fellow workers, but when they closed the doors to come home, he was a different man. He was sadistic, and I'm putting that mildly. He was like a man who didn't want a family, but had one anyway. On the day he left, we had a sing-song at our house to celebrate.

We learned later why we were so poor. My father worked on a run between Barrie and Hamilton, where he'd stay overnight and then come back. Ma somehow found out he had another home and another woman in Hamilton, and they had all the luxuries in the world while we were living on the poverty line. I was about 11 years old at the time, too young to know everything that was going on. I guess Ma finally got suspicious of where his money was going and had someone follow him in Hamilton.

After he left, I only saw him a couple of times. He stayed in Allandale at the YMCA or in a CNR caboose when he wasn't in Hamilton. I'd run errands between my mother and him, taking him things he'd left in the house and needed, and so on. I feared him so much, I'd just drop off or pick up whatever it was and run. I never saw him after I left Barrie. He came around a couple of times years later to places where I was playing football or hockey, but I refused to have anything to do with him. I heard he died when he was 84, but it was like he was a stranger with the same last name as mine. I had no feeling for him at all.

After he left, our relatives—my aunts and uncles and others—wanted my mother to put us children in an orphanage. But Ma, who was the most courageous and strong-willed person I've ever known, said absolutely no way. She told us that we'd make it through somehow. And we did, in the middle of the Great Depression—and in those days, there was no welfare and no unemployment insurance. My father was supposed to send so much money each month, but it wasn't coming in. Ma did every job imaginable, like laundry, cleaning houses and scrubbing floors.

We children tried to earn extra cash or help out in other ways. I can remember standing beside the railroad tracks that ran near our house and throwing stones at the engine cab. The fireman would get mad and throw pieces of coal at me. I'd pick them up and take them home for the stove. I used to fish in the stream on our property—for food, not fun—and that almost cost me a year in school once. I'd mistakenly thought our final exams in June were over and got my pole and some worms and gone fishing. I was sitting on the bank when Ma rudely interrupted my daydreaming to tell me the school had called and I'd missed the last exam that morning. A very caring teacher named Miss Loth let me take the test in the afternoon.

I was not the best fisherman in the family. Ma had a wonderful cat named Belinda who would lie on the bank of the stream, letting her paws hang down above the water. She'd see a fish, reach down and flip it out onto the ground behind her. One day she brought back a large sucker, 17 inches long, for her kittens. That got her mentioned in the local newspapers and even made Ripley's "Believe It Or Not" column. The cats may have eaten better that night than the Storeys did.

I had a bike and rode miles making deliveries and doing other errands. I took any odd job I could get. The youngest kids, George and Helen, were just babies, so the only guaranteed money coming into the house was the $8 per week that Irene earned working for the Bank of Nova Scotia.

It was Irene who made me realize that sports could be more than just something to do when I wasn't in school or busy with chores around the house. It was when she came home from the inaugural British Empire Games in Hamilton in 1930. She had won the 60-yard dash in the junior division and tied the Canadian senior record. They had a hometown parade for her and here was little me, aged 12 or so, with my eyes wide and my mouth open, taking it all in. The officials all came out to our house and presented Irene with a watch, and made a big fuss. I thought it was terrific that she was so popular. I also thought I'd enjoy something like that.

Irene ran on Canada's relay team at the British Empire Games in London in 1934, but—in a preview of things to come 50 years later—they lost to German girls who were more like men. "We never saw them in the showers," Irene told me when she came home. In 1936, she was selected to be on the Olympic team for the Games in Berlin. But she was told by the bank that if she took time off to go, she would be fired. She sacrificed that opportunity to make sure the rest of the family had food on the table.

While Irene wasn't the only athlete in the family, it took me ages to develop. And without her encouragement, I may not have gotten very far. I was very small as a child, with not much co-ordination and no reflexes to speak of. In fact, I showed no athletic talent at all. No one wanted me to play on their team. I'd be the last guy chosen, and then only because they didn't have enough players. But that certainly wasn't because of a lack of interest or effort on my part.

I had tried, without any success at all, to play all the sports kids my age did when I was growing up, and I had sports idols like everyone else did. The first I remember was Jack Dempsey, because the heavyweight champion was the biggest man in sports in every way. You'd hear people everywhere talking about the Manassa Mauler and his fights. George Young, the champion marathon swimmer, was another hero because he was a Canadian who did something internationally and proved we were as good as anyone in the world. Everyone in the schoolyard would pretend they were Dempsey or Gene Tunney. In Kempenfelt Bay, part of Lake Simcoe, we'd be Young.

I didn't really have any hockey heroes until about 1931, when we got an old Atwater Kent radio and would listen to the games broadcast from the brand new Maple Leaf Gardens by Foster Hewitt. Those were the years of the Kid Line—Joe Primeau, Charlie Conacher and Busher Jackson—and Hap Day and King Clancy on defence. We imitated them after they

won the Stanley Cup in the spring of 1932. Football didn't get
the coverage then, but I knew that Balmy Beach from Toronto
won the Grey Cup in 1930 because my cousin, Phil Newman,
played centre on that team. I spent a while after that hiking
small rocks and even big snowballs back between my legs. But
I seldom was able to play any game for real.

Irene, however, saw some future for me in sports. I don't
know where the genes came from, because my mother and
father were so unathletic they couldn't run for a bus. But the
ability was there. George, who was 10 years younger than me,
became a schoolboy champion runner and a helluva football
player. He would have made it in the Canadian Football
League if he'd been there before the American coaches took
over and wanted imports at all the skill positions. He also
could have played baseball for any team I ever saw. Helen, the
baby of the family, became one of the best basketball players
in Ontario after overcoming a terrible accident that shattered
her leg when she was just a child and left her unable to walk
for many months.

I had trouble catching the ball in both baseball and football, having what they called "cement hands." Irene made me
play "Jacks" with her. It's a game in which you try to pick up
one tiny metal-pronged object out of a pile of them without
disturbing the others, and do it before a rubber ball you
bounce in the air comes down. Then you try to get two in one
sequence, then three and so on. Those prongs in the game we
played were really sharp, so you had to have a light touch. I
got so I could do it with both hands, over and over again. I
developed what they call "soft" hands, and never again had
any trouble catching any kind of ball.

Not only did I need some work on hand-eye co-ordination,
Irene also noted that I was clumsy on my feet. To cure that,
she made me take her dancing at the Odd Fellows' Hall on
Saturday nights. I can still remember how embarrassed I'd be,

dancing with my sister, but eventually I did become very light on my feet and, if I say so myself, not a bad hoofer.

If Irene provided the inspiration for me in sports, my mother provided the encouragement and character. She always taught us that nobody in the world was better than us, and not to let them believe they are. I never did. I wasn't really a rebel, but I was stubborn. I always stood up for my rights. Treat me well, and I'd treat you well. When I was five years old, Ma opened an account for me at the Royal Bank to teach me thrift. I had to deposit a nickel every Monday morning, and she'd make up the difference if I didn't have enough pennies from running errands. The people at the bank were so nice to me right from the start that I've banked there ever since—71 years and counting.

Ma also involved herself in our sports. She made me take our lawnmower and cut a 100-yard pathway in the field across the street from our house so Irene could practice sprinting. Irene had to have someone to train with and I was elected. I couldn't stand the thought of my own sister being a better athlete than I was, and I got faster and faster. But I never beat her, because she was so good she had to run against boys her own age to find any competition in Barrie. She was invited to join the Silverwoods-Lakeside Athletic Club in Toronto, under the famous Bobbie Rosenfeld, Canada's best female athlete. Irene went on to set Canadian records in the 220-yard run and as a member of sprint relay teams.

Meanwhile, I was still a skinny little punk when I went out for football my first year in high school at Barrie Collegiate Institute. The coach, Alex Cockburn, looked at me and said, "Kid, you'd better go home before you get killed." I weighed 105 pounds. Because I wanted to play something, I turned out for track and field. A teacher named Bill Bell taught me how to high jump and I wanted to practice at home. We had a sand pit in a field across from our house, so I went to a lumber yard and I can't recall whether I bought or stole the wood to build my own standards. I worked hard and improved quickly as I grew bigger and stronger every year. In my fourth and final year of high school, I set a schoolboy record for Northern Ontario that stood for several years.

The training helped in another way. I went from 105 pounds to 160 in 12 months. I was growing so fast that all I wanted to do was sleep. I made the football team my second year at B.C.I., although I was no star. But by the time I was 17 and in my senior year, I was above six feet tall and weighed about 175 pounds.

I also got a new nickname, Toar, after a big strong guy in a comic strip. I'd been Buster or "Bus" since Old Doc Little called me that, and I was Toar until I got to the Argos. They couldn't call me Red, despite my hair, because they already had a player named Red Vail, so I became Ginger Storey there until Vail retired. None of those nicknames bothered me at all. The one thing I didn't want was to be called by my given names. My father was known as Roy, so I wanted no part of that, and Alvin was hardly a name you wanted fans yelling. I've used Red ever since my time in Toronto, even for legal documents.

In my last year at B.C.I., we won the Georgian Bay senior school football title for the first time ever. It should have been two years in a row. The season before, the officials said I had come up one yard short on a plunge on the final play of the game that would have given us the victory. I know I was across the goal line, but they said no. During my last season, *The Barrie Examiner* printed an anecdote: "A small B.C.I. pupil was absent from school for several days. The teacher asked him why he was away, and he said: 'I went out to rugby practice and Toar Storey stepped on me.'"

Barrie had a great tradition in the sporting world. It always had fine athletes for a town of about 8,000. I couldn't have asked for a better place to play sports anywhere and I played them all. Except for track and field, I always played team sports. I liked the idea of a bunch of individuals trying to do the best they could with their ability within the team concept. I wanted to be a big-league hockey player, football player and baseball player, but in high school I did everything.

I was a defenceman with the Barrie Colts Junior B hockey team when I was 16, and a couple of things about that stand out in my memory. We imported Ab DeMarco from Northern Ontario. On the first day of training camp in the arena, he seemed very uncomfortable. I asked him what was wrong. He said it was the first time he had ever played with a roof over his head and he had claustrophobia. I don't think I've ever seen a better stickhandler than Ab. When he walked down the street, he always had a stick in his hand and stickhandled with a ball or even a tin can in place of a puck. He later made it to the NHL, and so did his son, Ab Jr.

Our team doctor was Frank Maxwell. If anyone got hurt, we were in trouble, because he was a veterinarian. We always wanted to travel with him for road games because his car had a radio and a heater, which were not standard equipment in those days. There was one problem, however. The doctor chewed tobacco and was constantly opening his window to spit outside. In the back seat, we'd see him start to do it, but sometimes we couldn't get the blanket we had around our knees up fast enough and the spray would hit us in the face. We'd be covered with little brown spots. I'm sure fans in some of those towns thought the boys from Barrie had the most freckles of anyone in Canada.

I also played basketball in high school and was on B.C.I.'s first-ever championship team in that sport, as a senior in 1936. Basketball was my first sports love because it was the first sport I played well. Alex Cockburn told me later he was surprised I never turned pro in basketball because he thought it was my best sport.

Finally, when I was 14 or 15, our end of town had a junior lacrosse team called the Allandale Excelsiors. I didn't have a stick and couldn't afford one but even if I'd had one, I'm sure I wouldn't have been invited to play because I was still pretty small. I became their water boy because I just wanted to be involved in some way. I think even now I'd have to say lacrosse is my all-time favorite game.

But at the age of 18, that part of my life was ending. Even with the success I'd had in high school basketball and football, I couldn't see how I could make a living in sports. At that point, earning money to help out at home was the most important thing.

4

The Toronto Years

When I left Barrie for Toronto in the late winter of 1936, having just turned 18, I had no thought at all of playing for the Argonauts of the Interprovincial Rugby Football Union, commonly called the Big Four. I had no thought of playing sports at all. I was just going where the work was, to try to help the family. I didn't even wait to graduate from high school. The father of a friend of Irene's was superintendent of the railroad junction at Allandale and he arranged a job for me at Canadian National's Leaside shops in Toronto.

I started there on April 1 and the straw boss, a man named Jimmy Rainbow, was right when he told me: "Kid, this is the worst April Fool's joke you'll ever have played on you." I got up at five o'clock in the morning and being young and big and strong, I got all the heavy lifting. But I was just glad to be working, because there were no jobs in Barrie. I did, however, get a little tired of being a human crane.

One night I was out with my buddies, walking around in the east end, where we lived, and we ran into a tough-looking little guy they knew, Teddy Morris. I'd never heard of him but he turned out to be a halfback with the Argos. We were introduced, and he said, "My friends tell me you were pretty good in football in Barrie." I said I'd played some, and he asked, "Would you like a tryout with the Argos?" I said, "My

God, are you kidding?" This was like being chosen to go to the Olympics or something.

I'll never forget the day Teddy first took me to the Argos' camp. I had a windbreaker on, a black eye from a collision on the baseball field and hay growing out my ears. Lew Hayman was the coach and he was tough, parading around dressed in big jackboots up to his knees. There was nobody like him, and he knew what he was doing. In his career, he won five Grey Cup championships, as many as any coach ever, and never lost one. He only came up to my shoulder, but he frightened me. Even his whistle from the bench was like a knife in your ear. At the beginning, I tried to keep as far away from him as I could because I was afraid he might send me home. But I found out quickly that I could do all the basics, and I could run faster than any of them. I was 6′3″ by now and weighed 195.

I was very shy, however. The other players noticed this and decided to get me out of my shell. About the third day a big lineman named Len Staunton called me over. "Say, kid, how would you like to get in good with the rest of the fellows on the club?" I said, "Boy, I sure would," and he explained: "There's a guy in there taking a shower who's been causing a little trouble among the fellows. Sort of a smart aleck, know what I mean?" I nodded, and he continued: "Take that pail of cold water and throw it over the top of the wall. The fellows will really like you after that." Well, I did. I emptied the bucket over the wall and in seconds the dressing room was bedlam. Then everybody cleared out. The victim came out of the shower and it was a little tough standing there alone trying to explain it, since it was Hayman. But he took it pretty well, realizing I'd been set up.

Everybody played two ways then—both offence and defence. The Argos started out by making me an end because of my speed and tackling ability. I could see there wasn't going to be much future in that, so I went to Hayman and said: "I'd like a shot at the backfield, because I played that in school. I've looked at everybody you've got trying out and, to tell you the truth, I don't see anybody out there better than myself." He just looked at me coldly, and barked, "Who in hell ever told you you could play football?" Then he turned and walked away. The wind went right out of my sails. But the next day they gave me the ball to carry and I never looked back. The only thing that stayed with me from my brief time as an end was the number I wore. They'd given me 64, an end's number, and I never bothered to change it.

My coach at Barrie Collegiate, Alex Cockburn, used to tell us that school football was child's play compared to senior football, and some of us didn't believe him. But now I was finding out. Hayman's practices were murder, three hours every day, with no fooling around. The harder you hit, the better they liked it. This was after I'd worked a full shift at the railroad yards, and I'd end up so tired that all I could think about was going to bed.

The first exhibition game in 1936 was against the Sarnia Imperials, an Ontario league team that would go on to win the Grey Cup that year. I got to play only because Teddy Morris broke a hand in practice and missed his first game in six seasons. The Sarnia star was Ormond Beach, a 240-pound all-star fullback from Kansas. On one play, he had the ball in the open field. I hit him head on and stopped him dead. The coaches said they'd never seen anybody hit that hard. He just sat there. I think that one tackle gave me a spot on the team. When they told me I'd made it, you can believe I wasn't very long saying adieu to the CNR.

I had a decent first year with the Argos on the field, but I couldn't help feeling I didn't belong. With only a couple of exceptions, the other players were either college graduates or professional men, working in brokerage houses and so on. They were from a different world than I was, so I didn't see them off the field. I was accepted as a football player, but making $15 a week I didn't even have the clothes to go out with them if they'd asked me. I didn't have a social life, and it was a lonesome time. Whenever I wanted a job to earn extra money for home, the Argos would get me something menial, like in the Simpson's warehouse, hauling boxes around. I got so I loved to be at practice. That's where I enjoyed myself the most because I could outdo everybody at that level. I felt that way as long as I was in Toronto.

Before the 1937 season, Bill Strachan, my best friend in high school and a kicking halfback, was looking for a tryout. There was no chance for him with the Argos, who had one of the best in Bob Isbister. But I arranged for Bill to go to Hamilton and then I said to myself: "Hey, that's a lunch-bucket town, my type of people. I'm going over there, too." I was with the Tigers for three weeks in training camp that summer, but the Argos wouldn't let me transfer and I had to go back to Toronto. Bill made it, so we played against each other instead of as teammates again.

We had a great team in 1937, beating Ottawa and then Sarnia in the Eastern playoffs. In the six years I was with the Argos, the Rough Riders were our toughest opponent. We met them in the playoffs all six years. In the Grey Cup game, we edged Winnipeg 4-3 on a field that was just like cement. It turned into a running and kicking game, with a single by Isbister being the difference. I remember coming out of that game physically beat and I'm sure everybody was the same way. We had chunks of flesh taken out of us from hitting the dirt. We won because we stopped the great Fritzie Hanson, the hero in 1935 when Winnipeg had beaten Hamilton to become the first Grey Cup winner from the West. I was proud to be part of that defence. Many years later, I was speaking in Winnipeg and met Fritzie in the hotel suite before dinner. He said: "If you want, I'll take off my shirt and show you the cleat marks you left on me. I still have them." It was that kind of football. I gave Fritzie a pretty good mauling and he gave

me the same. Over two Grey Cup games, we held him to a
rushing average of minus one yard.

The Argos were even better in 1938, when almost all of our
top offensive stars made all-star teams, including quarterback
Annis Stukus, running backs Art West and myself, Isbister at
kicking half, Morris at flying wing, and ends Wes Cutler and
Bernie Thornton. We won the East once more, beating
Ottawa and Sarnia again. Winnipeg, meanwhile, wanted
revenge and was advertised as the best Western club ever. East
and West didn't play interlocking games as they do now, so
there was always a great element of doubt as to which was the
better team. The Blue Bombers practiced in secret out at
Appleby School near Oakville, which just added to the mystery. We'd scan the papers to see what these guys looked like
and to read their histories; I'm sure they were doing the same.

The buildup in the papers for the game was fierce. Art
Evans, our captain and a middle wing (now tackle), was
quoted as saying: "Anytime a gang of sailors can't kick the
stuffing out of a corral of cowboys then we'd better stick to
rowing." No, we didn't really talk like that; the press took
some liberties back then, too. Public interest was higher than
ever before. Varsity Stadium didn't sell standing room, and
thousands milled around outside the gates, unable to get in.
The number of people who did, officially 18,778, set a record.
So did the receipts of $17,545.75. That doesn't sound like
much compared to figures like 68,318 people at Olympic
Stadium in Montreal for Edmonton-Alouettes in 1977, and
$3,787,400.00 in revenue for Saskatchewan-Hamilton at
SkyDome in Toronto in 1989. But it was a big deal then.

As for the game itself, it started like a hard-nosed continua-
tion of the year before. At the end of three quarters, the
Bombers led 7-6. That made the total score 10-10 for seven
quarters over two years. There wasn't much to choose
between the two clubs. We were keeping Hanson under control again and we had a touchdown from West, my opposite

number at outside half. Hayman alternated two offensive units during the regular season, with each playing half the game, a quarter at a time. For the Grey Cup, however, you could play a total of only 20 men, instead of 24, so we couldn't afford to use two full backfields. I was also drilled as an inside runner on the famous Argo end run, an extension play with one man lateralling to another, with West to be the outside or last man. It actually was an option play, before they started using that term.

In the fourth quarter, the Bombers started to double-team West, and that's how the fun started. We had the ball on their 28-yard line when our quarterback, Bill Stukus, Annis's brother, called the end run. He got the ball from our centre, George Hees, the future cabinet minister, and pitched it to Teddy Morris, who lateralled to me. They were covering West closely, so I kept the ball, cut in, managed to score and we led 12-7. It's funny, what I really loved was to gallop in a straight line flat out; the shortest distance between two points, etc. Hayman had been after me for three years to cut inside, teaching me how to shift and sidestep and cross-step and reverse and all that, and finally he put me in a position where I had to do it.

A few minutes later, I intercepted a pass and ran it back about 40 yards to set up a one-yard plunge for my second touchdown. Then as Winnipeg, trailing 18-7 and trying to get back into the game, marched down the field deep into our territory, Isbister intercepted another pass near our goal line. Seeing he was trapped, he lateralled to me and I took off tiptoeing down the right sideline. A lot of guys had the angle on me, but I beat a few of them and finally was pushed out of bounds inside the Bombers' five-yard line. I got creamed, in fact, and landed right in the laps of some of the 40 fans from Barrie I'd found tickets for. I'd been upset with the location, down near the end of the field, but it turned out they were in the right place after all. When I got into our huddle after the

102-yard run, Bill Stukus said, "Red, we'll rest you a play and then give you the ball." But we scored right away as Stukus passed for a touchdown to Thornton and it was 24-7.

My third and final touchdown of the quarter was a run from about their 10-yard line. It was a lot like the first one. They were watching West outside, so the middle was there for me. In all, I had run for something like 190 yards in 12 minutes. Ted Reeve of *The Toronto Telgram* wrote, "That could win any football game and most track meets." More lyrically, Ralph Allen of *The Winnipeg Tribune* said that I combined "the most spectacular features of an angry rhinoceros and a frightened gazelle." I was carried off the field on the shoulders of the fans. The strange thing was that I played better games than that and didn't score at all. That was just my lucky day, and the three touchdowns in one quarter remain a Grey Cup record.

Afterward, I spent some time with my mother, who saw all our games that year, even going on the road with us, before I went to the Argos' big dinner-dance. For winning a second Grey Cup in a row, we were presented with a little gold football from the City of Toronto, a windbreaker with the Argos' crest on it and a picture of the team. I had kept my sweater in 1937, which I wasn't supposed to do, and in 1938, I traded it for the jersey of one of the Winnipeg players, which I wasn't supposed to do either.

My Grey Cup game caught a lot of people's attention and I heard from several teams interested in having me join them, including Ottawa and Sarnia. But the most serious offer came from Winnipeg. The Bombers' general manager, Joe Ryan, promised me a big job with the Maytag Company at $175 a month, plus $1,250 for playing football, far more than I was making with the Argos. I thought I needed an advisor. I didn't have a father, so I talked to Charlie Carson, an older friend in Barrie and a bright man. He had a White Spot outlet, one of the first fast food chains, and he also drank. A lot. He went

with me to Toronto to see Ryan and they got into an argument, with Charlie finally saying insulting things like, "If
you're so goddamn big, how come you're wearing that cheap
suit?" and so on. We got out of there, and that was the first
and last time I ever used an agent. I don't feel agents—male
pimps, to be impolite—are necessary since everyone knows
what everyone makes now anyway. If you can read a paper,
you can figure out the money you're worth and get it. I
decided to stay with the Argos.

One thing my sudden fame did was to make it easier to get a
ride when I hitchhiked home to Barrie. That was something I
did every week the whole time I was with the Argos. I lived in
a boarding house in Toronto and couldn't wait to get home.
I'd leave right after the game Saturday and not come back
until Tuesday, because we didn't practice Sunday or Monday.
My teammates used to kid me about it. I might have had the
best thumb in the east. "One-Car Red," they called me, but I
froze my butt off a lot of days. Sometimes I'd wear my Argos
sweater, because there was always a football fan around
who'd give me a lift. The sweater really meant something. It
was gold on the highway. Today, they might run you into the
ditch for wearing one.

I only had one bad hitchhiking experience. I was thumbing
a ride back to Barrie at night and a man stopped and waved me
in. I smiled, thanked him and settled into the front seat beside
him. The next thing I knew, he pointed a gun at my head.
"Son," he said, "you just sit there and be a good boy and we'll
get along okay. Make one move and I'll blow your head off." I
was only 18 at the time, and scared stiff. We didn't say two
words to each other the whole trip. I just looked straight ahead
at the road. I didn't want this guy to get even the least bit
nervous. Of course, if he'd known I'd be a referee in the NHL
someday, he might have shot me on the spot. But when we got
to Barrie, he let me out and I never saw him again.

Back in Barrie, I was playing both hockey and baseball in

the football off-season, and I soon added lacrosse. That came about one summer when I was playing senior baseball. Because I was a local boy, they wouldn't pay me any money, even the few dollars I wanted. So I said, "In that case, I'll go and play lacrosse." I'd seen the Orillia Terriers play one of the games in the Mann Cup series for the Canadian championship, which they won, and I'd fallen in love with the game. I'd never even had a lacrosse stick in my hands, but I had the confidence of youth. I went up to Orillia, got a tryout and worked like hell. Every day, I used to practice an hour-and-a-half with the team and then five or six hours by myself. The playing coach was Bucko McDonald, a great body-checking defenceman in the NHL and one of the many hockey players who played lacrosse in the summer for conditioning. He was the best man I ever saw with a lacrosse stick. He would sit in the dressing room, opposite an old corner sink, and he'd flip the ball and hit the tap and turn the water on, flip the ball again and turn it off, and do that over and over. He helped me learn the game.

The evening of the season opener, I went into the dressing room and my sweater was hanging on a nail, which meant I was in the lineup. I'd made the best team in Canada in one month and I didn't have to go back to Barrie to play baseball for nothing. What a thrill it was, with all the lights out in the arena, when they announced each name and a spotlight would follow you out onto the floor. I was three feet off the ground. Then in the warmup, the tradition was that the youngest rookie took the first shot on goal. That was me, so they threw me the ball and I ran in on our goalkeeper, Teddy Hall, who was No. 1 in Canada. I wound up and took a shot and broke his bloody jaw! I wanted to die right there, but they forgave me and I went on to play with both Orillia and the Hamilton Tigers, the latter at top dollar of $15 a week, out of which I had to pay all my expenses. Nobody made much money playing sports in Canada back then.

I had played baseball with the Barrie senior team from the age of 16, as a pitcher and an outfielder. I remember once having a no-hitter with two out in the ninth inning, before an error opened the floodgates; I couldn't get anyone out after that. I got mad, lost my concentration and just tried to throw it past the batters. I couldn't. All this came a few months after my mother had helped me overcome a problem. I had smashed up a shoulder playing football with the Argos in 1937 and, even though it was supposed to have healed, I was still babying it near the end of winter. Ma knew I had to start using it and one day when we were out hanging the wash on the clothesline, she hit me right in the puss with a handful of snow. I always had the explosive temper that goes with red hair and I made a snowball and fired it back at her, and then another and another. I realized suddenly that I was throwing with no pain. I was the opening day pitcher that season.

In the summer of 1938, I went to two training camps run by Dan Howley, a veteran baseball man. The first was right at home in Barrie and I didn't impress anybody because I had a sore arm. But a guy from Penetanguishene, Phil Marchildon, who was at that camp, was invited to spring training with the Toronto Maple Leafs of the International League and eventually became an outstanding pitcher with the Philadelphia Athletics in the majors. The second camp was in Owen Sound; this time I was offered a contract by those same Athletics. I was tempted, but I added up the figures and I was making more money year-round from amateur baseball, hockey, lacrosse and, of course, the Argos. None of those leagues or teams was considered to be professional; only the National Hockey League and American football and baseball were.

In those days, if you turned professional in any sport, you were automatically a pro in every other sport, too. It took you three years to get your amateur card back. That made it too big a gamble. If I'd signed with Philadelphia in baseball and failed or been hurt, I was out of all my jobs in amateur sport in Canada for three years. That also kept me from accepting tryouts later with both the Chicago Bears and New York Giants of the National Football League.

I've always thought I could have made the grade there. Lew Hayman agreed. "I'd say he could be developed into a great pass receiver as well as a ball carrier in the pros," he told *The Globe and Mail* in 1940, when I received the Giants' offer. "He's got the greatest pair of hands I've ever seen on a footballer on either side of the border and he wouldn't be lost in the shuffle, even among those professionals." But if anything had happened, how would I have fed myself for three years? So I always backed off.

At one point in the late 1930s, I was making money in four sports and I remember one holiday weekend when I played all four of them. It was Thanksgiving. I played baseball for the Barrie senior team, lacrosse with Orillia, hockey in Toronto in a good industrial league and, of course, football with the Argos.

The Argos didn't get back to the Grey Cup during the last three seasons I was with them. I'm sure people expected great things from me, and even though we finished second and lost in the playoffs to Ottawa, I thought I was a better football player in 1939 than ever before. I got off to a good start and went on to win the scoring title. The real pressure, near the end of the Great Depression, was simply to earn money, to go out and do the best you could, to keep your job. I was able to do that for two more seasons.

I remember a game against Montreal in 1939. I had played hockey with Bill Davies, a good friend and one of the stars of the Montreal team, then called the Cubs. I wanted to find out his plans for the next winter so I went down to the Royal York Hotel to see him that morning. The next thing I knew I was in a big crap game with the whole Montreal team. When their coach came in to tell them it was time to get the bus to the stadium, I didn't have a nickel left. I figured I'd just get on their bus and go with them, but they wouldn't let me. They were laughing and cursing at me. I asked Bill to lend me a half-dollar for taxi fare. He laughed, flipped me a quarter and said, "Take the street car." I had the last laugh. I scored three touchdowns and we beat them easily. Years later, when Bill was dying in hospital in Montreal, the last words he said to me were, "Red, you never paid me back that quarter."

I tore up a knee against Hamilton in 1940, and that was the beginning of the end of my football career. In the six years I was with the Argos, the team's record was 27-8-1, with two Grey Cups won. The Argos had a lot of money and fine players, but they never let the two of them get too close to one another. The Argos had been formed originally as a rowing club and the football players en masse hated the rowers. The club took all the money we made for it, bought the rowers new shells, new this and new that, and all we got was a party on Saturday night after the game. So there was a lot of hate there from people like me. I finished up getting $50 a week from the Argos and not as much from the other sports I was playing. That meant I had to do other things to earn a living. Some of those were a little strange because in those days, if you saw a 10-cent profit, you grabbed it.

One summer in Barrie, I worked with Jack Farquharson, a photographer. He'd go over to Camp Borden, the military base about 14 miles away, and take group pictures. I'd help him frame them, which was a rush job because the group might be transferred out any time. Then we'd run back with the photos and sell them for $2 each. The cash register was my big sweater. I'd just stuff the bills down the front. Jack also had a monkey that we used to take into the men's bar in the Queen's Hotel in Barrie. We'd sit in the middle of the room and, when the guys at another table went to the can, the monkey would run over and steal the beer bottles off their table and bring them back to us.

I almost became a wrestler once. The promoter, I think his

name was Playfair Brown, wanted me for the off-season. I
told him: "Look, I don't even weigh 200 pounds. How am I
going to be a rassler?" And he said, "Give us two months
with you at a camp and we'll have you up to 235 or 240." It
was good money, and the next time I went home to Barrie, I
happened to mention it to my mother. Ma said right away, "If
you go in as a rassler, we don't want you here any more." That
was that.

Another time I went into business with a school friend
from our street named Bud Kashner, who had as much natural athletic ability as anyone in town. Bud starred with Baltimore of the Eastern Hockey League, and we were both home
during the summer of 1938. We had no money and jobs were
scarce. We decided that Bud, his wife Doris and I would pick
dew worms at the local golf course at night and then sell them
along the highway the following day. We held up signs reading
"WORMS FOR SALE," but when any car looked like it was
going to stop, Bud and I would jump down into the ditch and
let Dorrie do the selling. We were just too proud and embarrassed to let anyone we might have known see us doing that.
Dorrie soon got fed up and we folded the business.

My parting of the ways with the Argos came at the end of
the 1941 season. We'd finished tied for first with Ottawa and
were going to meet them in the playoffs. The contracts we
signed in those days were for the regular season only, so I
asked Herb Boynton, the general manager, how much I was
going to get for the playoffs. He said, "You're not getting
anything." I asked him what he meant, and he said, "Just
what I said." I protested again; he refused to budge. He said I
had been paid for the whole season, including playoffs. I said,
"Okay, I have a contract to play hockey in River Vale [New
Jersey, in the Eastern League], and I'm going to play hockey."

I went back to my boarding house, packed up all my stuff
and got on the train. When we got to the U.S. border, the
immigration man who came into my car asked, "Is there a

guy in here named Red Storey?" I said that was me, and he brought over a telegram from Boynton that read: "COME BACK. WE'LL PAY YOU WHAT YOU WANT." But no one gets two shots at me, not ever. I always mean what I say, I always back up my word and nobody pushes me around. So I said they could tell Boynton what he could do with his contract. All he'd had to do was keep paying me at the same rate. I think he'd been bluffing, figuring, "This guy loves the game so much he'll play for nothing." Now I wouldn't have gone back if they'd doubled my pay because they had shown their true colors to me.

I never played football again.

5

A Career Change

I guess, like a lot of people did back then, you may be wondering why I wasn't in uniform two years after the Second World War had started. Believe me, it wasn't for lack of trying. All my buddies were in the service and I went to the recruiting office seven times trying to enlist. I always failed the medical. The last time, the army doctor asked: "Who in hell keeps sending you down here? The enemy?" As an athlete, I may have looked great, but my body was shot. The shoulder I'd smashed with the Argos prevented me from firing a rifle and my legs were held together with tape.

Not being in uniform brought a lot of insults, which I managed to ignore most of the time. But not always. I remember being in the club car on a train in Michigan just after the U.S. got into the war, enjoying a quiet beer, when an American Army officer sat down. As the evening and the drinking wore on, he became more belligerent over the fact that a healthy guy like me wasn't in the service. We all tried to ignore his insults, when he suddenly stood up and challenged me to fight, calling me a draft-dodging coward and worse. He took a swing, which I avoided, and I grabbed him and flipped him face down on the floor in a hammerlock. We called the conductor, who notified the next station, where four big MPs came aboard. The man in charge thanked me for not harming the guy and they took him away. I thanked the Lord I was able to control my temper. Usually I just swung. If I'd slugged an officer, they might have put me in front of a firing squad.

Another time I was riding on a streetcar full of ladies going downtown to shop. One of them, who probably had family members in the service, took exception to a healthy-looking guy standing 6'3" being in civilian clothes. "What's a big strong man like you doing out of the service?" she asked in a voice loud enough for everyone to hear. "Why aren't you fighting for your country?" I told her I wasn't in uniform for the same reason she wasn't in the Ziegfield Follies. We were both physically unfit. That quietened things down.

The closest I got to the service was at Camp Borden, where I played hockey one winter before the war for the RCAF. The team was allowed to have three civilians, and I worked in the base hospital. Then when I was hurt and couldn't play hockey during the 1940-41 season, I worked there as a range warden. The camp had a $250,000-per-week payroll for civilians. One morning the commanding officer got all of us on parade, and said, "All single men step forward one pace." I figured, "Here we go for a promotion," but what he said was, "You're all fired." People had been complaining about single men having jobs there and not being in the service.

For the 1939-40 season, I had gone to play hockey for the Atlantic City Sea Gulls of the Eastern League. They were coached by an old-time NHLer and perfectionist named Bert Corbeau. He was a tough guy who had played with the old Montreal Maroons. The first thing he taught me was how to break a man's ankle and not get caught. He also told me no one ever got by him twice. "A guy passed me once and the next time I broke every muscle in his stomach." I couldn't play that way and I had no respect for him. Neither did a lot of guys.

We had 68 players through the revolving door, so we had a big sign made and tacked up on the dressing room wall: COME AND GO WITH BERT CORBEAU. TRAINS ON THE HOUR FOR CANADA. Bert, who had a mop of fluffy white hair, would knock back a quart or two on bus trips. One night, on the way back from a game against the New York Rovers, the Rangers' farm club, Bert had some beers and fell asleep. Someone put a match to his hair and it went up in a puff of smoke. A few of my teammates were on their way back home the next day.

From Atlantic City, I was traded to River Vale, New Jersey, also in the Eastern League, and then to Sault Ste. Marie, Michigan, of the Northern Michigan League early in 1942. When I got there, I said to myself, "This is a dead end." I was starting to worry about my future. With the shape I was in from injuries, I wasn't sure how much longer I'd be able to play sports. It was time to think of the future. In New York one time, I met a Canadian businessman named Len Peto, a sportsman who had an interest in the Montreal Royals of the Quebec Senior Hockey League (QSHL). He asked me what I was going to do after the season. I told him I had no plans at all, and he said, "Come to Montreal and we'll take care of you." So I did.

Mr. Peto was the head of Canada Car and Foundry, a big munitions manufacturer. I was to work there and make extra money playing hockey for the Royals and football for Montreal in the Big Four. He asked me, "What kind of job do you want?" I told him, "I grew up in a railroad town. Every man I ever saw in my life had overalls on and carried a lunch pail. I don't care what I do as long as you let me wear a shirt and tie." He said, "If that's your wish, you've got it." I worked myself up to being CanCar's stock transfer agent, with six to eight people under me. I was with them until a couple of years after their war business ended and they were forced to scale back.

The most important thing that happened to me at CanCar was meeting my first wife, Helen St. Pierre, who worked in the office. We had a two-year courtship and were married in December, 1944. Our older son, Bob, was born in October, 1945, and Doug came along in April, 1947. We were married for 37 years, until Helen died in 1981. People had said it wouldn't last because I was an English Protestant and she was a French Roman Catholic. There weren't a lot of mixed marriages back then.

The Big Four suspended play because of the war before the 1942 season. I was just as glad there was no football because I didn't think my legs could stand up to the pounding. I did line up on defence with the Royals. We had a terrific team. Bill Durnan, who later played with the Canadiens and made the Hockey Hall of Fame, was in goal. We also had the Razzle Dazzle Line—centre Buddy O'Connor, Gerry Heffernan and Pete Morin, all slick passers and fancy skaters—who went up to the Canadiens together. O'Connor was a marvel, and later with the Rangers became the first man to win the Hart and Lady Byng Trophies in the same season. He fairly danced on the ice. I asked him one time how he'd learned that. "On the St. Lawrence River," he said, "dodging and stickhandling past all the rocks." You could have taken that Royals team and put it in today's NHL and been very competitive.

I was playing well enough during the 1942-43 season that the Rangers were interested in me. But the day I was supposed to sign the contract was the day following a particularly rough game when I hurt my leg so badly that I couldn't get out of bed. So I thought, "Goodbye, NHL." But it was even more serious than that. They had to operate on my right knee, the one I'd originally hurt with the Argos in 1940. The surgeon was supposed to be the top man in Canada. I was in St. Luke Hospital for three months. Thank heaven the Royals and their insurance company took care of the bills. This was a long time before medicare.

They put me on the overnight train to Toronto to go back to Barrie to recuperate. I was 6'3" tall and the sleeper berth was 6'2". When the train made a sudden stop, my leg hit the end wall hard and the impact split open the spot where the stitches had been. I didn't realize it then, but when I woke up in the morning, there was blood all over the place. I phoned the doctors and they said to come right back to Montreal and they sewed me up again. They also told me I had played my last game. If I damaged the knee again, I wouldn't be able to skate, and possibly not even walk. Worse still, the leg might then have to be amputated. That destroyed any hopes I had for a further career in football or the NHL. I was 23 years old.

Bill Head was the physiotherapist at the Montreal Forum for many years. When I went to see him to start rehab, he looked me over and said: "Red, get as much use out of your leg as you can because you'll be in a wheelchair when you're 50 years old." I was horrified. "What are you talking about? I just had a great operation." He just looked at me sadly: "Red, you had the worst operation I've ever seen. It was a horrible job they did on your leg." The knee always hurt. Fifty years later, in 1992, it got so bad I couldn't stand it. An outstanding orthopedic surgeon in Montreal specializing in athletic injuries, Dr. Larry Coughlin, did an arthroscopy on it. He came around to see me the next day, and asked who had done the previous surgery and the circumstances. I told him and asked why he wanted to know. "Well," he said, "they butchered it. They operated on the wrong side of the knee."

I still have pain. The second operation couldn't be a success because the first one was such a failure. The problem was that they were just starting to learn about leg and knee injuries in the 1940s. They didn't know much about tendons or ligaments. Today, they'd have reconstructed the knee completely and probably saved my career. They've been able to do it with many top athletes, who've gone on to be as good as they ever were, or even better. Todd Brooker in skiing comes to mind. So do Cam Neely and Pat Lafontaine in hockey; Larry Walker and Darren Daulton in baseball; Dan Marino in football; and Danny Manning in basketball.

But that's now, and I was then. I loved sports so much, and to be through in football and hockey really hurt. I was not, however, through in lacrosse. As the knee became stronger, I found I could still run, so I signed with the Lachine-Ville St. Pierre team of the Quebec league at $20 a game. I could still play and led the league in scoring. I had 12 goals in one game, an all-time record. Another time I scored three times in nine seconds, right at the start of a game. Our centre, Henri Payette, and I had a special play. As soon as they signalled for the faceoff, I'd race for the other goal. Henri always won the draw and would get me the ball in full stride. The other team finally wised up.

But my knee still wasn't right and I retired after that season. I thought that was it for me and sports. But the next spring, I was sitting at home when a man from the lacrosse league called and asked if I'd like to referee. I told him I'd never refereed. He said, "I didn't ask you that." I loved sports and didn't want to be out of them entirely, so I said, "Sure, I'll try it." I got out on the floor and realized I had one very important asset. While there were some things I had to learn, I found I could keep control of situations. Lacrosse actually looks a lot dirtier than it is. You were pretty well padded where they were hitting you, but there was always slashing and that provoked retaliation. There were no offsides, which made it simpler. But you had to stay on top of the game all the way because it could erupt in seconds. Basically, it was tougher to control but easier to referee than most other games.

You had to be in better shape to officiate lacrosse, however. In football, they stop after every play. In hockey, there are whistles, and skating is easier than running. There is no gliding in lacrosse; you run and run and run. As in every sport I ever refereed, I had a favorite partner in lacrosse. Tommy Shore and I were a perfect team. He also was the only official I ever saw fight with a player on the floor, or the ice, or the field. There was a guy named Desrosiers playing for the Lachine-Ville St. Pierre team, which his father owned. There'd been some friction between him and Tommy in the past. One time, all of a sudden, Desrosiers challenged

Tommy, dropping his gloves. Tommy threw his whistle down and they went at it right in the middle of the floor. I've never seen anything like that in my life, before or since, and I'm very pleased to say that my man won.

After the lacrosse season ended, I got a call late that summer from the Protestant school board wanting to know if I'd like to referee football. It didn't appear to matter to them either that I'd never done it. Then Loyola, a Catholic high school, asked me to do its games. After the football season, it was the junior hockey people who called. I would referee in any game where the pay was more than a quarter, even though it cost me more than that to get there and back on the streetcar. The main thing was that I was learning, always learning. Some of the amateur officials in those days were real characters. I remember working a hockey game one night with a guy who had a mickey of rye in his back pocket. He slipped and fell on his behind going out through the gate and, sitting on the ice, surveying the liquid spreading around him, he looked at me and said: "I hope that's blood."

In football, I went through the ranks just like a player— from high school to junior to intermediate and, finally, to the Big Four when it resumed play after the war in 1945. I worked in that league for 11 seasons as part of a fine officiating crew from Montreal, along with Harold Platt, Pean Bennett and Ralph Harrison. We had great chemistry among us, we backed each other up and no calls fell through the cracks, not even the two hardest you had to make in football. The first was deciding if a man had crossed the goal line in a pileup. That was a call for the linesman; if his view was blocked at all, he asked for help. Someone would have seen it.

The second tough call was deciding who had committed interference on a pass play, the defender or the receiver. I remember a game in Montreal against Hamilton. Bruce Coulter of the Alouettes was covering Ron Howell, an all-star flanker. Howell missed a pass and I thought there was something wrong, because he didn't jump very high. But I didn't see anything and didn't make a call. Three or four plays later, here they came again. Howell, who could really dangle, seemed to have Coulter beaten. But he didn't go high enough again and missed the ball again. This time I noticed Coulter went up with only one hand in the air, and I saw his other hand had Howell by the belt and was pulling him down. I called it. Coulter didn't beef, but the Montreal crowd, which hadn't seen anything, gave me hell.

Red O'Quinn, the great wide receiver of the Alouettes, was tricky. He'd line up at tight end and often run a route over the middle. He knew exactly how far he had to go downfield to make a first down. If there was a linebacker there, he'd just run right into him. If he didn't make the catch, down he'd go, looking for the interference call. If the game was in Montreal, everybody would be waiting for the flag. If we didn't call it interference, we'd be in hot water with the crowd. It was a tough decision because it could be called either way, or not at all.

As an official, I found football easy for a couple of reasons. First, I'd played the game. I remember one time Seymour Wilson, then the referee-in-chief, held a seminar in Hamilton. Because we had played against each other and were great buddies, he called me aside the night before the final day: "Red, I hope you're up on your rules. We're running a test tomorrow with 100 questions." I said: "Seymour, I'm going to let you in on a little secret. I've never read the rule book. Players do something right, or they do something wrong. I just work automatic." He said: "I hate to tell you this, but I'm not marking these exams. And the guys who pass them are the guys who are going to be hired by the league this year. If I were you, I'd go up to my room and cram tonight." I thought that he was right, but when I started to read the rule book, I knew that if I studied all night I was just going to confuse myself. So I went out for a few beers instead. I took the exam the next day and passed with 98 percent. I guess my whole background gave me the basic rules and technicalities without realizing it.

The second reason I think football is easy to officiate is because the fans are a long way from the field in most stadiums, and they don't know the rules. After every play, they turn to each other and ask: "What happened?" or "What's the flag for?" They haven't got a clue. You could then, and still can, call holding along the line of scrimmage on almost every snap of the ball. When I'd see it, my next look would be to see if it affected the play. For example, if it was holding on one side of the line and the play went the other way, I didn't make the call—but I let them know I'd seen it, for the future. To me, the important thing was not to affect the flow of the game if you didn't have to.

I think having been a player let me anticipate what would happen and keep out of the way. I can remember being hurt only once officiating football. That was at the old baseball park in Montreal, Delorimier Downs, in the early 1950s, when I stepped in a hole and hurt an ankle. I finished the game, but then the ankle stiffened up. The doctor told me it was cracked and would have to go into a cast. I had to open the NHL season in three weeks, so I said no way. I went home and propped the foot up on some pillows. For the first week it was so bruised it was as black as the ace of spades.

The second week, I got out of bed, leaned my back against the wall for support and made myself move my legs by sliding up and down the corridor, putting as much weight on the ankle as I could. The third week I went over to the park around the corner, before anyone was around to see me, and I started moving around more normally. On opening night, I was out on the ice and did the game.

I officiated in the Big Four for 11 seasons, the last seven from 1950-56 when I was also working in the NHL. In fact, I can remember doing a Big Four game at Varsity Stadium on a Saturday afternoon and a hockey game at Maple Leaf

Gardens the same night. But my hockey commitments meant I had to leave football before the season ended. When Cam McFadden took over as referee-in-chief in the summer of 1957, he decided he didn't want any part-time officials and told me to make a choice. The Big Four only played a 14-game schedule then so, financially, it had to be the NHL. I'd also worked too hard to get there to give it up, spent too many years on streetcars and buses and in small, cold arenas while learning my trade.

The first hockey game I ever did was at the Montreal Forum, which was starting at the top before working down. On Sundays, they'd have a doubleheader, with a senior league game first and then the juniors. The two refs for the senior game were Kenny Mullins and George Mallinson. When I arrived in the dressing room to do the junior game, they found out I was so much of a rookie that I didn't even have the right stuff to wear. They flipped a coin to see who would have to work with me. Mullins lost, and it was one of the best things that ever happened to me because he taught me the ropes in a very short time. He was up front about everything and he was tough. Lord, he was tough! I did lacrosse with him later and one night he went right up into the crowd to belt a guy. I asked him why. "No one's gonna throw a stone at me and get away with it," he said.

We refereed together for five years in the QSHL, and we had some times. The fans in that league were crazy, bordering on insane. They were far more dangerous than any in the NHL, and we didn't get much protection. Once we went into Quebec City where the Aces were playing Sherbrooke with first place at stake. With four seconds left, I disallowed a goal that would have given Quebec the win, and the roof fell in. The fans swarmed out of the stands like the apes in a Tarzan movie. The Sherbrooke players were using their sticks like bayonets to hold them off, and Mullins and I were throwing the occasional punch when we were threatened. We got the game finished about an hour later, but we heard the rumble start again while we were showering. We had time to lock the doors and pick up a couple of chairs. We were standing back-to-back like lion tamers when the police arrived just as one of the walls collapsed under the weight of the fans trying to get at us. We were kept safe by the police until it was time to catch the train to Montreal.

The same two teams were to play in the same rink the following week. Although we weren't scheduled to work the game, Mullins and I made a special request to be switched to it, to prove we weren't intimidated. George Slater, the league president, understood and said okay. Surprisingly, it was a quiet game until near the end of the third period, when a Quebec player tried to fire the puck along the boards from deep in his own zone. That one had my name on it and I vaulted up on the rail to avoid being hit. The puck bounced off my skate blade right in front of the goal and a Sherbrooke player snapped it in. All hell broke loose. A few people were hurt and this time we passed up our showers and headed straight for a squad car, still in our striped shirts and with every cop in town clearing a path for us through the mob.

The next day, Slater received a wire at his office in Montreal, which read: PLEASE DO NOT SEND MULLINS AND STOREY TO QUEBEC AGAIN THIS SEASON. WE DO NOT HAVE ENOUGH POLICEMEN TO GUARANTEE THEIR SAFETY. It was signed by the mayor. But when the Quebec team was asked to indicate the referees it would accept for the playoffs, the two names on the list were Mullins and Storey. They said we were the only ones they could trust because we stood behind our decisions.

Other people were noticing my work, too. During the summer of 1949 I had a call from Clarence Campbell, the president of the NHL, to come and see him in his office in the Sun Life Building in Montreal. He wanted me to sign with the league. I was all for it until he said, "Of course, you'll start as a linesman." I thought about it for a moment and felt that if I got in that rut, they'd never move me out of it. Anyway, I was making more money with all my amateur refereeing than he was going to pay me. It wasn't my cup of tea. I told him: "Mr. Campbell, I'm not a linesman. I'm a referee. If you want a linesman, my mother is a beautiful skater." Well, Campbell got so mad he picked up a sword he had as a souvenir from the war, and started waving it around. He was missing my nose by inches but I wasn't blinking an eye. I'll tell you, if he'd touched me, somebody in there would have died.

I went back to what I'd been doing. The next spring Ernie Mundey and I from the Quebec league were picked to referee the 1950 Allan Cup final, with the Toronto Marlboros playing in Calgary. On the morning of the first game, we met a guy named Bill Heron, the Calgary Stampeders' fan who had brought the horses into the Royal York Hotel in Toronto in 1948 and started the Grey Cup on its way to becoming a national festival. He invited us out to his ranch to ride. I said I wanted the oldest, most lovable creature they had, but Ernie said he'd been riding all his life and there'd be no problem. I got an old mare with a swayback who wasn't going to go very fast or very far. In the barn next door, meanwhile, we could hear a lot of banging and stomping and snorting. Bill explained they were just trying to saddle Ernie's horse which, when we finally saw it, seemed to have flames coming out its nose.

After he got up on this beast, Ernie crossed himself. They wanted to take some photos. To get the horse's ears to stand up and make a pretty picture, they threw a hat in the air. The movement startled Ernie's horse, which bolted and, before they got it under control, Ernie had ripped his groin. He couldn't even walk and there was a game that night. We went back to the hotel and up in the freight elevator because we didn't want anyone to see the shape Ernie was in. We were each getting $50 per game for the series and didn't want to blow it.

We had checked the arena earlier, and the gate where the

officials came out was right beside one of the blue lines. I told Ernie, "We're going to bluff our way through this. You're going to take one step out onto the ice and one step left to straddle that blue line and you're not going to move. You don't pick up a puck, you don't do anything. You just stand in that one place, watch that blue line and all you do is call the offsides there. I'll get all the pucks, look after the other blue line and do all the rest."

We went through five games that way. I refereed the whole thing alone and Ernie never left the blue line. Hap Day, the coach of the Toronto Maple Leafs, was on hand because they had some prospects on the Marlboros, including George Armstrong. Hap apparently was impressed by my work because I heard later that he went back and told his boss, Conn Smythe, that the only guy he had seen who was assured of a job in the NHL was the referee, Red Storey. I think Smythe forced Campbell to sign me for the next season, 1950-51, because I don't think he ever would have done it himself.

Even with the pressure of going into the NHL, my life was about to get a little less hectic and better organized. I'd had times in the late 1940s when I'd make a round trip of 700 miles, risk my neck, pick up a couple of new specimens for my collection of choice insults and come home less than $10 richer than I had started out. I remember one weekend when I officiated in four games. I did an Eastern playoff lacrosse game in Alexandria, Ontario, on a Friday night, drove home to Montreal, then drove to Kingston for a Queen's college football game Saturday afternoon, drove to Ottawa for a Royals-Senators senior hockey game Saturday night, drove home, and did another hockey game between the same two teams in Montreal Sunday afternoon.

That's four games in three sports in four different cities in less than 48 hours. I didn't need a Hawaiian orchestra to lull me to sleep after that.

6

Nine Years In The NHL

I had a difference of opinion with Clarence Campbell on my first day as a National Hockey League official. I'd gone to his office in Montreal to sign my contract—$4,500 base salary for the 1950-51 season, with an extra by-the-game payment after a certain minimum. There was added pay, too, for playoff games and for work in the American Hockey League, which NHL officials had to do from time to time.

After the formalities, Campbell gave me a general outline of how things worked. Then he got personal. "Never be seen in public having a drink," he warned me. "You'll have a hotel room on the road, so do any entertaining you want there." I'd always lived my own life and I wasn't about to change. "Mr. Campbell," I said. "I'm over 21. I'm married and I've got two children. I will live exactly how I wish to live. I will not hide from the world, so you might as well know that right now." And I never did.

In any case, you couldn't drink all that much on the NHL's expense allowance of $10 per day. It had been at that level for years and it was laughable. King Clancy once told Campbell at a pre-season meeting, "Christ, Clarence, it costs me $10 just to plan my day." From that, you were supposed to pay your hotel, meals, taxis and incidentals, including laundry. Officials had to wear white shirts and ties and, after three weeks on the road, there were lots of shirts that could have got home on their own. The per diem was still $10 when I finished up, nine years later.

I soon learned that there was never an easy night in the old NHL. My first game was in Toronto and, even though I'd signed as a referee, I was there as a linesman working with George Gravel. They had me do that for a few games while I found out where the arenas and hotels and so on were in the different cities. I got an introduction right away to Conn Smythe, who ran the Maple Leafs. We had just got into our dressing room after the first period when—BANG!—the door burst open and here was Smythe, his face red and his eyes wild. He got right after Gravel, really tearing a strip off him for a call. Sitting there listening, I realized he had the wrong guy. It was a call I had made. I said: "Excuse me, Mr. Smythe. May I have a word? I made that call, and do you want to know something? I made a mistake. I shouldn't have blown it, but I'm admitting it. Now how would you like to go back to your dressing room and ask all your 18 players if any of them made a mistake in that period and see what happens?" Smythe said, "That's fair enough for me." He turned and walked out the door.

As might be expected, the players would test a new official. In the first game I did in Detroit, I had trouble with Ted Lindsay over something; when he kept arguing, I gave him a penalty. Before the faceoff, one of the Red Wings said: "Don't you know who that is? That's Lindsay. He's a star." I told him, "Hey, you're all stars to me." Usually the guys who gave you the most trouble were the guys having a bad night. Lindsay would give you a hard time during the greatest games he ever played. He'd be on your back all night long, just griping and snarling. But I respected his will to win.

Overall, however, the players were awfully good to me. I just tried to use common sense and keep my temper. Maybe I didn't always go by the book. A cop doesn't stop every car for every little infraction, he has to keep the traffic moving. If you had control of the players and kept the flow going, you were a good referee. I always felt that you set the mood in the first period. If you didn't catch things right away, you could have a riot on your hands later. You were also letting them know what kind of a game they could play, what they could do and what they couldn't.

I also believed in listening to a player's beef. Once in a while it might even be a legitimate beef. I used to get crap from the league for that but, hell, we made mistakes. If a referee was working 70 games a season, there'd be five or six he wasn't proud of. It was better for me to take 15 seconds to listen than to shut a guy off and then have him turn around mad as hell and club the first player on the other team he saw. It made sense to let them blow off steam and I did as much as I could not to give misconduct penalties. I wanted to keep players in the game because I figured there'd be folks who'd driven 100 or 200 miles and paid money to see them play. I probably called fewer penalties than anyone in the league. I tried to call only the ones that might interfere with the outcome of the game—unless it was something really obvious.

One night in Toronto, there was a big schmozzle with some Detroit players and the fans near the boards, and I saw Lindsay rushing over there with his stick up. I knew he was going to clobber someone, so I got out of there in a hurry. In those days, if a case against a player went to court, it would usually be dismissed if no penalty had been called on the play. When the period was over, I told the linesmen: "We were following the puck. We didn't see what happened." Campbell did something to Lindsay, but not nearly as bad as it might have been. Even though we didn't care for them sometimes, we always protected the players.

There'd be times, like when a player was cussing you out, that it was tough not to react. The language could get real thick. I could always use the convenient excuse that I was hard of hearing, which I am. But I did hear it, and then I would cup my hand to my ear, and ask the player what he had said. If he was stupid enough to repeat it, he was gone. Like I said, we tried to protect the players. After all, they were the most important people in the game.

Once the players learned to trust you, they'd protect you, too. One of those times came after I was hit in the eye by the stick of Wally Hergesheimer of the Rangers during a game against Toronto one Sunday night in March, 1956. I suffered a laceration of the upper lid, contusions of the eye and a slight hemmorhage. It was the only time in my career I was forced from a game in any sport in more than 1,000 times officiating. The Madison Square Garden doctor stitched me up and wanted to put me in the hospital, but I decided to go back to Montreal, with the help of the two linesmen—Curly Davies, who had taken over as referee, and Bill Morrison. Before we left, Hap Day, the Maple Leafs' general manager, came over to find out how I was. I told him I couldn't see out of the injured eye. He said, "That won't bother you none. You only call half of what you see, anyway."

Back home, the league sent me to a Dr. Nicholls, who told me to read the first line on the eye chart. I couldn't even find the chart. He said in amazement, "You can't see." I told him, "Doc, only two people in town know that. I want to keep it that way." He said, "Well, I'll have to write a report." I said, "You write a report that will protect your ass because I'm refereeing here on Thursday." He wanted to know how I could referee if I couldn't see. I said I didn't tell him how to check eyes. He covered for me and when the time came, out I went. I was skating around, feeling okay, but then I looked down and I couldn't find the ice. I couldn't see it. I couldn't see my feet.

But I always figured you had to bluff and I thought I could fake it. I'd drop the puck, someone would pick it up, everybody else would start to chase him and I'd follow them all. We started and I saw everyone heading for the Montreal end so I took off after them. Suddenly—WHAM!—I'm lying on my back, seeing stars, with both teams gathered around me. I asked, "What the hell happened?" One of the Blackhawks said, "Dolly St. Laurent got the puck and started back the other way. You were in his road and he went right over the top of you."

Then someone else said, "Look, Red, we heard you can't see. You go and stand over by the penalty box out of the way and we won't hurt you." I went over there for the rest of the game. I could see movement and the red light come on for goals, but I couldn't tell who scored. Luckily, the public-address announcer always wanted to be in charge of that part of it. I'd turn around, and he'd say, "Geoffrion from Beliveau and Harvey," and I'd say, "You're absolutely right." I couldn't call any penalties, of course, and the next day the Montreal writers all said it was the best-officiated game of the year.

In Chicago one night in the early 1950s, I got belted and hurt my side. I finished the game and went on to Detroit, where the Canadiens were playing the next night. I went to see the Red Wings' team doctor; X-rays showed I had two broken ribs. I told him to just tape me up and keep quiet about it. I got to the Olympia and Gordie Howe and Bob Goldham were around, so I called them aside and said, "Tell your guys to try not to hit me." They said they'd heard I'd been hurt the night before. I said I didn't want any favors, "but if you can miss me, miss me." They spread the word, even to the Canadiens. Nobody bothered me all night. Both teams just stayed away.

I had a frightening experience after Eddie Sanford of the Bruins knocked out two of my teeth one night in Boston. I went in for repairs and finished the game. Then I went back to Montreal to see my dentist before leaving for my next job in Toronto. He gave me painkillers and I took so many of them I didn't remember working the next game. When I came to my senses, I was walking down the street in Detroit with George Hayes. "What the hell happened last night in Toronto?" I asked him. "I don't remember anything." He said he'd found me walking around in a snowstorm without a coat on outside the King Edward Hotel early in the evening and had gotten me to the game. "You know," he said, "I was wondering. You didn't call S.F.A. last night." One of the Toronto columnists called me "Old Redibus, with the snow hair and the ice in his whistle." That was a combination of my nicknames, Red and Buster.

The toughest call for me always was the disputed goal. Did it go in or didn't it? When you were wrong, you were better off admitting it. One night in Toronto in 1954, Harry Lumley was well out of his crease and got just a piece of a Detroit shot. I watched as the puck slid behind him toward the net and I was sure it was going in so I stuck up my hand to signal a score. But Lumley made a sensational dive and stopped the puck just in time and one of the Toronto defenceman swept it out of danger. The rules say the puck has to be all the way over the line to be a goal, and it wasn't. I'd had no business signalling a goal before I was sure it was in and I was looking for a hole in the ice to fall through. I brought my arm down and waved it off and the Red Wings, led by Lindsay who, unfortunately, was on the ice at the time, went crazy. But I kept telling them I had made a mistake and they finally calmed down.

I went to Boston for a game the next night, and I was resting at the hotel in the afternoon when Carl Voss, the referee-in-chief, called me. He wanted to know what had happened the night before in Toronto. I had the happy faculty of being able to forget every game right away, so I asked him what he was talking about. Jack Adams, the Detroit general manager, had been phoning all over the league about the call I'd made on the non-goal. I explained the whole thing to Voss and, being honest, said I'd pulled a rock. He said, "That rock will cost you $50." That was a lot of money in those days, so I said, "I beg your pardon?" He repeated, "That rock will cost you $50." I exploded. "You mean to tell me that when you ask me a question and I tell you the truth, I'm fined?" He said I had heard him right, so I told him, "In that case, don't ever talk to me for the rest of your life," and hung up. I never spoke to him again until the day I told him I was quitting.

The one thing I never wanted to see was a stick fight, but one night in December, 1953, in Madison Square Garden, I had one of the worst in hockey history. It started when Ron Murphy, a rookie with the Rangers, and Bernie (Boom Boom) Geoffrion of the Canadiens tangled near the boards. Geoffrion dropped his stick, ready to fight, but Murphy didn't. When linesman Dom Baolto got between them, Murphy reached over his shoulder and whacked the Boomer on the head several times. Geoffrion touched his scalp as Murphy kept slashing at him, and saw blood on his hand. I could see his eyes change and he went berserk. He picked up his stick and chased Murphy toward the middle of the ice. He took a wicked overhead swing that would have cut Murphy in two, but it missed by inches. Then Geoffrion took a full baseball swing, hit Murphy in the temple, and he went down like a limp rag. I thought he was finished when they brought out a priest to give him the last rites. But the medics worked on Murphy for several minutes and took him off on a stretcher.

There was a big hearing afterward, with about 20 written reports—from some of the Canadiens and Rangers, various league employees, the two linesman and myself. Both players were suspended. Murphy recovered and came back to play in the league for several more years. Geoffrion continued as one of its greatest stars well into the 1960s. I remember that, as quickly as he had snapped, he was back to normal just as fast. He threw his stick away before Murphy hit the ice and had a look on his face like "My God, did I do that?" His teammates gave him an escort to the dressing room when the enraged fans started throwing beer cans and other stuff.

While we were standing around as they treated Murphy on the ice, I was next to Butch Bouchard, the Canadiens' captain.

I said what a terrible thing this was and that it was going to be a black eye for hockey. Butch said, "I don't know, Red." He looked around and pointed to some corners of the Garden with empty seats. "We have five more games here this season, and I'll bet you every seat will be full when we come back." He was right.

Geoffrion was part of a funny incident I had in Montreal in his rookie year. The language of conversation on the ice in the NHL was English. That had been ordered after there were complaints that Gravel, who spoke French with some of the Canadiens, was somehow giving them secret information or some such nonsense. This night, I gave Boom Boom a penalty and he was so mad he threw his gloves and stick away and started yelling at me in French. I couldn't understand what he was saying, and he knew that so he figured he was safe in trotting out the swear words. I had a pretty good idea of his meaning and, after he ran out of breath, I mustered all of my French, and told him, "Et dix minutes pour vous, Monsieur." He was stunned. He was gone with a 10-minute misconduct and for years warned new French players that Storey understood their language.

When Henri Richard came into the NHL with the Canadiens in the fall of 1955, he was the only guy in the league who never said anything to me at all. I asked Toe Blake, his coach, "Can the Pocket Rocket speak English?" Toe said, "He's so quiet I don't even know if he can speak French." About three months later, Detroit was playing in Montreal and I allowed a disputed Red Wings' goal. One team and 16,000 fans, who began throwing things, didn't agree. After we got the ice cleaned, Henri was getting ready for the faceoff at centre, and it was all too much for him. I could see the color coming up into his neck, his face, his ears, his forehead. He was steaming. He turned, pointed his finger and used English for the first thing he'd ever said to me. "Storey, you're full of shit, you." It was so funny I didn't even give him a penalty. I had to skate away. Years later, I told the story to his brother Maurice just like that. The Rocket had never heard it and almost collapsed in laughter. Then he asked, seriously, "Why would you give a man a penalty for that?"

The oddest thing that ever happened to me was during the third period of a Canadiens-Red Wings game in Detroit. It was a close one, as they always seemed to be between those two teams. The Wings had the pressure on in the Montreal end when I saw the red light go on and some of the Detroit players raised their sticks in front of the net in celebration. I was over in the corner where two or three other players were fighting for the puck. I thought there was something wrong about all this and blew the whistle. I looked down and what was in the corner was half the puck. I skated over to the goal and there was the other half. The whole puck had to be over the line for a goal to count and that hadn't happened here, even though this situation wasn't what the rulemakers had in mind. I wiped out the goal and there was a huge argument. Amazingly, Toe Blake, the coach of the Canadiens who was usually in the middle of every row, didn't get into it at all. I asked him about it later, and he said, "I didn't know if you were right or not." I told him, "Toe, that never stopped you before."

We did have some fun, and there were some funny lines. Lindsay was the best needler. One night in Boston he was calling the linesmen everything he could think of over an offside. "Break it up," I told him. "You can't talk to them like that. They're not dogs, you know." He agreed, sort of. "They aren't dogs," he said. "They need dogs, seeing-eye dogs."

Johnny (Goose) McCormack, a centre who had a decent career with the Maple Leafs, Canadiens and Chicago, said to me one time as we waited for a faceoff, "I'm always sticking up for you, Red." I took the bait. "Oh, yeah?" He smiled. "Yes, the other fellows say you're a big red-haired buffoon. But I always say you're not so big."

Coaches were forever sending the captain out to give you

crap, but I didn't mind. It was better than having to talk to the coaches, who couldn't help any situation but only make it worse. With the captain, I could say, "You ask me a question, I'll give you an answer, we'll both skate away, and that'll be the end of it." And it usually was. Sometimes the captains weren't very enthusiastic about coming out at all. One time Tommy Ivan of the Blackhawks dispatched Gus Mortson to bitch about something. Gus started waving his arms and the crowd loved it. But what he was saying was, "Where are you taking the kids this summer on their holidays?" I said, "I don't have a clue. Got any suggestions?" Now he was really whipping his arms around and the crowd was hollering even louder as he told me, "There's a great place northwest of Peterborough in the Fenelon Falls area. It's a great camp, just fabulous for families. You'll love it." I said, "Terrific. Thanks. Now let's get out of here," and he went back to the bench. We were both laughing inside but Ivan was happy, which was the main thing.

The best official I ever worked with was George Hayes. He had been the best in the Ontario Hockey Association and was hired as a referee by the NHL. Clarence Campbell ruined that part of his career. One night in Toronto, George gave a rare misconduct to Syl Apps, the Maple Leafs' captain and resident saint, for coming off the bench to get into a brawl with the Canadiens. Campbell caved in under pressure from Conn Smythe and, after the fact, removed the penalty entirely—from the game summary, the record books, everything—to save Apps's name as a gentleman player. It was like it never happened, although George had a photograph of it. George was a man of principle and when Campbell wouldn't back him, he quit as a ref immediately and became a linesman. I used to love to work with George because we had the same approach. Campbell thought officiating was a serious business and nobody was supposed to even crack a smile out there. But George and I had fun, and we showed it. Hell, we used to boast about it. Campbell got so he'd have as little to do with us as he could, which was fine with us.

There was a downside to all this fun and games, of course. I spent most of my time out of town for more than half the year. I'd be at home in Montreal with my family only four or five days a month, and never on weekends. It was tough on my wife, Helen, who had to hold everything together at home. She completely ran the house—budgeting and finances, any school problems involving the boys, dealing with servicemen, everything. She even signed my cheques because I was never home. In fact, after I quit the NHL, the bank at the corner didn't want to cash the ones I'd write because they didn't recognize the signature.

The most difficult time for the family was around Christmas. When Bob and Doug were small, they couldn't understand why all the other kids on the street had received their gifts and they hadn't. I was always away, so we waited to celebrate until I got home. We didn't tell the boys what I did for a living for several years. It wasn't that I was ashamed of it. I just thought I'd be discreet. But we couldn't keep the other kids from seeing me on television.

The older, Bob, was about eight the afternoon he came home from school when I happened to be there. "Is it true, Dad, that you're a no good, bleeping blankety-blank?" he asked me. "Repeat that," I said rather sharply, a little shocked that he even knew words like that. He did, and I decided it was time to have a heart-to-heart talk with the boys. I told them about my work, about how important officiating was in any game, and that ugly remarks and insults by ignorant people were an occupational hazard. We let them see me referee only once. I didn't think it was good for their morale to put them in a place where they could hear 15,000 people yelling "You're a bum" at their old man.

But most of them never went beyond that. There was, however, one chilling experience during my NHL years, when

I was sitting in the kitchen having a bite to eat and a brick came through the back window. We called the police but they never found out who threw it. I just got the window fixed, and wondered who around there really hated me that much. Helen sometimes was approached on the street by people who knew who she was, and they'd ask her how she could stand to be married to a man like that, and how could she live with me.

Even inside the family, though, it was tough to shake the natural hatred that everybody seems to have of officials. Bob arrived home one day when he was about 11 and just threw his skates down in the hallway. His mother guessed his team had lost its game. "We didn't lose," I heard him holler. "We got robbed by a lousy referee." Now it was my turn. "Enough of that," I told him. "You've been eating off a lousy referee's salary for 11 years. Let's have no more knocking the officials."

When I quit the NHL in the spring of 1959, I don't think I had an enemy among the people in hockey who counted, the players. Ted Lindsay was the exception who proved the rule. I wasn't always the greatest, but I was always as honest as I could be, and as fair. I don't think anyone could ask for more than that in a game full of judgment calls. I tried to let them play, figuring that if you called everything you'd be there until four o'clock in the morning. I think they appreciated that and I took pride in knowing I'd done a job I loved to the best of my ability.

And I felt satisfaction in knowing that I'd fooled them all for all those years. My knees were so bad I could only turn one way on my skates, and nobody realized it. And you never saw me standing at centre ice before a game while they played the national anthems, because my legs simply wouldn't support me in one place for that long. I had to go and hold onto the boards.

7

The Worst Night Of All

In a quarter-century of playing and officiating top-level sports filled with highlights and great memories, I can remember only one night when nothing good happened, when there was absolutely nothing to smile or laugh about. That was the night of March 17, 1955—St. Patrick's Day—in the Forum in Montreal. It was the night of the Richard Riot, after Clarence Campbell had suspended Maurice (Rocket) Richard of the Canadiens.

The league had been lenient, too lenient, with the fiery Richard over the years, letting him off lightly for incident after incident—even an attempted throttling of referee Hugh McLean in a New York hotel lobby. That came the Sunday morning after a Saturday night game in Montreal in which the Rocket had taken exception to McLean's work. The NHL tried to overlook Richard's outbursts because he had become the Babe Ruth of the sport, the only player who packed them in wherever he went.

The roots of his latest problem were planted about two and a half months earlier in a game in Toronto just before New Year's. The Canadiens and Maple Leafs were not exactly in a holiday mood, but I was managing to keep control of things as they headed into the final minutes in a 1-1 tie. The Rocket had scored for the Canadiens and as a goal often did, that seemed to spur him on—and the Leafs, too. If there was one

team Conn Smythe loved to beat, it was the Canadiens. If
there was one thing he really hated, it was the Rocket scoring
in his building.

The trouble started when Bob Bailey cracked Richard into
the boards with a painful check, but one that didn't deserve a
penalty. The Rocket had been taking abuse all night, which
was nothing new. You were going to be abused if you were that
good a goal scorer, and he would take as much as he could.
Then, without warning, he would explode. I guess the Bailey
check was the last straw for him that night. He got up and
chased after Bailey for 50 feet. Richard had his stick up when
he slammed into Bailey and it caught him in the mouth,
breaking the tops off two of his teeth. They hit the ice together
and the Rocket said later that Bailey tried to gouge his eyes,
which really set him off.

We had an awful time containing the situation. Referees
usually let linesmen deal with fights, but this one was soon
too brutal for that. George Hayes and I kept taking his stick
away from the Rocket and getting him out of there, and he
kept coming back into the brawl with another one. We didn't
find out until we looked at the film later that the Canadiens'
coach, the late Dick Irvin Sr., was giving Richard a new stick
every time we got him disarmed and over to the bench. That
happened five times. The Rocket also slapped George once
while he was trying to break it up, and he got his glove into my
face a couple of times. The Rocket had a temper but he really
wasn't a bad guy and hadn't done much damage, so George
and I tried to soften it up in our report.

Campbell fined the Rocket $250—on top of the automatic
$50 in fines for two misconducts—and warned him he'd be
suspended for any future outbursts. He behaved himself until
a Sunday night in Boston, March 13, when there was a lot at
stake. The Canadiens were in a dogfight with Detroit for first
place with four games to go, and the Rocket was leading the
league in points. The scoring title was the one honor he'd

never won, and he really wanted it. He was clipped by Hal Laycoe, a Bruins' defenceman, and lost control when he discovered he was bleeding from a cut that would take five stitches to close. The Rocket charged Laycoe, hitting him in the face with his stick. The officials grabbed him, but the Rocket got away and attacked Laycoe twice more, still swinging his stick. Cliff Thompson, a rookie linesman, tackled the Rocket, who punched him in the face twice before they got it stopped. The Rocket said later he felt Thompson had gone too far in manhandling him.

Hitting an official was the one thing that couldn't be overlooked. Campbell held a hearing in Montreal with all the principals. On the Wednesday, saying "the time for probation and leniency is past," he handed out his stiffest sentence ever. The Rocket was set down for the last three games of the regular season, and for all the playoffs that spring. Since Richard was bigger than the Pope in Quebec, the reaction was more than angry. The mayor of Montreal, Jean Drapeau, criticized Campbell and said the suspension would ruin hockey, which didn't exactly calm anyone down. Some of the Montreal newspapers and broadcasters said Campbell's actions were anti-French Canadian and accused him of taking his orders from the other club owners. That helped whip up feeling, too.

Detroit was coming to Montreal to play on the Thursday night, with the two teams dead even, and I was looking forward to refereeing it. I always loved to work the big games. I didn't have any idea how serious the situation might be until I was eating breakfast at home and listening to the radio. The deejay said something like, "Well, this is St. Patrick's Day. Or is it blow up the Sun Life Building day?" I thought it was a pretty funny line, until I heard the news and they said there had actually been bomb threats against the NHL offices.

I realized just how serious it was when I got to the Forum maybe an hour before the game, and a crowd was already surrounding the building, chanting and yelling. I got inside with no trouble, but someone came to our room about 15 minutes before game time and told us he'd had to hold his coat over his head to get into the Forum. The people were throwing bottles at the building and the glass was falling down on the sidewalk and the street. But I didn't get the feeling we might be in a bad situation until I went out on the ice. It was like being in a vacuum that was going to blow apart. It was so quiet it was scary.

We started play; it was a dead game. You could feel and hear the murmur when Campbell arrived midway through the first period to take his seat a few rows up in the south end behind the Red Wings' goal. But there was no trouble right then. People later criticized Campbell for going to the game, but I think he had to. Otherwise, he'd have shown no guts at all. But it would have been better if he'd arrived on time. Meanwhile, the Canadiens were flat and the Red Wings took a 4-1 lead.

As we went back to our dressing room after the first period, you could feel the electricity. You knew something was going to happen. Suddenly smoke started to come in under the door. It was tear gas, so I yelled at Bill Roberts and Curly Davies, the linesmen, to grab some towels, get them soaked and get them over their heads. As soon as I said that, the door burst open. It was the cops. They grabbed all our towels for themselves and left us there to suffer, and we began to cry from the gas. We didn't know exactly what was going on, except they weren't ready to start the second period.

The cops told us that garbage—eggs, fruit and vegetables —had been thrown at Campbell. A guy in a leather jacket had come down and punched him and someone else had thrown the tear gas bomb. It was one of the few times in his life that Campbell didn't go into the directors' room between periods. I don't know why he didn't, but it wasn't very smart. If he'd gotten out of there then, we might not have had the riot that followed.

They'd ordered the building cleared. Once I heard that, I

went out into the hall to look for my wife, Helen. I mean, to hell with anything else. There was a riot going on. I couldn't find her, and tried to ask a guy standing there, but he was yelling in French and I didn't understand him. Bill Roberts, a French-Canadian despite his name, literally pushed me back into the dressing room. I was frantic, telling him I had to look for my wife, and he said: "Look, you stupid bugger. He's telling you he's going to shoot you. He's a cop on duty and he's a little trigger happy."

We yelled over the transom for the police officer in charge. Eventually Captain Bill Leggett, whom I knew, came in. We told him what had happened and he didn't believe us for a while. But we finally convinced him. He had them take the plainclothesman and put him in a taxi and send him home. By now an hour had gone by and I still hadn't found my wife. I was getting really worried. Then Bill Leggett came back and told us the game was over. I learned later that Campbell and Frank Selke Sr., the Canadiens' general manager, had written a note to Jack Adams, the Detroit GM, forfeiting the game. A while after that I heard that Helen had come down from her seat and was safe in the directors' room with Campbell and some other hockey people, so I went over there. Now we had to get out of the building, but it was too dangerous to leave just then. People were rioting all along Ste. Catherine Street, burning and looting. There was still a mob around the Forum and some bullets had been fired. It took hours to disperse them, and we finally went out the back way about 1:30 in the morning.

As fires continued to burn and merchants began to board over and clean up their looted stores, the Rocket had gone on the radio to appeal for calm. But the fury seemed to be pretty well spent by then. I also refereed the final game of the season between the Canadiens and the Red Wings the following Sunday night in Detroit. They went into it tied for first place again. The Canadiens played better than the score indicated, but they lost 6-0 as Terry Sawchuk was unbelievable in goal. The home ice advantage that victory gave the Wings was important because three and a half weeks later, the Canadiens took them to the limit before losing the seventh and last game of the Stanley Cup final at the Olympia in Detroit.

In retrospect, I think Campbell—who had a bodyguard for the rest of the season and the playoffs—made one mistake. There's no doubt the Rocket deserved a long suspension. He'd had a lot of incidents, three or four that year alone. But he should have been allowed to play in the playoffs. Don't let him play the last three games, fine, and then suspend him for the first 10 or 20 games or whatever the next season. But by keeping him out of the playoffs, Campbell cheated the whole hockey world, including the Red Wings, whose victory in the final seemed a little hollow to a lot of people.

Another person affected was Bernie (Boom Boom) Geoffrion, who overtook the Rocket to win the scoring championship. Montreal fans never felt the same about him afterward. I think it really hurt Geoffrion's popularity through the years. Even in 1960-61, when he became only the second man, after the Rocket, to score 50 goals in a season, the fans didn't make a hero out of him the way they did some others.

The only good thing to come out of it all eventually was that only one-sixth of the fans who had been at the game picked up the refunds they were offered. The money that wasn't returned—close to $25,000—was turned over to Paul Meger, a Canadiens' forward who earlier that season had suffered a severe head injury that ended his career.

Irvin, the coach, said afterward, "I've seen the Rocket fill a lot of rinks. This is the first time I've seen him empty one." I was told later the comment upset the Canadiens' brass and was one of the factors in their deciding to let Dick Sr. go at the end of the season. The day after the riot, however, I thought it was about the saddest thing I'd ever heard.

8

The Golden Age

The 1950s, the decade when I officiated in both the Big Four (later the Canadian Football League East) and the National Hockey League, was the Golden Age in those two sports. Our distinctive Canadian brand of football has never been played better; the NHL has never had so many great stars being allowed to play the game the way they could.

Let's start with football. Every team in Canada, even the losers, had great players during the 1950s. In the East, Hamilton was rock solid on defence with guys like Vince Mazza, Vince Scott and Pete Neumann, and had great offence with Bernie Custis and later Bernie Faloney and Cookie Gilchrist. Ottawa always had outstanding Canadians, led by Bobby Simpson. Toronto won Grey Cups with Al Dekdebrun and Nobby Wirkowski at quarterback, where Tobin Rote played later, and had running backs like Ulysses Curtis and Dick Shatto. Montreal had a gang of all-stars on both offence and defence.

In the West, Winnipeg had quarterbacks like Indian Jack Jacobs and Jim Van Pelt, with Tom Casey and Leo Lewis running, Ernie Pitts catching and Herb Gray and Buddy Tinsley on defence. Calgary had fullback Normie Kwong before he went to Edmonton and Don Luzzi on the line. Saskatchewan had Ron Atchison and Martin Ruby on defence and Ken Carpenter and Bobby Marlow on offence.

B.C. had all-stars By Bailey, Tom Hinton and Norm Fieldgate. Edmonton made it to the Western final every year in the decade.

The best years, I think, were those from 1954-56, when Edmonton and Montreal met for the Grey Cup three years running. It was the last time that two teams in Canada took full advantage of the wide Canadian field at the same time, the Alouettes by passing the ball and the Eskimos by running it. The coaches were Americans, but they played the Canadian game. It was also, not coincidentally, the last time all the fans, East and West, got the kind of entertainment they were paying for.

The Alouettes of that era were the most exciting football team I've ever seen anywhere. When Doug (Peahead) Walker arrived from Wake Forest University in North Carolina to coach them in 1953, someone asked him what he'd do about the extra man that Canadian football called for. "Oh," he said in his Southern drawl, "ah'll just put him way out theah as a flankuh. The othuh club will have to covuh him and then we'll get on with playin' football." His Alouettes did use every yard of the field in the best passing attack ever in Canada, with Sam Etcheverry throwing to the likes of Hal Patterson, Red O'Quinn and Joey Pal. In the three years they went to the Grey Cup, the Als won 30 regular-season games and lost only 10, averaging better than 30 points per game. They scored a remarkable 478 points in 14 games in 1956, most ever by a Canadian team then. Officiating their games was like being in a track meet.

Peahead knew, however, that you needed more than just passing to win. The Alouettes had a fine running game to set up the pass and vice versa, with Alex Webster, Pat Abbruzzi and the ill-fated Chuck Hunsinger, who threw away a Grey Cup game. Their defence was outstanding, led by Tex Coulter, Herb Trawick, Tommy Hugo and Doug McNichol. In 1954, they allowed an average of only 10.6 points per game.

Edmonton was coached by Frank (Pop) Ivy, who brought the split-T formation with him from Oklahoma and was 36-12 in his three seasons in Canada. The split-T was similar in a way to the old Argos' extension in that it used the whole width of the field and forced the last defensive player to make a choice. The Edmonton quarterback—first Bernie Faloney, then Jackie Parker and Don Getty—would take the snap and start down the line. He could hand off to either Kwong or Johnny Bright inside, or keep it and either pass or lateral to the outside man or turn upfield himself. For the last defender, it was like swallowing a cup of scalding coffee. Whatever he did next was wrong.

Like Peahead, Ivy realized he couldn't win without a solid defence and some sort of passing to go with the running. His quarterbacks could throw well enough to receivers like Rollin Prather, Rollie Miles and, occasionally, Parker. The defence allowed an average of just 10.7 points per game through the three great years, and held the opposition to an incredible 7.3 point average in 1955.

In their first Grey Cup meeting in 1954, the Alouettes lost on perhaps the most famous play in Canadian football history. They were ahead 25-20 and driving for the clinching touchdown or field goal in the dying moments, down about the Edmonton 20. Hunsinger started on an end run, was trapped and either fumbled or tried to pass the ball. Parker scooped it up and raced 90 yards for the five-point touchdown that tied it. Despite protests by the Alouettes that the play was an incomplete forward pass, it was ruled a fumble and Bob Dean's convert won it for the Eskimos 26-25. In 1955, the Eskimos blew open a tight game in the second half and won 34-19 after Etcheverry and Patterson had set pass-and-catch records. In 1956, the first season a touchdown was worth six points, the Alouettes scored more than ever, but Edmonton had its biggest winning margin, 50-27.

After that one, someone asked Peahead about the three

straight losses. "Ah wanna tell yuh somethin'," he said. "If we win the Cup, it's a bonus. The fust thing ah was hired to do was to fill them seats and that's the fust thing ah was gonna do." And he did.

Because they won the national title three times in a row in the best era our game ever had, I have to say that those Eskimos were the best team in Canadian history. But being part of a Montreal officiating crew, I saw the Alouettes often and, believe me, they were more entertaining. I used to wish they could play three-hour games. You never got tired of watching them. Pop Ivy once told me, "I'd love to play the same style as Montreal. It would be fun. But I just haven't got the talent so I have to grind it out."

One last note: I'm sorry Sam Etcheverry, the greatest passer I ever saw, never got the chance to play in the U.S. when he was at his best. His arm was about shot when he finally got to the St. Louis Cardinals in the NFL in 1961, although he was still an effective short passer. One guy who was even sorrier was Sam's first coach in St. Louis: Pop Ivy, who always said that the old Sam would have been absolutely sensational in the NFL.

Just as two teams dominated the years I consider our Golden Age of football, the 1950s in hockey belonged to the Montreal Canadiens and the Detroit Red Wings. In the decade, the Canadiens won the Stanley Cup six times and lost in the final the other four years. The Red Wings won three Cups and finished first six times to the Canadiens' four. The two clubs also combined to place at least four players on the first all-star team each year, including all six on two occasions. Their players won all 10 scoring titles.

But two franchises can't make a Golden Age. Even the other clubs had great players. In the 1950s, Toronto and Boston each had seven different men named first or second all-stars; the Rangers had six and Chicago, three. Those teams also included more than two dozen future Hall of

Famers, including goalies such as Harry Lumley, Chuck Rayner and Gump Worsley; defencemen Leo Boivin, Fern Flaman, Harry Howell, Pierre Pilote, Bill Quackenbush and Allan Stanley; and forwards Andy Bathgate, Woody Dumart, Bobby Hull, Stan Mikita, Bill Mosienko, Milt Schmidt and Harry Watson. I think the worst club in the six-team league then could win the NHL today.

There were only 120 or so players in the league—almost every one of them a Canadian—and they were the best in the world. Americans were few and far between and no foreign country, even the Soviet Union, was playing the game at nearly this high a level at that time. It was tough to make the NHL in those days. Almost everybody had spent time in the American Hockey League or senior hockey learning how to play the game the right way—even future Hall of Famers like Rocket Richard, Doug Harvey, Gordie Howe and Jacques Plante. Those minor leagues had prospects stacked up, just waiting for a chance.

Because they won five consecutive Stanley Cups from 1956-60, when no one else had ever won more than three in a row, I have to choose those Canadiens as my greatest hockey team ever. En route to those five Cups, they had an incredible record in the playoffs of 40 wins and only nine losses. Living in Montreal, I used to referee their pre-season exhibitions, so I got to know them well. The Red Wings of the 1950s would be my second choice. They played some unbelievable games against each other. One year I was the referee 12 of the 14 times they met. You couldn't relax for a second, but the hockey was beautiful.

Frank Selke Sr. built the Canadiens' dynasty. He came to Montreal to take charge before the 1946-47 season, after being Conn Smythe's assistant in Toronto for many years. It's true that the Canadiens had won the Stanley Cup in the springs of 1944 and 1946. But that was in an unbalanced league with wartime hockey players. The Canadiens had some

age and they didn't even have a farm system then. That began
to show when they missed the playoffs in 1948 and went out in
the first round the next two seasons. Selke was building stead-
ily, however, and the Canadiens started the 1950s by losing
twice in the final and then winning it all in 1953. They lost to
Detroit in the next two Cup finals, both times in seven games
—the latter without their emotional leader, the Rocket. Then
they started their great run in 1955-56.

The two missing pieces were Toe Blake, who took over from
Dick Irvin Sr. as coach, and an 18-year-old centre named
Henri Richard, Maurice's kid brother. Toe had been coaching
successfully in the Quebec league and he was tougher in practice than anyone else was in games. Compared to him, guys
like Mike Keenan and Pat Burns are a week at the beach.
Henri had been playing with the Junior Canadiens and was
very small and very shy. They invited him to training camp
just to please his brother. But he wouldn't let anyone else play
with the puck, so they had to keep him.

Throughout their history, people have always talked about
the Canadiens in terms of firewagon hockey—the Flying
Frenchmen, and so on. They've never realized the basic strategy behind the success: first, win the Vezina Trophy for
fewest goals allowed. They did that with Jacques Plante in
net every year during the five straight championships. I still
think he was the greatest goalkeeper ever. I remember so
many nights that the Canadiens would be tied or up by only
one goal late in the first period, and the other team would
get a breakaway. Plante would make the save, the Canadiens
would go back the other way and score, and it would end up
5-1 or 6-1. But what if Plante hadn't made that stop?

How good were the Canadiens defensively? At different
times I asked Bobby Hull and Gordie Howe, respectively the
highest-scoring left and right wings ever, who were the
toughest checkers they'd ever faced. With no hesitation, Hull
said Claude Provost and Howe said Gilles Tremblay, who

came along a little later. According to them, the two Canadiens did it without hooking or holding, but by skating and checking.

Offensively, the only word to describe the Canadiens was awesome. The Richards and Dickie Moore played on one line and Jean Beliveau, Bernie Geoffrion and Bert Olmstead on another. All six made at least one all-star team between 1956-60; together they were on a total of 13. Moore won two scoring titles and Beliveau and Geoffrion one each. Beliveau won a Hart Trophy.

They were all different. Beliveau was grace personified and the Rocket fire. Geoffrion, who invented the full-swing slapshot, fired the puck harder than anyone in the league. The two left wings, Moore and Olmstead, were character players. Moore won a scoring title while he had a cast on a broken wrist. One night I saw him jump the boards at the Olympia in Detroit to go after a bunch of U.S. Marines who were giving him the business. Olmstead was tough and demanding; after he was traded to Toronto, Punch Imlach told me there'd be nights when the Leafs weren't playing well but Punch wouldn't go into the dressing room between periods. "They're more scared of Bert than they are of me," he explained.

The Canadiens also had the best special teams ever. Their power play was so good it made the league change the rules before the 1956-57 season. Minor penalties used to be served in full, but the Canadiens sometimes would score three times in two minutes with the man advantage. The new rule allowed the penalized player back on as soon as one goal was scored. The power play usually had Doug Harvey and Geoffrion on the points, with Beliveau and the Rocket in front of the net or just to the side and Olmstead or Moore working the corners. Individually, they were better than anyone they were going against, and they just played tic-tac-toe until they worked it around for a great chance.

The Canadiens got a lot of power-play chances. They had so much talent that they always seemed to have the puck. The people who have the puck don't take penalties; it's the people trying to get it who commit the fouls. On the other hand, when the Canadiens were shorthanded, they were better than anyone else in that situation. Provost once scored 30 goals in a season when that was really something, and Donnie Marshall, a defensive specialist, once had 22. Henri Richard would just skate with the puck, and nobody could get it away from him. As they used to say, he had more moves than a cat in a roomful of rocking chairs.

Running it all—even strength, power play or a man short—was Doug Harvey, the best defenceman of them all in the time I call, with no insult intended, B.O. (Before Orr). A great hockey team is like a great baseball team. It has to be strong through the middle. The Canadiens had Plante in goal, and they had terrific centres in Beliveau, Henri, Kenny Mosdell, Marshall and later Phil Goyette and Ralph Backstrom. But the glue was Harvey, because there's no way any team is going to stay on top for long without a great leader on defence. You see it over and over again: Bobby Orr in Boston, Denis Potvin with the Islanders, Paul Coffey in Edmonton.

Harvey was a great athlete. One year right after the Second World War, he played for the Canadiens' farm team in Buffalo, he played halfback and punted for the Big Four team in Montreal and he played minor-league baseball as a third baseman in the Braves' organization. He eventually chose hockey and won the Norris Trophy for top defenceman seven of its first nine years. He was the best I ever saw at controlling a game. He never panicked; hell, he was never even flustered. He would get the puck, skate behind his own net, take his time, look for daylight and hit the open man in full stride right on the blade of the stick—every time. He paced himself so well that I think he could have played 60 minutes in today's hockey with its 18 timeouts per game for TV commercials.

Doug also was a physical presence, a punishing body checker, although he wasn't what was called a policeman. He was too smooth for that. But he did, as they say, take care of business—and he had a real mean streak. One incident I remember involved the Canadiens and Rangers playing a weekend home-and-home series. On Saturday night in Montreal, with the Canadiens well ahead late in the game and just playing out the string, Red Sullivan checked Harvey heavily into the boards from behind. Doug wasn't hurt, but it could have been serious. The game was over before he could get even, but I knew he wouldn't forget.

The next night, Sullivan tried one of his pet plays early in the game. He would carry the puck over the blue line and skate right into the defenceman to tie him up while dropping the puck back to a trailing winger who should then have an opening. I was behind the play and the defenceman in front of it was Harvey. Suddenly, I saw Sullivan crumple to the ice in agony, and I knew Harvey had done something I couldn't see. To protect myself, I gave Doug a minor penalty, but if I had known what I found out later, it would have been two five-minute majors for spearing and deliberate injury, plus a game misconduct. Sullivan was rushed to hospital and operated on for a ruptured spleen. He remained in critical condition for a time and didn't play for three months.

After the game, the New York writers went to the Canadiens' dressing room, told Harvey how serious the injury was and asked him if he'd visit Sullivan before going back to Montreal. Said Doug, "I hope the son of a bitch dies. Put that in your papers." He and Sullivan had long been enemies for another reason. Plante was the first goalie to leave his crease and play the puck to help out his defenceman. Once he was away from the goal he was fair game for a check, but opposing players seldom went after him, with one exception. That was Sullivan, who would hit Plante every time. I saw nothing wrong with that; in fact, if I were coaching today, I'd tell my players to do the same thing, or at least to get between the goalie and the net to make it tough for him to get back. It could be worth a goal or two over a season.

But Harvey didn't want anyone messing with his goalie—or anyone else on the team, for that matter. The Canadiens had that great spirit and pride. It's become a tradition, reflected in the most famous sign in any dressing room in sport, surrounded by pictures of the team's dozens of Hall of Famers. The sign was there to motivate the talented youngsters Selke kept bringing in, one or two at a time, to renew the dynasty. The words are from "In Flanders Fields," written by the Canadian poet John McCrae during the First World War. They read:

"TO YOU FROM FAILING HANDS WE THROW THE TORCH; BE YOURS TO HOLD IT HIGH."

9

Hockey's Best Ever

When I was refereeing in the NHL in the 1950s, one question I was asked wherever I went was: "Who's the best? The Rocket or Gordie?" Maurice Richard of Montreal and Gordie Howe of Detroit were the most important individual reasons that decade was hockey's Golden Age. They are still the two greatest right wings of all time (sorry, Guy Lafleur and Mike Bossy fans). For 14 seasons their rivalry led off every Hot Stove League discussion and provoked heated arguments (and worse) wherever hockey fans gathered. I'd tell anyone who asked that Rocket Richard was the greatest goal scorer and most exciting player the world had ever seen. Then I'd say that Gordie Howe was the best all-around player in history. I would say they're two different people and nobody had the talent of Howe and nobody had the scoring ability of the Rocket. I'm not sure if I pleased everybody, or nobody, but it's the way I felt.

By the late 1960s, I had to change the answer if the question was about the greatest player ever. I had retired as an NHL referee before Bobby Orr arrived in Boston in the fall of 1966, but I saw him at his peak from the best seat in the house—the bird's-eye view from the broadcast booth, when I was doing color commentary and analysis on both television and radio. Being so far away seemed to slow the play down, and being overhead let you see things you never could at ice level. You had to sit in that seat to really appreciate the players with exceptional talent. They would do things you couldn't believe, nobody more than Orr, although both Wayne Gretzky and Mario Lemieux have been almost unbelievable more recently. But I'll still take Orr, Howe and Richard.

It seemed like Orr had 16 different speeds and used whatever one he needed. He had terrific moves with his head and shoulders, and he was fantastic with the puck. You would see a play develop in a certain way, and expect a certain thing to happen because it always did. But suddenly Orr would do something no one ever had; he'd do something you'd never seen. He was like a ballet dancer. He mesmerized me. He had everything, plus leadership. The Bruins were absolutely pathetic when he joined them at the age of 18, but after they got him some help, filled in some holes, they finished first or second the next eight years. They won two Stanley Cups and he was the playoff MVP both times. He made the second all-star team his first year and the first team the next eight. He won the Norris Trophy as best defenceman in the league eight years in a row. Above all, Orr was a leader and a great competitor. He had that winning temperament and, believe it or not, he was mouthy with officials on the ice. He wasn't an agitator like Ted Lindsay was, but like Lindsay he had to win.

I'm only sorry that Orr's knee problems cut his career to just 12 seasons, the last four hardly productive at all. The first time he underwent surgery, after he hurt a knee playing charity softball in Winnipeg, they hadn't perfected the operation. They kept trying to reconstruct his knees, but they never got it right, even after operating another half-dozen times. I could sympathize with him from my own experience.

Orr will be remembered as a great hockey player, of course. But more important was that he changed the way the game was played. Hockey no longer was a goalie, two defencemen and a forward line. Defencemen became offencemen, too, mobile skaters who followed the puck wherever it went. I remember Doug Harvey telling me that there was a time when Dick Irvin Sr. would fine a defenceman if he crossed the other team's blue line. Orr changed all that, making the game more entertaining and paving the way for players like Larry Robinson, Denis Potvin and Paul Coffey. Someone once asked Gordie Howe what Orr's best move was. "Just putting on those bleeping skates," he said.

Gordie knew about that. Over 26 seasons, he put on the skates more often than anyone in history—1,767 times in the regular season and another 157 in the playoffs. And those are just his NHL numbers; they don't include his years in the World Hockey Association. He was a marvel, playing until after he was 50. He and Doug Harvey were the best natural athletes I've known. Gordie took batting practice with the Detroit Tigers, and pounded balls out of Briggs Stadium. He hit golf balls a mile. I think he could have been heavyweight champion of the world if he'd taken up boxing.

On the ice, you always got the impression that he was playing within himself. He was tall and fluid, and his elbows gave him all the space he needed. If he'd played in the league the way it is today, he'd have had 1,000 goals, instead of 801, and Wayne Gretzky never would have caught him. But Gordie was a totally unselfish player. In 1952-53, when he had 49 goals with a few games to play, he had a clear breakaway with an empty net in front of him. He passed the puck to Alex Delvecchio, giving up No. 50, which only the Rocket had done at that time. A game or two later, he tipped in a drive from the point but the referee didn't see it and gave the goal to Red Kelly. Gordie never complained. It didn't mean that much to him.

Gordie also cared little about money. For years, Detroit general manager Jack Adams would hand him a blank contract and tell him to fill it in. Gordie always gave himself a raise of only $1,000, even after six scoring titles and six MVP awards. Adams kept telling him he was the highest-paid Red

Wing. When Bob Baun came to Detroit from Oakland, he told Howe he was a sucker because Baun was making about $67,000 per year and Howe only $45,000. Gordie wrote in "$100,000" on his next contract, but got it only after a lot of argument.

Adams always took the credit for finding and developing Gordie, but he wouldn't have had him if Frank Selke Sr. hadn't been such a nice man. Selke, working his last year for Conn Smythe before going to Montreal, went to scout the Morrison brothers in Omaha, where Gordie was just starting his career in 1945-46. On the way back to Toronto, he stopped off in Detroit to see Adams about the Morrisons, and then said, "You have a young fellow in Omaha named Gordon Howe. Have you got him on your protected list?" Adams said he didn't. Selke told him, "Well, you put him on your list before midnight tonight or he'll be on the Toronto Maple Leafs' list, we'll win the Stanley Cup and you'll be out of a job." If their roles had been reversed, you can bet Adams would have stolen Howe with no warning.

After he retired the first time at the age of 43, the Wings gave Howe a title and nothing to do. He said he was like a mushroom: "They keep me in the dark and every once in a while open the door to throw manure on me." He finally made some real money in the WHA, after signing with Houston so he could play with his sons, Mark and Marty. In 1973-74, when he was 45 years old, he weighed 206 pounds, exactly the same as when he was a Detroit rookie in 1946. He scored 100 points and was the league's MVP.

The next fall, Gordie and his boys played for the WHA allstars against the Soviet Union. I was watching on TV and in one of the games I saw a Russian take Mark into the corner and really cream him. I turned to my wife and said: "That is going to be evened up sometime. The old man's in this game." The puck went down to the other end, there was a stoppage of play and the camera moved back to centre ice where there was a Russian on his hands and knees crawling toward his bench. We didn't see what had happened, but I knew. I spoke to Gordie later and told him I was sure it was going to happen, but I didn't think that fast. "Red," he said, "in an international series, you don't get too many shots at it."

Gordie was mean. I remember he scored a milestone goal in Montreal, his 700th or something, and came back to the bench and said, "Now all I've got left to do tonight is get J.C. Tremblay." The next shift, he broke J.C.'s jaw. Nobody knew why. His wife, Colleen, explained one time: "Gordie doesn't elbow someone in the jaw out of anger. He does it to teach them a lesson if they've embarrassed him on the ice. He's a tremendously prideful person." Gordie generally had a reason. He always gave a receipt back for anything that happened to him. He could also fight. He went at it one night with Lou Fontinato and three uppercuts later the Rangers' tough guy was in the hospital with his battered mug on the cover of *Life*. Phil Watson, the New York coach, kept insisting to the the press that Gordie hadn't won the fight. "Oh, yeah?" said Gordie. "Well, I hope I lose 'em all that way."

Age hasn't mellowed him. A few years ago, I refereed at a fantasy camp in Brossard, across the river from Montreal. Fans paid to come and learn hockey from men who had played the game at the highest level. We divided them into teams, with each allowed to have two ex-pros. There was a regular schedule, with playoffs and even a miniature replica of the Stanley Cup. I was refereeing a semi-final game with Gordie and Bill Gadsby playing for one of the teams and they scored. This guy on the other team, a chronic complainer who was paying perhaps $2,500 for the privilege of being on the ice, huffed and puffed over to me before the faceoff and, pointing to Gordie, said, "We're only in the second period and already I've got two beefs against the big guy." I called Gordie over and repeated to him, "This guy says we're only in the second period and he's already got two beefs against you." Gordie said, "No kidding," and gave him a left hook that knocked him on his ass. Then he said, "Now he's got a hat trick."

The Rocket, on the other hand, did mellow after his retirement, although it took a while. When we started with old-timers' hockey, he was playing and he was every bit as competitive as ever. Part of our show, of course, was comedy —absurd penalties and so on. The Rocket would get mad at me. "Hockey's not a funny game," he'd say. "You shouldn't be doin' stuff like that." I'd tell him: "Rock, if you guys were good enough to play 60 minutes of hockey, you'd all still be in the NHL. But you can't, so I've got to entertain the people." He would never be convinced. Then he stopped playing, started officiating and stole all my gags.

There was nothing funny about the Rocket when he was playing. He was born to do one thing, and that was to score goals. He had the greatest desire and determination to do that I've ever seen, and he did it with more flair and drama than anyone before or since. He changed when he got out on the ice. He had an incredible focus. The first time Kenny Reardon, a teammate, scrimmaged against him, he recalls, "I see this guy skating at me with wild hair and eyes just out of the nuthouse." Harry Lumley, who played goal for several teams, once said the Rocket's eyes in the heat of a game were like a pair of headlights. In high gear, he moved like a runaway train and he could be almost unstoppable from the blue line in, no matter how much they interfered with him. He'd carry two guys on his back if he had to. If the Rocket were playing today, I think he'd score 100 goals every year because against some of these teams there'd be nights when he'd get five or six.

Because of the trouble he kept getting into, most people thought the Rocket was hard to handle. I don't buy that, and I knew him pretty well in those days. He just thought everyone who wasn't wearing a Canadiens' sweater was the enemy, including the officials. His coaches never had any difficulty with him, nor did his teammates. All he wanted was to score goals and when he felt he was being kept from that unfairly, he'd blow up. No player in history was held or hooked or high-sticked the way he was. He'd take it as long as he could, but then watch out! He had great individual pride, but he was also a tremendous team man. He loved to win. When his linemate, Elmer Lach, scored the overtime goal that beat Boston and won the Stanley Cup in 1953, he was so happy that he leaped at Elmer to give him a bear hug. He broke Elmer's nose and knocked him over backwards. They had to patch Elmer up before they could start celebrating.

Usually it was the Rocket who scored in overtime, which was used only in the playoffs back then. He had a remarkable six game-winning sudden-death goals during his career, and the first two I saw will remain in my mind forever. In 1951, at the end of my first season in the NHL, I was assigned to the first two games of the Canadiens-Red Wings semi-final series in Detroit. I was the standby for Bill Chadwick in the first game and it went into a fourth 20-minute overtime period before the Rocket shifted around Red Kelly, walked in and beat Terry Sawchuk for a 3-2 win. I refereed the second game, which was scoreless after regulation time and through two overtime periods. Then the Rocket shifted around Kelly almost identically and beat Sawchuk for a 1-0 victory.

He also did more than score goals to win that series. He got into a fight with Ted Lindsay and kayoed him with one punch. Lindsay went down cold as a mackerel and that took most of the steam right out of the whole Detroit team. The Canadiens won the series in six games, but went on to lose to Toronto in the final. All five games of that series went into overtime and guess who scored the goal that gave the Canadiens their only win?

I can hardly recall the Rocket ever starting a fight. But he finished almost every one he was in. One exception was a night in January, 1956, when the Canadiens were in New York and he clashed with Lou Fontinato at the Rangers' blue line. The Rocket very seldom lost a fight, but this time Fontinato really connected on his jaw. His arms went limp and his legs buckled, although he didn't go down. Fontinato, seeing he was out on his feet and defenceless, backed off and ended the fight after just the one punch. To this day, the Rocket claims he was blindsided by someone else, but I tell him, "Rock, there was only one other person in the vicinity, and that was me, and I sure as hell wasn't going to belt you."

The one criticism you would hear about him was that he didn't check. I used to tell the people making the noise that when a man could score 50 goals like the Rocket, he didn't have to check his man. His man had to check him. His man had to stay with him, he had to try to go wherever the Rocket went. If you could score goals like that, I'd tell them, I wouldn't want to see you in our end of the rink, either. The Rocket frustrated a lot of people. Hap Day told me the story of a playoff game he coached for the Maple Leafs at the Forum in March, 1944, when Richard scored all five goals as the Canadiens won 5-1. Bob Davidson, a rugged left wing, was the Rocket's check. When Hap got into the dressing room after the game, he said to Davidson, "I thought I told you to watch Richard tonight." Davidson said: "I did. He played a helluva game, didn't he?"

I was there for some of the Rocket's most memorable times, good and bad. I was refereeing in Toronto the night he scored his 324th goal to tie the career record of Nels Stewart, and I was refereeing a few days later, on November 8, 1952, when he scored his 325th at the Forum against Chicago's Al Rollins to set the new mark. I got the pucks from both those goals and gave them to him. He had tears in his eyes. I was involved in the Richard Riot game, of course. I also was on the ice in Toronto in November, 1957, when the Rocket went into the game leading the scoring race, at the age of 36. It was his last chance to win a title he had missed twice by one point—to

Max Bentley of Chicago in 1946-47 and to teammate Bernie Geoffrion in 1954-55. He fell over the skate blade of Marc Rheaume of the Maple Leafs and partially severed his Achilles tendon. Everyone thought he was through forever, but he returned four months later and scored twice in the first few minutes of his first game back. He never talked to anyone on the ice, especially officials. But after his first goal in that game, he was so happy that he skated by me and said, "Not bad for a rookie, eh?"

Dick Irvin put a poster up on the wall of the dressing room while he was coaching the Canadiens. It was a quotation from Abraham Lincoln: "I do the very best I know how—the very best I can—and I mean to keep on doing so until the end." The Rocket told me once, "I read that almost every game." After he came back from the Achilles tendon injury, the Rocket was a major part of three more Stanley Cup winners. He retired just before the 1961-62 season because he wasn't happy with his play—right after a training camp game in which he scored three goals.

The Rocket still has the magic he had when people would lean forward in their seats every time he came on the ice and stand up every time he touched the puck. They didn't know what was going to happen; they just knew something was. The Forum fans had a love affair with him. After every goal, even meaningless ones, there would be long cheering, and then newspapers, overshoes and hats would be thrown. There'd be a delay to clean the ice and the Rocket would skate around looking a little embarrassed.

I travel with him across the country now and they still remember him, and not just people from our age group. Kids whose parents weren't born when he finished in the NHL want his autograph. Henri Richard once was asked who he thought was better, his brother or Gordie Howe. "I'm not going to answer that," he said, "but I'll tell you one thing. If they were playing in two different rinks across the street from each other, the building Maurice was in would be the one that was full."

Let's give the last word to an unlikely source. One night in Toronto late in 1954, the Rocket had a terrible stick-swinging fight with Bob Bailey. After we got peace restored, I threw him out of the game and an ugly mob of really angry fans was lying in wait for him. Conn Smythe, who ran the Maple Leafs and had no time for the Canadiens in general and the Rocket in particular, came rushing over and I thought, "Oh, oh, here we go." But what Smythe did was urge the police to "protect that man. He's the greatest hockey player in the world."

10

Storey-Book Characters

N o one ever played harder on the ice than Milt Schmidt did
from the mid-1930s to the mid-1950s—19 years in all
with three seasons lost to World War II service—and no one
was a nicer guy off it. He's the best all-around centre I've ever
seen. He had size and strength and speed, and great leadership qualities. He'd play it any way you wanted. And he was
tough, more guts than a canal horse. No wonder they wor-
shipped him in Boston for 16 years as a player. He wasn't as
successful after he moved upstairs to coach the Bruins in 11
different seasons and serve as general manager for five more
years, but they still loved him.

His Hall of Fame career speaks for itself, along with the
two Stanley Cups the Bruins won before he went into the
service for three years during World War II. How tough was
Milt? One night he fell on a skate and cut his rear end badly.
He had them sew him up and went back out on the ice. The
first time he was hit, the stitches popped, but he said, "To hell
with it," and kept going. Every time he'd leave the bench for a
shift, the trainer had to get some towels and soak up a pool
of blood.

Milt had a longtime feud with Black Jack Stewart, whose
nickname tells you all you need to know about him. I was
doing a Bruins-Blackhawks game in Chicago during the 1951-
52 season and Stewart high-sticked Milt and ripped his nose

open. Milt went away for repairs and I gave Stewart the automatic five-minute major. I got that straightened out and came back to the faceoff circle. Who was standing there waiting but Milt. He had a band aid covering this dreadful cut. I told him, "I've just given Stewart five minutes for deliberately injuring you and you're making a fool out of me. Get your ass out of here." He didn't want to go but finally did —under protest. I looked over a couple of minutes later and they had three guys trying to tape him up to stop the bleeding.

Milt also had an explosive temper when he was riled. One night in Detroit I gave him a penalty he didn't like and he threw his stick or something. That's a misconduct, but knowing Milt, I didn't give the signal right away. I went over to the penalty box and told the timekeeper, "He's got two minutes for whatever and a 10-minute misconduct, but don't announce it until I get out of here." I was in the corner of the rink when the announcement was made and Milt was fit to be tied. Not only was he in the box for 12 minutes, but the misconduct carried an automatic $25 fine. When his time was up, he came out still steaming but under control. He asked me where I'd be having a beer after the game. That would be the Bagley Bar, as always. He said, "Don't you dare move until I get there."

I was sitting on a stool and I heard BANG as the front door slammed open. I looked up and it was Milt. He went to the back, sat down, called the bartender over and said, "Russ, give me a double shot of Scotch, give me a beer chaser, give me two of your best cigars and charge it all to that big bastard up at the front." I was watching him in the big mirror behind the bar and I didn't say anything as he downed the Scotch and the chaser and lit up one of the cigars. He called the bartender over again and gave exactly the same order. I was still watching him in the mirror and he caught my eye. He'd played a game, he hadn't eaten at all and the Scotch and the beer were having an effect. Suddenly he grinned, picked up what was left of his drink, came over and said, "I guess that's enough of that shit." I looked at him and asked, "Milt, what was on your mind anyway?" He said, "You cost me 25 bucks tonight and I made up my mind I was gonna drink every bit of it and you were gonna pay for it." That was about the way it worked out.

Milt used to have some great duels with Elmer Lach of the Canadiens. Each centred the best line in the league—Milt from 1936-42 on the Kraut Line with Bobby Bauer and Woody Dumart, all boys of German extraction from the Kitchener-Waterloo area of Ontario; and Elmer from 1943-48 with Rocket Richard and Toe Blake. That was the Punch Line, which set scoring records that stood until the schedule was lengthened. In 50 games in 1944-45, they combined for 105 goals and were 1-2-3 in the scoring race, with Lach leading with 80 points; the Rocket second with 73, including 50 goals; and Toe third with 67 points. Elmer told me years later that Toe could have scored 60 goals that season, instead of 29, if he'd cashed in his chances.

Elmer wasn't strong enough to muscle Milt, but he had some great tricks. When he was back-checking, he'd flick the toe of his stick into the calves of the man he was chasing. It was almost impossible for a referee to spot, and it hurt like hell. Even cuter was the trick he'd use on people swinging around the goal in front of him. I'd see guys fall down in pain and couldn't figure out what was happening. Elmer and the net were usually blocking my view so I wheeled off to the side and saw it perfectly the next time. He was lifting his stick up between their legs and giving them a couple of little taps. That would destroy anybody's concentration.

Kenny Mosdell also had some wars with Milt. They were of a size and there was no backing away in either of them. Mosdell played one season as the Rocket's centre after Elmer and before Henri Richard. He was one of the most under-rated players in history. He came into the league with the old

Brooklyn Americans as a kid in 1941 and joined the Canadiens after two years in the service during the war. At some
point, he had a falling out with Frank Selke Sr. and was
dispatched to Chicago. He was there for only 25 games in
1956-57 and then quit in disgust, fed up with his teammates
singing in the shower after a defeat. You wouldn't find a guy
doing that today. The Blackhawks' voices were in good shape
since they lost 39 of 60 games that season. Mosdell came back
to Montreal, joined the senior Royals and made it back to the
Canadiens the next season.

Ted Lindsay also had some great duels with the Rocket and
his line. He was the best left wing I ever saw, even though we
never got along. Lindsay didn't have any more use for officials
than he did for the opposition. If I was starting a team
tomorrow and could get him in his prime, he'd be my first pick
for left wing. He wasn't a big man, but he was fearless, he was
talented and he had the same kind of desire to win as the
Rocket had to score goals. But in his own way, he could be a
joker, too.

I remember being in Chicago to do a game being televised
on a U.S. national network, which was—and still is—a rare
thing. In those days, when the teams and officials came out
on the ice to warm up, they stayed, so there was no time to
change any of the arrangements. The first thing I saw was a
microphone in the penalty box, sort of sticking out toward the
ice. I went over and asked about it, and this guy who turned
out to be the TV producer said, "Today we would like you to
announce the penalties through the microphone so that the
millions of fans watching this game will know what you're
doing out there." There were a lot of times when *I* didn't know
what I was doing, but he insisted it would be all right.

I told him that he was taking a chance with an open mike,
hockey players being hockey players. He said: "Oh, the boys
know they're on TV today. They'll be on their best behavior."
I rolled my eyes at him and tapped the boards, like for lots of

luck. I started skating around, and, when I saw Lindsay go past the microphone and do a double take, I knew we were in trouble. He had a bad mouth at the best of times, and he could be really foul when he put his mind to it. I knew he wasn't going to let an opportunity like this go by.

The game started, the puck went into the opposition's end and Lindsay took a baseball swing, I mean a real baseball swing, at the first guy he saw in the corner. There were 18,000 people in the building who saw it, and a few million more watching on TV who saw it, and since I was having a good day, I saw it, too. Ordinarily, you had to coax Lindsay off the ice after giving him a penalty, but not this time. The race was on to see which of us got to that microphone first. Lindsay won, and it was 10 years before they put it back on again.

Bob Goldham, the defenceman with whom I'd played lacrosse in Hamilton, Ontario, told me that one day just after he joined the Red Wings from Chicago, the rest of the team went to a Roman Catholic Mass. Bob was a Protestant, but he tagged along. He was in a pew beside Lindsay. With everybody else kneeling down praying, he looked up and saw the head honcho in the front with the gold headgear and golden robes. Bob was impressed and wanted to know what was going on, so he gave Lindsay a little shot in the ribs. Lindsay turned around, a little annoyed, and asked, "What do you want?" Bob said, "Who's that guy up there?" Lindsay looked up and said, "I don't know, Bob, but you can bet your ass he's no minor leaguer."

I'm happy to say that Lindsay and I buried the hatchet— and not in each other's heads—at the opening of the new Hockey Hall of Fame in Toronto in 1993. He gave me a big hug and said: "It's over, Red. It lasted too long." That was one of the nicest things that ever happened to me.

Another guy I got to know and like after spending years trying to figure him out was Eddie Shack. He was one of the most entertaining guys ever to play in the NHL, but it wasn't always like that. When he came up with the Rangers he was shy because he couldn't read or write, and he became the butt of a lot of jokes. Eddie wasn't happy with this treatment and finally decided that if the NHL wanted a clown, he'd be the best one anyone had ever seen. He came out of his shell, became Eddie the Entertainer, had a 17-year career with six teams and won four Stanley Cup rings with the Toronto Maple Leafs in the 1960s.

When he got the puck, the fans would yell, "Clear the track, here comes Shack," and he often didn't seem to be particular who he hit. He'd just bang into anyone in the road. One night in Eddie's first season with Toronto, he knocked down one of the Leafs. Teammate Bert Olmstead, who had little patience for nonsense, spoke to Eddie on the bench. "Eddie, what's the color of your sweater?" "Blue." "Eddie, what's the color of my sweater?" "Blue." "Eddie, what's the color of the sweaters of those guys we're playing against?" "White." "Then for God's sake, Eddie, stop knockin' down the blues. That's our side."

Eddie still entertains the people as one of the most popular attractions at old-timers' games. I have a lot of admiration and respect for him. He overcame his early handicaps so well that he might be the richest NHL player from the good old days, many times a millionaire. Don't let anyone ever tell you that you can't make good in Canada.

I remember a player with the Toronto Argos who also overcame obstacles to have a career in football. He was a lineman named Chuck McLean, called Bruiser, out of Queen's University where he had been the collegiate heavyweight champion and he was a frightening guy. He had arms that hung down to his knees, wasn't exactly handsome and proved to be a better boxer than football player. Lew Hayman, the coach, just a little guy about 5'7" or so, decided to cut him. He went over and asked him, "How much do you weigh?", figuring Bruiser would say 210 or 215 and he could say that wasn't heavy enough. Well, Bruiser looked him in the eye, and said: "I weigh 240. What do you weigh?" Hayman turned and walked away. Bruiser made the team.

He and I were roommates and we were asked by Nat Turofsky, who with his brother Lou did all of the photography for the Toronto sports teams, to pose for some publicity pictures at Varsity Stadium on a Friday afternoon, just before we were going to get a train to Montreal for a game the next day. Nat wanted one of Bruiser diving on a loose ball. This wasn't a smart thing to ask of a lineman who never touched the ball and wasn't familiar with it. Bruiser dove and dislocated his shoulder. I was in a panic, but he told me to help him get dressed and keep my mouth shut or he'd break my neck. He was a strong enough guy that I wasn't about to argue. We got to Montreal but Bruiser was in such pain he couldn't sleep, could hardly even rest. Nobody knew about it, so he couldn't even ask for a shot. He played the whole game and when the doctor came through the dressing room afterward to check on any injuries, Bruiser asked him to take a look at the shoulder. "On the last tackle, somethin' snapped," he said.

I don't know how he stood the pain, but he was the gutsiest man I ever knew. He was to prove that again later, during World War II. He was a pilot in Malta and was shot down in flames. The late Buzz Beurling, an early RCAF ace, spotted him and reported to the base. They went out and rescued Bruiser, but he had burned for 10,000 feet coming down, almost his entire body. He had three years of skin grafts and other treatment in hospital. I met him on the street in Montreal after the war and we talked for a while. He was sort of jittery on his feet and explained: "Red, I can't stand for too long. I can't stand in one position. I had to give up my dentistry practice because of that."

Not all of the "storey-book characters" actually played sports. Early in the war years, after the Argos had won a game in Ottawa on a Saturday afternoon, we were having a private celebration in the Grill downstairs in the Chateau Laurier while waiting to take the midnight train back to Toronto. We were having a helluva time, just the players and the people we'd invited. The maître d' came in and told us there was a gentleman at the door making a request to join us, a fine fellow from another country who liked the look and sound of our party. We said to send him in and he turned out to be a fairly stout man with a ruddy face. He thanked us in his English accent, and we said, "Sit down, you old bugger, and when it comes time to buy a round don't run for the can." He was there for three hours, bought his share and laughed at the insults. We called him all sorts of names and finally he stood up and said: "Ladies and gentlemen, I'd like to thank you very much for hosting me here tonight. But now I must beg my leave." We told him he wasn't such a bad old guy, thanked him for buying some drinks and said goodbye. A while later the maître d' came back and asked us if we knew who our guest had been. We didn't, and he told us: "That was Lord Beaverbrook, and he said it's the best night he's ever had in his life. He said that's the first time he's been at a party where nobody knew who he was and he really enjoyed himself." Beaverbrook, a newspaper magnate in Britain, had been born Max Aitken in New Brunswick. He was at that time Minister for Aircraft Production in Winston Churchill's cabinet, and was in Ottawa on war business.

I had another indirect brush with nobility years later in Maple Leaf Gardens. Col. W.A.H. MacBrien was one of the directors of the team and a rabid fan who would get on me every time I refereed there. Once at the end of a period he came down from his box seat and handed me an NHL rule book as I left the ice. Another night he had the former governor-general, Earl Alexander, as his guest for one of those games in which there was one rhubarb after another, with almost every call being argued. I went off after the second period and MacBrien threw his program right in my face. I stopped and looked at him. "For God's sake, Colonel, when you're sitting next to a gentleman, at least try to act like one." One of those old soldiers smiled. Years later, MacBrien came into the referees' room before a game and told me he was retiring as a Maple Leafs' director. "Red, it's been a good feud," he said. "I'm sorry it's over but it's time." We shook hands and I went out to start the game. The first penalty I called was against the Leafs and from his box came a bellow: "Storey, you're a bum."

I have a different read than most people on Harold Ballard, who wound up running Maple Leaf Gardens after Conn Smythe left and Stafford died. I liked him and even admired him. You know, any time he made an outrageous statement, it was because the team was going bad and he was trying to shake things up and take the heat off the players. Everything he did was calculated. The players might moan and groan, but you never heard of a salary holdout in Toronto. He gave them what they asked for. His hockey people, like Punch Imlach and John Brophy, used to tell me he never interfered with them. I'd hear people say Harold was an S.O.B. and this and that, and I'd ask them, "What do you think of King Clancy?" They'd say: "Oh, King. Greatest guy that ever lived. A fine gentleman. Very intelligent." I'd say, "Isn't it amazing he'd choose Harold Ballard as his lifelong friend?" Then I'd add: "You've got a lot of friends. You know any of them who gave $100 million to charity? 'Cause that's what Harold did."

Another guy I liked who took much of the same kind of heat as Ballard for being a little eccentric was Eddie Shore, who owned and ran the Springfield team in the American Hockey League after a great NHL career as a defenceman with Boston. He was a tough competitor and one night in Cleveland he went crazy when I disallowed what would have been the winning goal. Paul Bibeault was in net for Cleveland and the puck hit him square in the forehead. This was before goalies wore masks. His eyes crossed and he started falling forward, out cold. I blew the whistle, but the puck popped up into the air, hit Bibeault's back as he was falling and went into the net. I waved it off. Eddie was beside himself, but I told him, "No one's going to score on an unconscious goalie as long as I'm refereeing." Eddie kept raising hell, but I finally got out of there and went to New York. At about five o'clock in the morning I was sound asleep and the phone rang. It was a guy from the press and he wanted to know what I was going to do about the stuff that Shore was saying, that I stole a game from him and so on. I told the guy I didn't give a damn what Shore was saying, and the next time I saw Eddie, I started to give him hell. "You know damn well that was no goal." He grinned. "Yeah," he said, "but look at all the publicity I gave you." Of course, it was the wrong kind.

Eddie had a handle on most of hockey, but he could never figure out goalkeepers. He devised really weird drills for them that didn't work, never realizing that they are truly a breed apart. They were all pretty good guys, once you realized that most of them were frustrated because they couldn't skate or play well enough to be forwards and defencemen or had become goalies because they were the smallest guys around. A lot of them resented it and today in old-timers' hockey, you won't find a happier guy than a goalie who gets a chance to play up front.

That may explain in part why Jacques Plante of the Canadiens became a wanderer, playing the puck behind the net and even into the corners. He also invented the mask, which I thought was great. I had a soft spot for goalies because I'd seen so many of them hurt and I was all for anything that helped them. Plante was strange at times, and never more than in Toronto, where he hated playing. He had a bronchial condition and wouldn't stay with the team at the Royal York Hotel, which he thought caused it. Instead, he'd bunk down at the Westbury. One night, Toe Blake found Plante in the dressing room before the game, hacking and coughing and in no shape to play. "Didn't you stay at the Westbury?" the coach asked. Plante said he had, "but I dreamed I was at the Royal York."

The Maple Leafs always had great goalies. Johnny Bower had a marvellous poke check. I see guys come in on net now and they do a dipsy doodle and score. With Johnny, they'd have been on their ass in the corner. He'd not only check the puck, but he'd trip you at the same time. As long as he touched the puck, it was legal. Turk Broda was a great, great, great playoff goaltender. There used to be a rule that a goalie couldn't come out and argue about any referee's decision. One night I was standing in the circle beside his net and out of the corner of my eye, I saw him coming from the net to talk to me. He wanted to complain, like they all did, about being bumped by opposition forwards. I started screaming: "Turk, you can't come near me, don't talk to me. Go away." He kept coming, but at the last minute dropped to his hands and knees and started to dust off the red spot in the circle. He never said a word. I guess my warning saved him.

I wish Glenn Hall could teach all of the goaltenders in hockey how to play the game, instead of just in Calgary for the Flames. He was the first one to use the butterfly style, which today allows too many goals to get between goalies' legs as they go down. It's one reason why I think goaltending is weaker than it used to be. Hall always covered that hole with his stick. Gump Worsley, who also did some coaching, showed me something about the butterfly once. "Spread your legs like this, and then try to get them back together," he said. "You can't do it. You can't move. But you can't tell them. They won't listen."

Gump was a character. I refereed junior games around Montreal when he was so small he used the grab the crossbar to swing from side to side, just like a monkey. One night I got into New York from Syracuse and went down to a bar near the

Piccadilly Hotel, where we stayed. I was sitting in a corner about two o'clock in the morning, taking it easy because I was working the next night, just a sandwich and a couple of beers. I looked over at the bar and thought, "That looks like the Gumper," and I went over. He said he was glad to have the company and kept drinking his V.O. Canadian whisky. At about four o'clock, I told him that perhaps it was none of my friggin' business, but he had a big game the next night and maybe he should get to bed. "Red, you're right," he said. "It's none of your friggin' business." He stopped 53 shots, allowed only one goal and the Rangers won. I was just leaving the ice when he was introduced as the No. 1 star. He skated the usual little circle in front of the bench and then began chasing me, yelling, "You friggin' dummy, you didn't know what you were talkin' about, did you?"

One of the guys who played on defence in front of Gump was Lou Fontinato, who wasn't afraid of anything except a fine. He was a tight man with a buck from the start. During his first year in the league, I was refereeing a game against the Red Wings in New York and Marty Pavelich kept goading Lou into some pretty stupid penalties. Every time he would try to retaliate for something Pavelich did, he'd get caught. After about the fourth penalty, Lou came over and said, "Red, will you stop that guy from needling me into penalties?" The only player allowed to speak to the referee is the team captain, which was not Fontinato, so I had to give him a misconduct. That meant an automatic $25 fine and as I skated toward the penalty box, I saw his gloves and stick fly into the air. He got even madder when his teammates on the bench doubled up in laughter. They knew how he felt about money.

Fernie Flaman was a tough defenceman for 17 seasons in a Hall of Fame career with the Bruins and Maple Leafs. One night in the Boston Garden we had an odd episode. I was in the face-off circle ready to go and Fernie skated over. He just looked at me, not saying anything. The crowd started to clap for action but he just stood there. He pushed his chest out at me, so I did the same. We were both stubborn buggers and neither of us was moving. Finally, we were nose to nose and I said, "What the hell do you want?" He said, "I don't want nothin'." Well, why was he just standing there? He said, "I got the worst cold in Boston and I'm standin' here until you catch it." I laughed and told him: "That's the one I left here three weeks ago. I'm glad it was you that got it."

I'll always remember Marcel Pronovost as the guy who got caught on his own dive, rather than for playing on five Stanley Cup winners in Detroit and Toronto. One night with the Red Wings he skated in and split the defence, lost the puck and took the big dive. I mean, it was a huge dive. The only problem was he turned his head to make sure I was watching, and he didn't get it turned back fast enough. He landed on his face and cut his forehead for about 20 stitches. I skated over and told him, "Not only did you get cut, there's no penalty." He knew it and didn't argue too much.

I never had much to do with coaches. I didn't go near the benches during games unless there was a real good reason for it. Coaches weren't going to contribute anything to what I was trying to do. Dick Irvin Sr. of the Canadiens was the one man who knew every rule in the book. Most players knew very little and most coaches not much more. Dick was always thinking up new problems to stump referees. One day he asked me, "What would you do if I sent out my players with two sticks each?" I told him I wouldn't start the game. He said I'd have to because there was nothing in the rules about it. I thought for a while, and finally told him: "I'll handle it when it happens. But, Dick, you're doing such a lousy job with one stick, I wouldn't try two."

Eddie Powers Sr., who had been one of the greatest lacrosse players in Canadian history, was the most demanding coach I ever played for in any sport. Eddie Jr., who later refereed with me in the NHL, and I were playing lacrosse with the Orillia Terriers one summer in the late 1930s. The team wasn't going too well under Bucko McDonald and management decided to keep him as a player but bring in a new coach. We didn't know who it would be but we had an idea. Although I was a Protestant, I drove over to the shrine at Midland with Eddie Jr. six days in a row. He was lighting candles and praying his father wouldn't get the job. We went back to our rooming house the sixth day and I had my back to the door as we were having a beer. Eddie looked past me and said, "I'll never pray to St. Peter again as long as I live." I turned around and Eddie Sr. was standing there. Eddie Jr. pulled out a suitcase and started to pack. "My old man's too tough for me to play for," he said. But he stayed, his dad whipped the team into shape and we came within one goal of beating St. Catharines that season. They went on to win the Mann Cup, the national championship.

11

The Fighting Men

O ne thing I've noticed over the years about the truly great players in any team sport is that they seldom fight. They save all their energy for playing. When I was officiating in the NHL in the 1950s, the superstars took care of themselves. Rocket Richard, Gordie Howe, Ted Lindsay, Doug Harvey and Milt Schmidt were among the toughest guys I've ever known. Then came the so-called policemen or enforcers, who could play at least a little hockey, to protect and set an example for their teammates—Lou Fontinato, Reggie Fleming, Howie Young, John Ferguson and, more recently, Bob Probert come to mind. Finally, today we have the goons, who sit on the bench until a fight seems to be called for, play for 10 seconds, brawl for 20 seconds more and then are through for the night—and probably for a week. I'm not going to give them any publicity by naming them. I'll just say that even boxers have to fight three-minute rounds.

The difference between a policeman and a goon is that the former is on the ice to settle fights, the latter to start them. Winning teams do need some muscle. If some of your most skillful players are small, you must prevent their being mugged on the ice. That was the role filled by Dave Semenko in the 1980s in Edmonton, perhaps the last dynasty hockey will ever see in today's expanded, watered-down game. Semenko's physical presence and the respect he earned made room for Wayne Gretzky, Glenn Anderson, Jari Kurri and the Oilers' other speedsters. A team without some muscle is simply too vulnerable in today's game. Its skill players would take too much of a beating to continue to win consistently.

The first of the modern policemen was probably Butch Bouchard of the Canadiens. He was normally quiet and easygoing but when a fight started, he would be there to finish it. He developed a technique that has been widely imitated. He would grab the opponent by the sweater and pull it over his head, pinning his arms, which made it a one-way fight. Bouchard's role was a key one on the Canadiens who, even though they had scrappers like Richard and Harvey, always had a number of small, swift forwards.

Policemen like Bouchard and those who followed him were usually no special problem for the officials. They would drop their sticks in a fight and go at it with their fists. They earned respect. The real troublemaker, and too often that includes today's goons, tends to use the stick as a weapon. He's most often a fringe player, not good enough to play in the NHL on talent alone, so he feels he can't afford to lose any fight. Sometimes he uses his stick to try to make sure he wins. Officials can't stand him, because he's also the guy who protests the loudest and carries on the longest when he gets a penalty. He deserves no respect.

Fighting has always been part of hockey, even before Conn Smythe managed the Toronto Maple Leafs to seven Stanley Cups in three decades with a philosophy that included as its cornerstone the words, "If you can't lick 'em in the alley, you can't lick 'em on the ice." In the early days, a player literally had to be able to fight his way into the league and keep fighting to stay there. That has changed, and one of the reasons is the universal use of helmets and the number of face visors in the league. You can break your hands if you're stupid enough to hit someone up around the head, so there's a lot of grabbing, pushing and dancing. Fights just don't exist as I knew them. I remember crisp, sharp punching with both hands and not the scrums we see today.

John Ferguson of the Canadiens was a throwback to those days. After an unprecedented run of five straight Stanley Cup victories from 1956-60, Frank Selke Sr. saw his team bow out three years in a row in the first round of the playoffs. They finished in first place in two of those seasons but their under-sized forwards became worn down by springtime. Before his last season as GM, 1963-64, Selke bought Ferguson from Cleveland of the American Hockey League to add some toughness. He was probably the best fighter the Canadiens have ever had. He took the fear away from his teammates and he had other things going for him. He had some natural ability, and he had the same kind of desire to win as the Rocket. Later, he even proved to be too competitive for old-timers' hockey and had to give it up.

Fergy scored 145 goals in 500 regular-season games, and another 20 in 85 playoff games, decent production by the standards of the day. More important, however, the Canadiens won the Stanley Cup five times in his eight years in the NHL. In 1965, his second season, Ferguson kayoed Chicago's Eric Nesterenko with one punch in the early minutes of the seventh and deciding game of the final. The Blackhawks lost most of their steam and the Canadiens romped 4-0 for their first Cup victory in five years. Fergy's secret was that he would always fight with his back to the boards. He would dig his rear foot into the wood just above the ice surface, giving him far greater leverage than his opponent who had his skates on the ice. That was a trick discovered by Lionel Conacher, who was a professional boxer in addition to starring in several other sports.

The best fight—or the worst, depending on your point of view—I ever saw in sports didn't take place in the NHL. It came in the old Quebec senior league, which was just a step below the NHL in those days. This night, Sherbrooke was playing in Quebec City with Kenny Mullins and me as the referees. The teams were bitter rivals and trouble broke out when Ivan Irwin of Sherbrooke came to the defence of a teammate who had been involved in a skirmish with Dean McBride of Quebec.

McBride turned on Irwin and high-sticked him in the face, splitting his lip clean through so that you could see his teeth behind it. That started the battle. Players from both teams formed a circle around them, and Mullins and I decided to let them settle it themselves. They fought for a good 10 minutes, really fought, I mean sledgehammer blows. When one would go down from a punch, the other would wait until he got up and away they'd go again. They were a couple of heavyweights and they just pounded each other until McBride went down exhausted and Irwin fell on top of him. Mullins and I stepped in and all we had to do was say, "That's enough." Irwin had the split lip, a partially torn ear and a lot of lumps. McBride could hardly see, his face was so puffed up. If I'd had to award a decision, I'd have given it to Irwin, but not by much. He played in 155 games spread over five seasons with the Canadiens and Rangers, but McBride never made it to the NHL.

Irwin was the best fighter I ever saw in hockey. I never saw him lose one in any league he played in. He was the first guy I knew who didn't have palms in his gloves. He cut them out so he could grab your stick or sweater and nobody could see it. Others did the same thing later, notably Carl Brewer of the Maple Leafs. Ivan's also one of the nicest guys you'd ever want to meet, manager of a senior citizens' home in Ajax, Ontario, the last I heard. He plays a big role in old-timers' hockey and if you ever meet him, be careful how you shake with him. He laughs all the time, but he has the biggest hands I've ever seen. He told me later that even if Mullins and I hadn't stepped in that night, it wouldn't have mattered. "Neither of us could have lifted a finger," he explained. "I've never been through anything like that in my lifetime, but that's the way we were then."

Lou Fontinato was brought up by the Rangers in 1954-55 to give the team some backbone. We ended up sitting together one night at a basketball game in Madison Square Garden and I said to him: "Lou, what is the matter with you? Every damn game I have with you, you're in a brawl. We can never have a pleasant evening with you on the ice." He told me he knew why the Rangers had hired him, which was to fight. "But I'm gonna tell you something," he added. "Everyday I'm learnin' a little more how to play hockey and some day I'll be a hockey player." He was the only man I ever saw in the NHL who would be out on the ice between periods trying to perfect his skating and working on other little things. When he was traded to the Canadiens in the early 1960s, he didn't fight as much and developed into a pretty darn good defenceman before he suffered a serious neck injury and retired.

One of the best fighters I ever saw was Adam Brown, a journeyman forward with the Red Wings, Blackhawks and Bruins. Harry Watson, who played on Stanley Cup winners with the Leafs in the late 1940s, could duke it out pretty well but only if he was mad, so opposing coaches always told their teams not to wake him up. Boston's Milt Schmidt was tough and a great centre; Dave Schultz of the Flyers, of more recent times, was a great battler, but not that good at hockey. One of the best ongoing series of fights was between Ted Harris of Montreal and Orland Kurtenbach of the Rangers. I wouldn't have wanted either one of them mad at me.

Of course, there were other guys who couldn't really fight but thought they could, or should. I hadn't been in the league long enough to have seen a real brawl when I was given a game between the Rangers and Chicago in New York. Gus Kyle of the Rangers, a huge defenceman, tangled with Doug Bentley of the Hawks, a small forward. We got them separated, but Kyle kept waltzing around telling Bentley what he was going to do to him. Doug was mad, too, but Kyle was doing all the talking. This phony war must have lasted close to five minutes. All this time, Charlie Rayner in the Rangers' nets was leaning on his stick looking as if he'd like a book to read. Finally, Charlie became absolutely bored with Kyle's monologue, skated out, grabbed his arm, pointed him at Bentley and said, "Gus, for the luvva Mike, if you're gonna hit him, hit him." All the players laughed and we had no more trouble.

I'm certainly not against a tough hockey game. Rough hockey does not have to mean brutal hockey and, with a very few exceptions, in the days of the six-team league it didn't. I am against the kind of goons who have come into the NHL lately. I don't think there should be any room for them in the game. These guys are there purely to fight. I think there should be a rule that if a goon comes out at the end of a period or the end of a game, and then the other team sends out its goon, the referee should have the privilege of throwing them both out before he drops the puck. Make it clear that nobody's going to cause that kind of trouble. Of course, today's fights generally are half wrestling and half dancing— and practically no fisticuffs. To tell the truth, it's usually a huge exaggeration to call it a fight. They grab a sweater and battle, or try to, with one hand.

A more serious problem is that, except for occasional short crackdowns, the rules against hooking, holding and interference aren't being enforced and there is much too much stickwork in the game. There's very little room today for the little guys with talent, the Henri Richards, Stan Mikitas, Camille Henrys, Dickie Duffs and so on. I think eventually things will reach the point where the fans will sour on the style of hockey being presented now. The main thing that sets hockey apart from all other sports is the fact that you wear skates while playing it. You can skate faster than you can run. But the NHL game seems to have become determined to reduce the value of that strong point.

The trouble with hockey today is that we now have a whole generation of players, owners and referees who have never seen the game played the way it should be played. The players are wearing more protective equipment than ever, which makes them feel safe and secure. Thus, sticks keep coming up higher and skills keep getting lower. There are, or should be, only two functions for a hockey stick: stick on stick and stick on puck.

Tiger Williams, who was a willing brawler himself for 14 seasons in the NHL, sees fighting as simply another tactic. "It's like slowing the game down if the game isn't going the way you want it to. You try to alter the flow of the game by engaging in a fight with their so-called tough guy. It's an intimidation factor to give your team an edge." Williams, however, adds, "Too many guys want to fight today just to make the highlight clips. Fights are staged now."

That can be a dangerous business, as I know from personal experience. When I was playing lacrosse in Montreal in 1942, we weren't drawing very good crowds, which meant some nights we weren't getting paid. Before one game, I got the teams together and said: "We'll have a fake fight, everybody swinging at each other, a real free-for-all. We'll make it look like the punches are landing, but they'll be just missing. The fans will love it and after that we'll have big crowds." They all thought this was a great idea, so we set the whole thing up and as soon as the game was on, the fight started. It was the best act I've ever seen in my life, haymakers being thrown all over the floor. Two guys had hold of me when all of a sudden I saw Russ Wheaton, a goaltender who weighed about 220 pounds, charging at me. He was one brick shy of a full load at the best of times, and I remembered that he was the only sonofabitch who wasn't at the meeting. He didn't know this was all a fake and he almost killed me. That was the end of the planned fights.

Bob Gainey, the coach of the Dallas Stars, had it about

right when he said that hockey can stand fighting that erupts because there's no other outlet for frustration, anger or emotion between two players. What he doesn't like are the instigated fights, the ones that come from players being provoked or intimidated deliberately. But the very fact of fighting leads to an atmosphere in which the huge talents that fans are paying $20 and $25 and more to see don't get a chance to do what they do best. Ugliness is added to a beautiful game in which speed and grace should count the most.

Apologists for fighting, including my friend Don Cherry and NHL officials like vice-president Brian Burke, agree with Gainey that it provides a safety valve. If it weren't for fighting, their argument goes, there would be many more stick assaults. The problem, of course, is that we seem to have the worst of all possible worlds. We still have senseless fighting and we still have mindless stick crimes like spearing.

I don't really think there's going to be a change any time soon—not as long as the league is run, and most of the clubs are owned, by men who have never been on skates in their lives.

I'm about a year old here, with my mother in front of our house on Tiffin Street in Barrie. Ma was the most courageous woman I've ever known, keeping our family together during the Great Depression.

I'm posing here with my sister Irene, who became an Olympic-calibre runner and was largely responsible for my career in sports, seeing athletic potential in me when no one else did.

I'm about two years old here. I guess I climbed up on the chair for a better view of the wide world out there, which I began to experience in 1936 in Toronto, playing football with the Argos.

BARRIE CAGERS BATTLE WITH OWEN SOUND

MARCH 14, 1936

—(Copyright. 1936. The Evening Telegram) ✦
Winning their group for the first time in several years, the Barrie Collegiate Institute senior basketball players are fighting it out with the Owen Sound Collegiate Institute and Vocational School quintette for the championship of the Georgian Bay district of the Central Ontario Secondary School Association. The Owen Sounders gained a slight edge in the first of the home and home series games with total points counting in the first game at Owen Sound last Saturday, and carry a three-point margin in the return fixture here to-day. The local basketeers are confident that they will take the home game by sufficient points to annex the district championship, to advance into the provincial playdowns. The photo shows: Back row, left to right—"Toar" Storey, William Strachan, T. Mayhew, E. Parker and D. McCulloch; front row, left to right—F. Ryan, coach; A. B. Cockburn, Doug. Reynolds, manager; E. Smith.—(Photo by Bill Gilbert, Barrie.)

This is the championship high school basketball team I played on at Barrie Collegiate Institute in 1936. I'm at the far left; my buddy, Bill Strachan, is standing next to me in the back row; and our coach, Alex Cockburn, is the man in the shirt and tie. Canada Wide Photo

LOCALS TAKE CAGE HONORS

B.C.I. Srs. Win Georgian Bay Championship for First Time

For the first time in the history of B.C.I., a boys' senior basketball team became Georgian Bay champs. The 1936 team earned this right last Friday by defeating Shelburne by a score of 46-25.

The B.C.I. squad were never in difficulty from start to finish and kept piling up the score until in the final quarter it was very sloppy with the ball being thrown around with reckless abandon and every once in a while finding its way through the basket.

As usual, Storey, Strachan and Ryan were the big guns for Barrie with each scoring almost the same number of points. "Dangerous" Dan sank a couple from mid floor and missed other chances. All in all, the game was well played and a real workout for the Barrie "quints."

Shelburne kept trying all the time but were very inexperienced and their passing was not up to the high standard of B.C.I. However, maybe if these fellows had a little more training and a different gym to practise in they would have given Barrie a real run for the honours.

There was a large crowd out for the game and it is too bad that it is the last and that it was so much one-sided.

Barrie now enters the Central Ontario playdowns to be held in Toronto on Friday and Saturday, March 27-28. And if they do win these games they continue on for the all-Ontario championship. The teams left on the roll are Barrie, Peterboro, Niagara Falls, St. Mike's

The clipping about our victory is from *The Barrie Examiner*. Courtesy of The Barrie Examiner

Here I am in action as a running back with the Argos, for whom I played from 1936-41. The number 64 is a holdover from my earliest days with the team when they thought I might make a better end. Canada Wide Photo

Red' Storey of Argonauts (64) Away on One of His Marche

ARGOS ROUT BOMBERS IN SPECTACULAR

Barrie Boy Looms as Hero Of Thrilling Grid Panorama

Sorrel-Thatched Backfielder Electrifies 20,000 Thrilled Fans With Triple-Touchdown Show in Final Quarter—'Pegs Set Early Pace, but Lose 30-7 Game to Defending Champs

(By VERN DeGEER.)

Buster (Red) Storey, a flame-thatched gridiron gladiator from Barrie, was the pigskin swashbuckler who spark-plugged Toronto Argonauts to their second straight Canadian senior rugby football championship at Varsity Stadium Saturday afternoon. An estimated crowd of 20,000 and an official paid attendance of 18,846 watched Lew Hayman's inspired Oarsmen come from behind in an electrifying fourth-quarter barrage that produced 24 points and a 30-7 victory over the challenging Winnipeg Blue Bombers.

The final score told little of the gridiron story that was linked with the thrill-soaked football panorama. The Blue Bombers combined their own aggressive tactics with mistakes of the Oarsmen to lead 4-0 at the end of the first quarter by means of a rouge and a field goal. Then came a 56-yard pass and run that brought a touchdown for the Argonauts as well as the pacemaking honors, with the score 5-4 in their favor. Next was unveiled a second Winnipeg field goal to give the prairie raiders the edge in a 7-5 score at half time.

Victory March Begins

Early in the third quarter the Argonauts sliced the Winnipeg margin to a single point by marking up a rouge, but the Canadian title-holders had not yet set the stage for the most remarkable offense ever unfolded in the 17-year history of inter-sectional competition.

The Argonauts started the fourth quarter on the Winnipeg 43-yard line. They had been parked there on a forward pass from Bob Isbister cleared for action and the heavy Toronto artillery cut loose with a pigskin salvo that pitched the mighty throng into a state of wild-eyed excitement.

Rocketed into the limelight was Barrie's Buster Storey in the fourth quarter after a wide lateral sweep by Isbister and West put the ball on the Winnipeg 28-yard strip. Storey swung wide of the right side of the Toronto scrimmage line, to all intents and purposes, engineer-signed manoeuvre which saw Storey suddenly cut sharply to his left and weave his way through a befuddled Winnipeg secondary and tertiary. He finished his march behind the goal-line with a touchdown that put Argonauts in front 11-7. It was the turning point in one of the greatest football spectacles in the modern history of the Canadian game.

Storey rolled on for two more touchdowns. Bernie Thornton produced another. Altogether the steam-rolling Toronto shelling fashioned four touchdowns in the final chapter. Storey got three of them. All four were converted, two by Annis Stukus and two by left-footed Bill Stukus. The bombardment harvested 24 points. The fourth quarter stand of the Argonauts not only brought a second straight Dominion crown but definitely stamped the Haymanites as one of the greatest of Canada's championship football machines.

Stevenson Stands Out.

It was a sturdy, versatile Winnipeg team that bowed before the Toronto offense in the fourth quarter. It was probably the most formidable challenging Western Canada team ever paraded here. Art Stevenson furnished the Bombers with unexpected punting power and a tantalizing pass attack. Hard-charging Eddie James slashed the Argonaut line with vicious and effective plunges in the first half. A fast-moving Winnipeg line, with Martin Gainor and Bill Ceretti as the central figures, reached its peak in the third quarter. Here Ceretti got through to block one of Isbister's punts. Bud Marquardt raced in from the left side of the Winnipeg line to slap the ball with his hand and then dribble it far

SUMMARY

FIRST QUARTER.

1—Winnipeg, rouge (Stevenson's punt to W. Stukus) 1 point.
2—Winnipeg, field goal (Kabat) 3 points.

SECOND QUARTER.

3—Argonauts, touchdown (West) 5 points.
4—Winnipeg, field goal (Kabat) 3 points.
Half time—Winnipeg, 7; Argonauts, 5.

THIRD QUARTER.

5—Argonauts, rouge (Hanson after field goal attempt by A. Stukus) 1 point.

FOURTH QUARTER.

6—Argonauts, touchdown (Storey) 5 points.
7—Argonauts, convert (A Stukus; 1 point.
8—Argonauts, touchdown (Storey) 5 points.
9—Argonauts, convert (A. Stukus) 1 point.
10—Argonauts, touchdown (Thornton) 5 points.
11—Argonauts, convert (W. Stukus) 1 point.
12—Argonauts, touchdown (Storey) 5 points.
13—Argonauts, convert (W. Stukus) 1 point.
Final score—Winnipeg, 7; Argonauts, 30.

engagement if Marquardt had been able to gather in the bouncing ball and go over for a touchdown. But Ted Morris interrupted the Marquardt dribbling act by smothering the ball on Toronto's nine-yard line. Isbister relieved the pressure with a punt to midfield and Winnipeg's greatest moment of the second half was lost.

Reg. Threlfall's Bombers struck out at the Argonauts soon after the opening kickoff. From Toronto's 35-yard line Stevenson punted to Bill

nipeg point. Midway through the period Winnipeg recovered an Argonaut fumble on the Argonaut 10-yard line. Greg Kabat booted a field goal from that point and it was 4-0 for the invaders.

Old Pals Click.

Early in the second quarter Annis Stukus whipped a long pass to Art West and the big crowd roared madly as the snake-nipped Toronto backfielder tore 30 yards down the field for a touchdown. It was a 56-yard event, 26 on the pass and 30 more on West's run. Annis Stukus missed the convert, but Argos were on top 5-4. They stayed there until late in the period, when Bombers lashed out with a 82-yard advance from their own 10-yard line to the Toronto 18 on three passes. Stevenson passed to Hanson for 23 yards, and then twice to Marquardt for 59 more. Standing on the Toronto 20-yard line Kabat kicked his second field goal and the Bombers had a 7-5 edge at half time.

Bill Stukus set the Argonauts up for the only scoring point registered by either club in the third quarter. He completed passes to MacPherson and Thornton that placed the ball on Winnipeg's 20-yard line. Annis Stukus aimed at a field goal from the 29-yard line, but the ball was slow and wide of the mark. Fritz Hanson recovered in the Winnipeg goal zone and was rouged. The count still showed the visitors leading, 7-6.

As the third quarter ended Isbister passed to Annis Stukus on the Winnipeg 43. On the first play of the final period Isbister and West swung Winnipeg's right end for 15 yards. Then came Storey's victory-making drive of 28 yards. Annis Stukus converted. Storey's gridiron show was now under way. The big redhead intercepted one of Stevenson's passes, shook off Hanson and raced to the Winnipeg four-yard line. **Morris picked up three yards. Storey knifed over centre for another touchdown, which Annis Stukus converted.**

thrill for the customers. Probably the greatest of the countless events developed when Isbister intercepted a Winnipeg pass on the Toronto five-yard line. Isbister flicked the ball to Storey as Hanson tackled him. Storey steered for the eastern sidelines and was away on a 100-yard charge. He was brought down on the Winnipeg five-yard line. Bill Stukus lined a goal zone pass to Bernie Thornton for a touchdown and then converted it.

Toronto's scoring splurge was capped three minutes before the final siren when Evans intercepted a Winnipeg pass on the Winnipeg 21. Selkirk made a first down on the nine-yard line. Storey cut through Winnipeg's right middle for his third touchdown. Left-footed Bill Stukus booted the extra point to climax the 24-point title-winning march.

Inspired by the acceleration of the offense, Argonaut linemen contributed increased power as the second half grew older. The Bombers did not make a single first down through them in the third and fourth quarters. They made only two in the second half, both on passes. The Bombers tired under the strain of the fast pace and were dog-weary by the time the game ended. Superior condition played an important part in the fourth quarter.

As the game ended hundreds of excited, cheering fans rushed on the field. Red Vail snatched up the coveted pigskin and raced for the Toronto dressing rooms. Red Storey was lofted on sturdy shoulders of grandstanders and carried to the Argonaut headquarters.

Winnipeg — Flying wing, Kabat; halves, Hanson, Boivin, James; quarter, Stevenson; snap, Wilson; insides, Ceretti, Peschel; middles, Gainor, Mogul; outsides, Marquardt, Nicklin. Subs—Rosebrough, Kushner, Hatakin, Mobberley, Bieber, Nairn, Badger and McCance.

Argos—Flying wing, Morris; halves, West, Isbister, MacPherson; quarter, Bill Stukus; snap, Hees; insides, Staughton, Palmer; middles, Burt, Evans; outsides, Thornton, Cutler. Subs—Vail, Levantis, A. Stukus, Selkirk, Reid, Miller, Storey and McLean.

Officials — Hec Crighton, Toronto, referee; Eddie Grant, Winnipeg, um-

This was the coverage in *The Globe and Mail* in Toronto of the 1938 Grey Cup game against Winnipeg. I scored three touchdowns in the last quarter to help bring the Argos from behind for our second national championship in a row. Reprinted from The Globe and Mail

In the dressing room with coach Lew Hayman after winning the 1938 Grey Cup game. Lew was tough but there was nobody like him. He was a perfect 5-0 in national finals.

I always played hockey during the winter. In 1939-40, I was a defenceman with the Atlantic City Bulls of the Eastern League. I wound up my hockey career with the senior Montreal Royals in 1943. Photo by Lou Shumsky

I played senior lacrosse for several years, finishing up in the Quebec League in the early 1940s. Here I'm in the uniform of the Lachine-Ville St. Pierre team, with whom I set scoring records that still stand.

My ride on a horse came in Alberta in the spring of 1950, when I refereed the Allen Cup final in Calgary. I guess my work in the Canadian senior championship series was okay, because I was in the National Hockey League the next season.

This was my first formal portrait as an NHL referee in the fall of 1950. The sweaters were white then, with the league's logo on the left side of the chest.
Imperial Oil Archives

I'm with Bill Roberts (*left*) and Curly Davies (*right*), in the jerseys adopted before the 1953-54 season. In my case, the orange-red color made it tough to tell where the sweater stopped and my neck and hair began. Bill and Curly were my linesmen for the Richard Riot game of March 17, 1955.
David Bier Studios

This was a tough night in the mid-1950s, with Toronto goalie Harry Lumley and Detroit firebrand Ted Lindsay defending their interests. I had made a mistake and signalled what I thought was a sure Red Wings' goal, but Lumley dove at the last minute and kept the rolling puck out. I then had to wave the goal off, which didn't please Lindsay. Imperial Oil Archives

This is Dec. 29, 1954, in Toronto. Rocket Richard got into a no-holds-barred brawl with the Maple Leafs' Bob Bailey. George Hayes and I kept taking the Rocket's stick away, but every time, Canadiens' coach Dick Irvin Sr. handed him a new one. Dickie Moore of the Canadiens and Sid Smith of the Leafs are in the background. Toronto Star Photo

This was my official portrait after the NHL adopted striped shirts during the 1955-56 season. This led to the officials being known as "zebras," which is not the worst thing I've been called in my life.

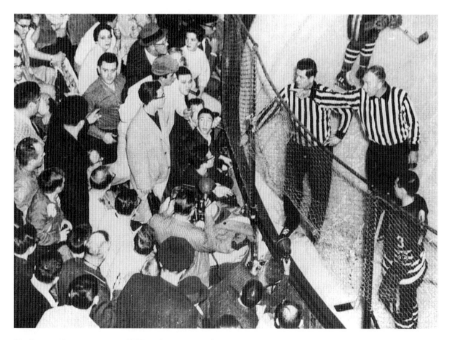

During my last game as an NHL referee on April 4, 1959, George Hayes (*left*) and I check the action in the stands as police move in on a threatening fan in Chicago. I quit after this game when league president Clarence Campbell refused to back me up, saying I had choked. The Blackhawks' Pierre Pilote is at the bottom of the photo. Bettman Archives

My wife Helen and sons Bob (*left*) and Doug were at Dorval Airport in Montreal to greet me when I came home from Boston after resigning from the NHL.

I saw a lot of great young players during the 17 years I refereed at the Quebec International Pee Wee Hockey Tournament. None was better at the age of 10 than Guy Lafleur, from Buckingham, Que., whom I first met in 1962. Courtesy Office du Film du Québec/Archives Nationales du Québec à Québec

I was the mystery guest on CBC-TV's *Front Page Challenge* shortly after I left the NHL and I stumped the panel. I did a return engagement on the show in the early 1960s when the subject was my three-touchdown fourth quarter for the Argos against Winnipeg in the 1938 Grey Cup. Photograph reprinted with permission of the Canadian Broadcasting Corporation.

This was one the proudest moments of my life. I was named honorary chairman of the Barrie Winter Carnival in February, 1964, and got to ride through the streets of my hometown in an open sleigh with Ma by my side.

I did television and radio work for several years during the 1960s and 1970s, including talk shows for CKGM Radio in Montreal. Here I'm interviewing Charlie Hodge, an underrated goalie who was a part of six Stanley Cup winners with the Canadiens. A.B.C. Studios Inc.

I spent a quarter-century with Seagram, selling and doing public relations functions. Here, I'm welcoming golfer Chi Chi Rodriguez to Montreal for the 1967 Canadian Open, a tournament Seagram sponsored for many years. Studio Alain Enrg.

At an old-timers' game in the early 1970s, we made it a pair by giving Milt Schmidt, the Boston general manager, an oar to go with his Orr (Bobby). Milt won two Stanley Cups as a Bruins' player and two as their GM. He also coached them into the finals twice. The Gazette

I share a quiet moment with Gordie Howe at the NHL meetings in June, 1972. This was before he un-retired from a front-office job with the Detroit Red Wings to play with his sons, Mark and Marty, for Houston of the rival World Hockey Association. The Gazette/George Bird

Much of the fun in my life has been the people I've met. Here I'm at an old-timers' game in 1988 in Winnipeg with Richard Dean Anderson, who was MacGyver in the TV series of the same name and played hockey for a team of Hollywood stars. I've refereed at least 2,500 games for good causes in the last 35 years. Albert Corbeil Photographe

This photo was taken in 1980 at a family Christmas dinner in Toronto. From left are my two grandsons, Bob Jr. (*standing*) and Mike, along with Ma, my son Bob, myself and my younger sister, Helen.

My older sister Irene was a champion sprinter as a youngster and continued running all her life. She is seen here at the age of 67 in a marathon in the early 1980s in San Francisco, where she lived with her husband and children. Irene died of a mysterious virus two years later.

Among the guests on hand when I was inducted into Canada's Sports Hall of Fame in 1986 was Wayne Gretzky. That's Jake Gaudaur, the former commissioner of the Canadian Football League, in the background.

The Storeys had a family reunion in 1986 when I became a member of Canada's Sports Hall of Fame. At the left is my kid brother, George, a fine athlete in his younger days. At the right are my two sons, Bob and Doug.

I've done this about 3,000 times since I left the NHL in 1959. As you can tell from the photograph, I've come to enjoy getting up on my feet after being very shy in my younger days.
Fednews Newsphotos of Canada

This is probably the most formal thing I've ever been involved in during my life. On April 29, 1992, I received the Order of Canada from Governor-General Ray Hnatyshyn.

This was one of the moments I enjoyed most. At the opening of the new Hockey Hall of Fame in Toronto in the summer of 1993, Ted Lindsay came over and gave me a big hug. Before that, our relationship had been no better than prickly for more than 40 years.

Here I am with my second wife, Bunny, in 1993. We were married in 1989, eight years after my first wife, Helen, died.

The Old Redhead turned 76 in 1994 and he's still on the go. I continue to referee up to 60 old-timers' and other charity games each year and carry out 50 or more speaking engagements. The Gazette/Len Sidaway

12

The Intimidators

A day or two after I signed my first referee's contract with the National Hockey League, in the summer of 1950, I was walking along the street in Montreal and I ran into Toe Blake, the former Canadiens' captain who was then coaching at Valleyfield in the Quebec senior league, in which I had been officiating. "Congratulations," he said, "but, Red, you don't know what a tough spot you're going into. This is the world's worst. You're gonna find what those people are like upstairs."

I looked at him. "Well, how tough can it be, Toe?" I asked. After all, I thought, this is a pretty good league I'm going to be working in. What am I going to see that I haven't seen before? How much tougher can it be than junior or senior? Toe just smiled, and said, "You'll learn."

Toe was right. What I hadn't known was that the whole league worked on intimidation, Jack Adams in Detroit and Conn Smythe in Toronto in particular. Adams worked for the Norrises, who owned the franchises in Detroit and Chicago and had influence over those in New York and Boston, through investments and loans; Smythe had one of the two most famous teams in the game, along with the Canadiens in Montreal. When they barked, there was a bite to it.

Clarence Campbell once told me, in my early years in the NHL: "I'm not the president of the league. I'm the manager for six owners and I do what I'm told." So they had him intimidated, too. I couldn't have taken the abuse he took from those men without telling them to go to hell. He was so enamored of his job and the title that went with it, I guess he'd have taken anything to keep it. The teams intimidated the players, of course, with the constant threat of sending them to the minors. The general managers and coaches would walk around with train tickets to their farm-system cities sticking out of their pockets as a daily reminder.

Campbell in turn intimidated Carl Voss, whom he called referee-in-chief while keeping the real power for himself. Voss tried to intimidate the officials, and wasn't alone. The players tried to intimidate the officials, the coaches tried to intimidate the officials, the fans in each arena tried to intimidate the officials and, above all, Adams and Smythe tried to intimidate the officials. The problem was that for people like me, the intimidation attempts worked in reverse.

Let me make one thing clear right off the bat. I am not lumping Conn Smythe and Jack Adams together. Smythe would fight you at the drop of a hat and if you turned your back on him, he'd hate you. But he was a very fair man. One story illustrates the difference between the two. Smythe told me once: "I have to work with Adams but I can't stand him. I'll tell you why. I went down to scout a game the Canadiens were playing in Detroit one night in the late 1930s and Toe Blake fell near the Red Wings' bench. Adams, who was coaching then, opened the gate and kicked him right in the face. I had no respect at all for the man after that."

Hockey has had some great nicknames: the Rocket for the explosive Maurice Richard; Terrible Ted Lindsay, a perfect description of his temperament; Boom Boom for Geoffrion's slapshot; and so on. Jack Adams was called "Jolly Jawn," and that was the most inaccurate nickname of all time. There was never anything jolly about him.

I remember a playoff game in Detroit in the spring of 1954, when the Canadiens had won 3-1 and Adams didn't like a couple of penalties I'd called against the Red Wings. He recalled that Montreal GM Frank Selke Sr. had said at a pre-playoff meeting in New York that he didn't want Frank Udvari to referee any of the Canadiens' games because he thought he was too high-strung. Adams then decided he didn't want Storey to referee any of the Wings' games, giving the reason that I was on Montreal's payroll. Selke, thinking he was joking, said, "That's right." Adams immediately made a big deal out of that remark. The result of all the charges and the publicity was that I had to have police protection to get out of the Olympia.

Another time in Detroit, also with the Canadiens playing, the Wings' Tony Leswick fell. As he was going down, with his head a foot or so from the ice, a stick hit him by accident and cut him badly. But it wasn't a high stick, so I didn't call a penalty. After the period, as we were walking down the 50-foot corridor to our dressing room, Adams was right on my tail, ranting and raving a mile a minute about the high stick. I opened the door to the room and he forced his way in right behind me and the linesmen. This was against the rules; team officials weren't allowed in there at all. He was yelling to see my boss, and all the time Carl Voss was right behind him, and the police were right behind Voss. We were all in there, and Adams started yelling personal insults at me. I was pretty good at that, too, and I challenged him right back. Finally, he said, "You redheaded bleep-bleeper," and tried to get at me. We were ready to go, but the cops held us back and got him out of there.

The NHL had a hearing about the incident at the Leland Hotel in Detroit about two weeks later. Campbell was running it like a trial. He was both the prosecutor and the judge, and you know who turned out to be the defendant. There were about 18 people from the Detroit organization there, including Adams; I got to say nothing while they all testified. Campbell asked each of them in turn, "At any time when Mr. Adams was in the referee's room, did you hear him say anything offensive to Red?" Each of them replied in turn, "Oh, no, Mr. Campbell, I never heard him say anything bad at all." This went on through all 18 witnesses, and I was thinking the only thing left was to bring out the rope and find a tree.

Finally Campbell said: "Well, there's only one more person to hear from. Mr. Adams, at any time when you were in Red's dressing room, did you use any bad language toward him?" And Adams said: "You're goddamn right I did. I called him a bleep-bleeper, and a blind bleep-bleeper, and a big stupid bleep-bleeper, because that's what he is." Campbell sighed, and said: "Case dismissed. Fine of $500 for Mr. Adams."

That incident was just the appetizer for the main course that followed in February, 1958. The scene again was the Olympia and the visiting team again was Montreal. I was known as a very vocal referee, shouting all the time. You could hear me all over the building. I'd be hoarse after a game from yelling at the players to break up scuffles before I had to give them penalties to keep the game flowing. This night, Alex Delvecchio of the Wings and Doug Harvey of the Canadiens were heading in my direction, both chasing the puck at top speed. I was next to the boards, but they were so intent that neither saw I was there. I realized that I was about to get run over. I worried about myself all the time and I wasn't going to let anyone belt me if I could help it. I yelled, "Look out," and they glanced up and veered off to miss me.

There was a fan in a seat right there who was a friend of Adams. He said to him: "You know, Storey is coaching the Canadiens. He told Doug Harvey to look out when Alex was going to hit him." Adams then started this big to-do about what he called my "directing the Montreal club during play." Adams said I was doing it because I was from Montreal. The Detroit papers were full of it the next day, the whole front page, quoting everything Adams was saying. If I was directing the Canadiens, I was doing a lousy job of it because the game ended in a 3-3 tie.

The league decided it had to have a hearing. They had the players in first, and Harvey told them, "The only time Storey ever did anything for me was last summer in the referees' golf tournament when he helped me find a golf ball I lost." Red Kelly, the Detroit defenceman, said: "I don't know what you're making such a fuss about. Red yells, 'Look out,' at everybody. He does it so he won't get knocked down. What's wrong with that? What's the big deal?" That stopped it right there and Campbell dismissed Adams's charge.

In the meantime, however, I'd been in the Bagley Bar in Detroit for a beer or two. The owner, a friend named Maxie Silk, introduced me to a fellow he called "the No. 1 lawyer in town." This man said, "I'd like to discuss the stories in the papers." I told him I'd read them and they bothered me because they weren't true. "How would you like to make some money?" he asked. I was getting $10 per day expenses and had never made as much as $10,000 in a year in my life, so I was interested. The lawyer said that because everything in the papers was quotes from Adams, there was no way we could lose. It was cut and dried. We could sue Adams, I'd get $100,000 guaranteed and it wouldn't cost me a cent. I guess the lawyer had it in for Adams or the Red Wings.

It sounded great until he told me that the one thing I would have to do would be to resign from the NHL before I could go after the money. I said, "You're asking me to give up my life. No, I love hockey more than I love money. Forget the lawsuit." It's times like that when you realize how much you must really love sports if you won't do anything to hurt them.

Bill Dineen, the former NHL player and coach, has the best story about Adams and money. He was negotiating a new contract in the mid-1950s, and it was going much more smoothly than he had expected. Adams kept praising him, and finally told him he'd be getting a $500 raise. Dineen had wanted more but decided he couldn't complain after hearing all those kind words. He found out later the minimum salary had just been raised from $5,500 to $6,000. Adams was able to pay him only as little as he had to for two years in a row.

Gordie Howe served as a pallbearer at Adams's funeral in May, 1968, and recalls everyone saying nice things about him. Finally, one of the other pallbearers couldn't stand it any longer. "I played for him, and he was a miserable sonofabitch. Now he's a bleeping dead, miserable sonofabitch." That's the way I remember him, too.

For Conn Smythe of the Maple Leafs, on the other hand, I had great respect. I fought with him verbally many, many times, but he was honest and if you stood your ground, you'd get 100 percent respect from him. No official could ask for more. But you had to be strong to resist him.

I remember a tough game in Toronto when I called 11 or 12 penalties, a lot for me, to cool things down in the first period. Voss came into the room to compliment me on the way I was handling it. On his way back out, Smythe met him down the hall and ripped into him over the officiating. Voss turned right around and came back, this time blasting me for the way I was calling it. Smythe just played pressure politics all down the line, and some people let him get away with it.

Smythe could be murder on his players, too. Gordie Drillon was a right wing who won the NHL scoring title in 1938, still the last Maple Leaf to do that. He told me he was playing the point on the power play one night when the puck hopped over his stick and the fastest player on the other team took off with it on a clean breakaway. Drillon was never known for his interest in checking, but he went after the guy and with a tremendous dive knocked the puck off his stick. There was only a minute or so to go and that play saved the game. He was happy afterward, undressing in his stall, "until I glanced up and saw this pair of spats that Smythe always wore, and then his eyes glaring at me. 'Drillon,' he snarled, 'I pay you

$5,000 a year to put the puck in the other net. I got dummies I pay $2,500 a year to stop those other guys from putting it in our net. I don't want to see you behind centre ice for the rest of your career with me.'"

Even the smallest detail might be controlled by Smythe. I had a game one night with the Canadiens in Toronto, a tight one as we got into the final minute or two. I was waiting in the corner for a faceoff and Cal Gardner came out to take it for the Leafs. Before I could drop the puck, Ted Kennedy came out and Gardner went back to the bench. Again before I could drop the puck, Kennedy left and Gardner came back. "Okay, Cal," I said, "what the hell's going on? Let's get this game over." He said, "They're all waitin' for the call from Mr. Smythe to tell 'em who to put out for the faceoff."

Smythe was a great believer in using game films to prove the points he was trying to make. For years, at least half the film clips coming into the NHL office protesting officials' decisions were from Toronto. I remember a Saturday night game when Paul Meger of the Canadiens had a breakaway from inside his own blue line. I was in the Canadiens' end, I couldn't skate as fast as Meger, and I admit I was behind the play. Howie Meeker of the Leafs was chasing him and, at the last minute, I saw Meeker dive and then Meger went ass over teakettle into the corner. I called a penalty and the Canadiens won the game because of it.

Smythe wouldn't let it go at that. He got the league to change my assignment, so I'd be back in Toronto the following Saturday. In the afternoon, they made me go to the movies. Smythe had his assistant, Hap Day, his coach, Joe Primeau, and, it seemed like, his whole board of directors there. Shanty Mackenzie, who played with me on the Argos, was running the projector and Smythe told him to start it up. I said, "Hold it, Shanty. Before you run that film, Mr. Smythe, I want you to know something. I'm not afraid of any sonofabitch in your league." I was looking him right in the eye. He huffed and snorted and finally said, "If you were, you wouldn't be in the league."

They ran the film five times, and it showed that Meeker hit the puck with his stick before it tripped Meger. Smythe was shouting, "What do you think now? What do you think now?" in the way he did when he was trying to intimidate you. I said: "Mr. Smythe, there was no penalty on that play, absolutely no penalty. But from where I was, if that same play takes place again, it will be the same damn penalty. How do you like that?" It didn't go on any longer.

Smythe wasn't above pulling a trick on you if he thought he could. One time, I had to go to see another film with George Hayes, who had made an offside call that wound up costing the Leafs a victory. We were watching and watching and suddenly George yelled, "Stop the film!" Smythe asked, "Why did you do that?" and George said: "Mr. Smythe. Max Bentley plays for the Toronto Maple Leafs now. Why are you showing us a game from the time he played for the Chicago Blackhawks?" Oh, they'd try to get you any way they could.

The part I remember most clearly of my induction ceremonies into the Hockey Hall of Fame in Toronto in 1967 involved Smythe. They had a little party and all the people from the Maple Leafs—Conn Smythe's son Stafford, Harold Ballard, Punch Imlach, King Clancy—were there, but early on they came over to me and said they had to leave. I said the party was just getting started so why hurry away, and they said, "Yeah, but Mr. Smythe is making a presentation and we have to leave before he'll come in here."

Tired of the grind in 1961 and wanting to spend more time in Florida and with his racing stable, Conn had sold his controlling interest in Maple Leaf Gardens to Stafford, Ballard and John Bassett, publisher of *The Toronto Telegram*. It wasn't long before he began to find fault with what they were doing. The first argument was over popcorn, which they wanted to bring into the Gardens for the first time ever. Conn told them,

"If you bring in popcorn, you'll bring in rats." They brought in popcorn anyway and, sure enough, the rats came.

Then, in the mid-1960s, they rented out Maple Leaf Gardens for a world championship heavyweight bout between Muhammad Ali and Toronto's George Chuvalo. Ali had been banned from fighting in the U.S. for refusing induction into the army after he was drafted. His handlers sidestepped that problem by bringing him to Canada. Conn didn't want his successors to have anything to do with it, saying: "I didn't build Maple Leaf Gardens to be a garbage dump." The fight went on, and the split deepened.

It was a shame he had to feel that way, but he wouldn't be in the same room. Sure enough, they left and about 10 minutes later he came in and gave me a painting. Smythe had been one of my strongest supporters when I resigned in 1959 after Campbell wouldn't support me, and I remember he referred to that in his little speech that day. He said: "The NHL was forced to fire bad referees, but Storey was not one of them. He, in effect, fired us and that was good."

13

The Good Guys

When you talk about the superstars who made sports so popular in this country, save a thought for the officials and, especially, for a man named George Hayes. They couldn't have played the games without us, after all, and George—the best and most colorful linesman ever to work in the National Hockey League—became an institution. I can remember him sitting in hotel lobbies, lighting up a cigar and talking with anyone who came along, telling stories one after the other. People loved him, and I did too. We worked together more often than not during my nine years in the NHL.

George was a huge man and his strength was legendary. He had come to hockey from baseball, where he had a bright future as a player until the day in Tillsonburg, Ontario, when he got mad at an umpire and literally picked him up and threw him over the fence. They barred him from playing, but he became a long-time scout for the Cleveland Indians.

He began officiating in junior hockey in the early 1940s and worked his way up to the NHL. Despite weighing 230 pounds, he was a graceful skater with great moves. George loved to put on a little show and the fans watched him as much as they watched the players in pre-game warmups.

I can remember only one source of friction between us in all the years we worked together. That would be if I was calling the game too strictly and he'd get mad because there were no fights. He loved to break up fights. He was the only man I ever saw who could grab two players by the front of their sweaters, one in each hand, and lift them both off the ice. He'd say to me: "I'm gonna phone Campbell and get all my assignments changed. There's no fun workin' with you anymore." I'd say, "Give me another night, George," and he always did.

Like me, George was never one of Clarence Campbell's favorites, because he lived a rebel type of life, but he was always ready for the hockey game. Sometimes that was difficult. We were paid only $10 per day for expenses during the 1950s. One time George was heading to Chicago from Detroit and the train he was on hit a car or something, leaving him stranded. In those days, you were ordered to get to a game any way you could and fined if you didn't make it in time. So George took a taxi. It cost him $65 and he nearly had to go to court to get the money back. He was getting $10 per day and made $2,500 in a year. He loved the game so much he spent his own money and the league, as rich as it was, didn't want to pay him back. That was one more reason for us to hate Campbell and Carl Voss, the referee-in-chief who carried his messages.

One way George and I found to have some beer money was to cash in our first-class train tickets, buy coach fares and keep the difference, which paid for incidentals like laundry, a good meal now and then, and a brew or two along the way. We also did a lot of walking from train to hotel to arena. George found another way to beat the system. He lived on a farm between Woodstock and Ingersoll, in southwestern Ontario, and at the start of a season he would buy one return coach ticket to Montreal. He would use it all year, because nobody ever got it off him on the train. One year, he had 39 return trips to Montreal and never surrendered the ticket. He had the nerve at the end of the season to try to cash it in for a refund, but it was so worn by then that they couldn't read the printing on it. George also would make enough sandwiches in advance for the first few days of road trips. It beat spending $4.50 in the club car for the same thing.

One year, George and I found ourselves in Detroit on a Friday morning and not working until Sunday. The Grey Cup game was the next day, and we weren't going to get it on television in Detroit, so I suggested to George: "We're not that far from your place. Why don't we go up there, watch the game on TV tomorrow, catch the midnight train out, we're back for Sunday morning and in great shape for the game." So we took a train to Woodstock and got there around 2:30 in the afternoon. George insisted we have drinks with everybody he knew in town, and there wasn't anybody he didn't know. It got to be 10 o'clock and we were sailing. It was time to go out to the farm, and it was pitch black when the cabbie dropped us off.

George had boarded up the house for the winter, saying "Nobody lives here without bringin' in any money," so his wife had gone to Toronto and taken a job with a bank. When we got to the front door, George started to swear. He couldn't find his key. We were miles from nowhere, the phone had been disconnected for the winter so we couldn't call another taxi, and it was starting to get really cold. I could see us freezing to death before morning. George said not to worry and stumbled off into the night. Now I was alone and I wasn't moving because I had no idea where I was. George came back in a couple of minutes with an axe, and he just about destroyed the front door to get us in.

He went into the front room to stoke up the old pot-bellied stove and I went into the kitchen to look for something to eat. The first thing I saw was an empty can of "Pard" dog food sitting on the kitchen table. I yelled to George, "I didn't know you had a dog," and he yelled back, sounding a little surprised, "I got no dog." I shouted, "What's this empty can of 'Pard' dog food doing here then?" He came into the kitchen and began to turn red. He said, "I was wonderin' why that meat was so cheap." I said, "George, you didn't make your sandwiches for your last trip out of that, did you?" He admitted: "I guess I did. And you know somethin'? Outside of being a little lumpy they weren't bad." He paused and then warned me, "If you tell anybody in the league about this, I'll break your bloody neck."

This was too good a secret to keep, however, and I could hardly wait to get back to Detroit. I saw my buddies Gordie Howe and Bob Goldham standing together during the warm-ups, so I skated over and told them the story. Usually, since I couldn't stand alone at centre because of the shape my knees were in, I'd stand beside one of the linesmen, supporting myself with my rear against the boards. Usually, I'd stand next to George, but not this night. In those days, the whole team stood at the blue line for the national anthems and once they were over Howe and Goldham, who weren't starting the game, headed for the Red Wings' bench.

Just before they got there, they made a sharp left turn and skated down to the blue line where George was standing. As Goldham got opposite him, he went, "Woof! Woof! Woof!" Gordie was right behind him and he patted George on the head, saying, "Nice doggie, nice doggie." George looked around wildly, yelling: "Where is that big bugger? I'm gonna kill him," and started chasing me. The fans in the Olympia must have wondered what on earth was happening. The game hadn't even started and they were seeing one of the great skate races of all time.

George had a sense of humor, which you had to have if you were going to officiate in the NHL for long. One time, Conn Smythe filed a complaint with the league, saying that any time there was a fight, George grabbed the Toronto player and let the other guy keep swinging. The old man could be pretty tough on you verbally, and he kept letting George have it from his box seat behind the penalty box every time he worked a

Maple Leafs' game. They were at home against the Canadiens one night and late in the second period there was a fight
between Teeter Kennedy, the Toronto captain, and Tom Johnson of Montreal. I gave them both majors, which carried over
into the third period.

The teams came out after the break and as Kennedy was
skating past, he said to me, "I've got a funny feeling Johnson
has been told to start something." The Canadiens were
behind, so maybe the coach, Dick Irvin Sr., wanted to stir
things up. I told George and he went over near the penalty
box. No sooner had I dropped the puck than Johnson made a
lunge at Kennedy and the fight was on. George barged right
into the penalty box to separate them. He got Johnson down
on his hands and knees, straddling him from behind and
holding him helpless. George looked up and saw Smythe right
there and hollered: "Grab your camera, Conny. Get a shot of
this one, baby."

George died a few years ago at the age of 67. There was no
reason for him to go so young, except that he just refused to
take care of himself and had a deathly fear of doctors and
dentists. In Montreal one time, I went down to the old Mount
Royal Hotel to see him the afternoon of a game and he was
walking around with one shoe on and one slipper. He had cut
his foot on a nail a week earlier. I told him to let me see it. He
pulled off his sock and the foot was all blue and black with
streaks running up the leg. I marched him right out into a taxi
and we went to see Doc Young, the Canadiens' team physi-
cian. He took one look, told George to drop his pants and
gave him a shot of penicillin. "If Red hadn't brought you
here," the doctor told him, "in another day it would have
been too late."

George died from gangrene after a foot became infected. He
wouldn't let a doctor see him, or go to the hospital. His wife,
Judy, told me he just went to bed and died. It took six weeks,
but he wouldn't let anyone do anything about it. If I'd been

there, I know I'd have picked the big S.O.B. up and carried him to the hospital. But I didn't even know he was sick.

George worked 1,544 games during the regular season and another 149 in the playoffs, and he loved doing every one of them. He couldn't wait for any game to start, one reason why he was probably the most respected guy who ever worked the lines in the NHL and why he was elected to the Hockey Hall of Fame in 1986. I'll always remember a radio show I did with George when I was with CKGM in Montreal in the late 1960s. STOREY: "The last 19 years must have been tough for you. Clarence Campbell hated your guts and hated your style of living and hated everything about you." HAYES: "And I hated every goddamned thing about him too." That was my guy.

Before I got into the NHL, my favorite refereeing partner was Kenny Mullins, with whom I worked in Quebec senior leagues in both lacrosse and hockey. I was just a kid then, and he tried to take care of me. We were doing the seventh game of a hockey final between the Montreal Royals and Sherbrooke, where the old barn of a building was jammed full to overflowing. It had these steel girders that came straight down from the ceiling to just behind the rink boards, which meant some of the seats were partially behind these poles. In the two-referee system used in that league, I was working one side of the ice and Kenny the other. Every time I skated by this particular spot, a fist would come out from behind a girder and almost deck me. I mean I was reeling. This happened several times and, at the end of the second period, Kenny told me I looked lousy. I explained what had been happening and he said, "Well, that's too bad, isn't it," meaning who gives a damn? "It's not only too bad," I said, "but it's starting to hurt."

About the 10-minute mark of the third period I skated by there again and the guy really hung one on my chin. I was staggered and when I recovered, I saw that the puck had been frozen against the boards at the other end of the ice. I blew the play dead and went to pick it up. I noticed all the players were looking back the other way so I did too, and saw the St. John Ambulance people coming in. They got to the spot where this guy had been reaching out and belting me, and they picked someone out of the seats. He was absolutely limp as they put him on the stretcher. I took a look at him and told Kenny, who was standing beside me: "That's the bugger who's been punching me all night. I guess he had a heart attack." Kenny laughed. "Heart attack, my arse," he said. "After he belted you the last time, he leaned out to watch the play and I snuck up and let him have it." Nobody in the building saw it.

Another time at the Forum in Montreal, Frank Carlin was coaching the Royals and the other referee missed a call. Kenny was skating past the Royals' bench and Carlin reached out and grabbed him to tell him about the other official's mistake. Kenny just swung around in reflex and belted Carlin before he even saw who it was. He broke his nose, broke his glasses, cut his eye, and who do you think was suspended by George Slater, the league president? Carlin. You had no business touching an official and Slater backed us up every time.

Another official I worked with in Quebec was Ernie Mundey. One night we did a Mercantile League game together in Verdun, a Montreal suburb. It was real amateur hockey, but they had all the things better leagues did, like boys selling refreshments through the stands. At the end of the second period, we were in our room and there was a knock on the door. This little kid, with a shoulder strap and a basket, came in and said, "You guys owe me 20 cents." I said, "What for?" The kid motioned at Ernie. "He ate my popcorn. I was standin' by the boards watchin' the game and he ate a bag of my popcorn." I looked at Ernie, and he blushed a little and said, "I was watchin' you work and I got hungry. The kid wasn't movin' so I ate it." He paid.

We were in Ottawa one time and Ernie came off afterward, raving about what a great game it had been. I wasn't that impressed, and said "Yeah, it was pretty good." Ernie said,

"No, no. I didn't mean it that way," and explained. He sold cars for a living at that time, and while the game was on he had managed to sell one to a guy sitting along the boards at the blue line.

The first year I was in the NHL we had some part-time referees. One of them was Bill Knott of Seattle, who came from the Western League, a little guy with baggy pants and a 25-game contract. Despite being a referee myself, I was working with George Hayes as Bill's linesmen his last night, because he really needed the support. It was the Maple Leafs playing in Montreal and he didn't have any control of the game at all. About halfway through the second period, George and I looked at each other and started flexing our muscles, like a chicken waving its wings. That meant that all hell was going to break loose soon. We were right, since the brawl involved everybody except the two goaltenders, Turk Broda of the Leafs and Gerry McNeil of the Canadiens. Bill had a very tough night. Afterward, Campbell came into the room, and told him, "Mr. Knott, your 25-game contract is up and you're free to go home." Just like that. Bill turned around and said, "You know, that's the biggest load off my shoulders I've ever had."

Then he added: "But I'm happy for one thing. I'll be able to tell my grandchildren that I worked in the National Hockey League." He was always so proud of that. George and I checked into the Hotel Manger in Boston with him another time when the league had us going around with him. The bellhop was taking us upstairs to our rooms, and Bill turned to the boy and said: "I want you to know I'm the referee. These two guys are only linesmen." He meant it. He was on a little ego trip, but I liked him. He was a nice guy.

I've always had respect for people who could thumb their noses at authority. We had a good referee in the NHL in the 1950s named Jack Mehlenbacher. He was also an outstanding trainer and driver in harness racing, No. 1 in Canada one

year, and he felt the same way most of us did about our boss—
he hated Carl Voss. Jack was running his horses at Green-
wood in Toronto, night racing, and Voss went down one
afternoon to the stables, looked Jack up and asked him to
mark his program. Jack gave him 10 dead-last finishes. Jack
later quit after the league wouldn't support him in some
controversy, much like my case later. But I've always thought
that losing that money for Voss was the thing that started Jack
on the way out. He went back to the harness tracks and did
very well.

There are very few men who have both played and officiated
in the NHL. Of the current crop, only Paul Stewart and Bill
McCreary qualify—just barely. Stewart played in 21 games for
Quebec during the 1979-80 season; McCreary in 12 games for
Toronto in 1980-81. A more famous Maple Leaf, Hap Day—
he won Stanley Cups as a player, coach and untitled general
manager—also served as a linesman briefly. His finest
moment came in Toronto, where a Dr. MacPherson sat at the
end of the Leafs' bench right at the blue line. On the same blue
line, directly opposite, a well-known funeral parlor owner
named Bill Myles had his seat. One night, the good doctor
second-guessed every offside call Hap made. Finally, Hap
turned to him and said at the top of his lungs, so everyone
could hear: "Dr. MacPherson, when I make a mistake out
here, 16,000 people can see it. When you make one, you get
that guy Bill Myles across there to bury it for you."
Silence reigned.

14

The Fans (As In Fanatics)

During my career as an official, starting in 1943, I have never been intimidated by any building or any crowd. My attitude was always fatalistic: "The worst thing that can happen to you is you die." Booing? Who cared? I always felt that the day they stopped booing me was the day I'd start worrying. As long as they gave me the raspberry, I knew I was doing my job and I'd be eating steak. When they quit booing, it would be hamburger. And, boy, I loved steak!

So I never let fans bother me. In fact, I usually couldn't hear them because most times there was a steady din at games I've done. When everything was quiet, of course, you had to hear them. But I tried to think of it from their point of view. Most of those guys went to work every day and got hell from their bosses. They went home and were jumped on by their wives and kids. That went on week after week. So they paid a few bucks for tickets and came out to the game where they could give us referees the devil. They needed that chance to let it all out. Anyway, they were cheering for one team, they were biased and they didn't know the rules. They also forgot—and still do—that officials don't make the rules, they only enforce them; they don't commit the fouls, they simply detect them. So their insults never bothered me.

I was probably booed more than any other official in the history of the NHL. In New York, for example, it got to the point that the linesmen asked if they could be introduced before me, so that the people would hear their names. The booing was so loud and so long at the mention of "Red Storey" that everything that followed was drowned out. When I was working football in Montreal, we used to play a little game. A dollar was a good bet in those days, so all the officials would put one into a hat and the one that got the most boos during introductions got the money. I won all the time, so they changed the bet so the other officials got to count the boos for the most hated player on the other team, too. But I still won, so they dropped it.

I think I was booed for two reasons: first, I did a lot of important games, where emotions ran high; second, my style of refereeing was to take charge of a game, which was like a red flag to many players and fans. No matter how abusive they became, there was one thing I always tried to keep in mind: the fans were the greatest people in the world because, in the end, they were the ones who paid my salary.

Hockey crowds were, and are, pretty much the same everywhere. There isn't much difference in how they react to things. It all depends on the tempo of the game and, of course, on how the home team is doing. Partisan fans have always been an important and colorful part of hockey. But here and there in every arena were pockets of people just waiting for an excuse to become hoodlums. In some rinks, the pockets were small and seldom heard from. If they were, the trouble-makers would be tossed out on their ears and the genuine fans could enjoy the game. The pockets were larger in other places, like Chicago Stadium, where they sometimes seemed to take over the entire building. I once asked a Blackhawks' official when they were going to start cracking down on the thugs. "We've got enough trouble getting people in here," he said. "We aren't about to start throwing them out."

Here's a rundown of how I remember the fans in the cities in the six-team league, starting with the fact that the most knowledgeable fans were in Montreal, Toronto and Detroit. The first two were the only Canadian cities in the NHL then, and the Red Wings drew thousands of their fans from southwestern Ontario cities like Windsor, Sarnia, St. Thomas, London and so on. Montreal's crowds were wildly demonstrative, to say the least; Toronto's were the league's best behaved; and Detroit's were much the same, unless things went against them. Elsewhere, Boston's fans were very impatient and the most critical; Chicago's were the most unruly at times; and New York's were the zaniest of all.

Physically, for officials, the two Canadian rinks were the best. They had the shortest exposed distance between the ice and the officials' dressing rooms. With angry crowds sometimes throwing things, including punches, that made a difference. In the other four buildings, it was a long walk, 50 or 60 feet through a gauntlet of fans in both Detroit and Boston, for example. Chicago was the worst, because you had a flight of stairs to go down to the dressing room and you always felt you were a target.

In the 1950s, *The Toronto Star Weekly* called Montreal "the world's most hysterically enthusiastic hockey city." Not much has changed. Hockey still is bigger than the church in Quebec. For example, the French-language tabloid *Le Journal de Montréal* routinely carries 10-page hockey coverage. In the Forum—which has assumed the mantle of a shrine since it opened in 1924—an official could feel like an early Christian tossed into the Colosseum to wrestle with the lions. The Forum was famous for things of some value being tossed on the ice. At one game, a total of 500 rubbers and galoshes were thrown, along with hats, belts, nails, watches and coins. The footwear and headgear always went to charity. With anything else, it was a matter of "finders, keepers." It helped to keep me in pocket change.

Perhaps the oddest littering in Montreal came during a playoff game against Detroit. I was forced to call a penalty against Rocket Richard. It was a really flagrant offence, but the crowd went crazy and started tossing stuff. One item was a bag of split peas, which just missed me and then scattered all over the ice. As the scrapers came out to clean up the mess, Butch Bouchard skated over with his arms waving and I stopped him cold. "Butch, I don't want to hear any guff from you. Not one word or I'll throw you out. The Rocket deserved that penalty." Butch grinned and said: "I know, Red. I just came out to tell you that if you can get that guy to throw out some bacon, I'll make you the best French-Canadian pea soup you ever tasted." He could have, too; for many years Butch owned a very successful restaurant in Montreal.

At a charity golf tournament in 1957, a female Canadiens' fan asked me to autograph her program. I did and she thanked me. But then, as I was turning away, she said: "I still hate you when you're refereeing a hockey game. You stink!" With all that, the Montreal fans knew hockey and they were fair. Often after a game I'd go downtown to have a couple of beers in a restaurant or bar. It didn't matter whether it had been a good night or a bad one, I'd go out to relax. People would come over and most times they'd say something like: "Geez, did we hate you tonight! But do you want to know something? You were right."

Toronto, on the other hand, had the deadest crowds I ever refereed before. Oh, I'd get them stirred up occasionally, but usually you thought you were in a morgue. The fans seemed more interested in the mechanics of the sport and less inclined to become bored or impatient than in other arenas. That may be the way Conn Smythe wanted it, because there was a rigid set of rules at Maple Leaf Gardens. If you hurled even harmless things like programs or paper cups, you were warned once and evicted the second time.

I'm going to tell a secret now. As I've shown many times in my own career, a referee can make a mistake. But you never see a referee make a deliberate bad call. I'll admit now that I did that a few times. The Toronto audiences used to be so quiet, I'd say to myself: "Where the hell is everybody? Have they all gone home? " On those nights, if one team was well in front and a bad call wasn't going to hurt anybody, I'd call one against the Leafs. That would wake everybody up. They'd be yelling that Storey was a bum and blind and a thief. I loved it, and at least I knew they were still alive.

There was one night they got really worked up. It was Detroit at Toronto in the playoffs, with some nut threatening to shoot both Gordie Howe and Ted Lindsay. It was a good, tough game and the Red Wings won 3-2, eliminating the Maple Leafs. Lindsay just had to rub it in, turning his stick around to pretend it was a machine gun, and going, "Rat-a-ta-rat-a-ta," while spraying the crowd. They were mad enough to start with, but now they were ferocious and not too pleased with me either. George Hayes, one of the linesmen, and I had to catch a train so we undressed, showered, dressed, packed our bags and were ready to go in seven minutes. We went outside and the lobby was wall-to-wall with angry people who absolutely hated our guts at that moment. I started to push my way through, with George shoving me from behind, but we were hardly moving.

Suddenly, this young lady was in front of me and she was hysterical. She began to scratch me on the chest with her fingernails. I could feel the blood running down across my stomach, but I didn't know what to do. The woman had gone totally bonkers. I looked her right in the eyes and there was nobody home. The crowd had no idea what was going on, but if I slapped her to bring her out of it, they were going to lynch me. I reached out and grabbed her by two parts of her anatomy I won't mention and just picked her up and moved her to the side. She absolutely went into a trance, never opened her mouth, never said a word. George and I went out of there in a helluva hurry. When I got on the train, I took my clothes off and they were all bloody from the waist up.

Toronto is the only city in which the NHL rink I worked in is either still in use or not about to be retired. The Olympia has been replaced in Detroit by Joe Louis Arena and there's been a new Madison Square Garden in New York since 1971, with yet another one planned. There's a new Chicago Stadium for 1994-95 and they've started construction on a new Forum in Montreal and a new Garden in Boston. Maple Leaf Gardens soon will be the only one left, and I think I'd miss it most of all. Opened in 1931, it's been declared a heritage monument, so it can't be torn down. They'll have to build a new one on another site, and who has that much money?

Detroit became famous for the things thrown onto the ice. The fan who threw the first octopus was named Pete Cusimano and, as far as I'm concerned, he goes down in history right beside the people who invented airline food, junk mail and elevator music. It was in the spring of 1952, during a playoff game between the Canadiens and Red Wings, and all sorts of people in Detroit began to copy him, and still do. More octopuses, three dozen in one night, some fish, some chickens and even a three-foot eel have flown out of the stands during games there in the years since. Cusimano once was asked why he did it in the first place, and explained that an octopus had eight legs and the Wings needed eight playoff wins for the Stanley Cup. The arithmetic at the time made sense, and the Wings won it all in three of the first four years after he started. But the magic rubbed off after that.

For some reason, I usually seemed to do the first playoff game in Detroit each season and that damn thing would come out of the stands in the first five minutes every time. It was really weird-looking coming through the air and I got so I couldn't concentrate on anything else until it appeared. If you check the records of those games, you'll see there were never any early penalties. I used to drop the puck and then just skate around looking for the bugger with the octopus. I never touched them. No, sir, I was afraid of them. Marcel Pronovost, the Detroit defenceman, had no fear of them at all and he became the designated guy to go and pick them up off the ice and put them in the garbage.

Another time I had better luck with something thrown on the ice at the Olympia. I was roaring down the side, chasing the play, when something shiny suddenly caught my eye going through the air. I reached down with one hand like a short-stop, still skating like hell, and—THUD!—I had an American half-dollar in my hand. I had caught it on the first bounce, although I guess it could just as easily have hit me on the head. Believe it or not, I didn't spend it on beer after the game. I still have it somewhere.

Boston had the narrowest ice surface in the NHL and it could become a little congested, particularly since the two teams didn't have their benches on the same side. That meant that whichever side of the ice a referee was on, he could run into traffic going and coming from the bench. I can remember a lot of collisions in the Boston Garden, in the old Madison Square Garden in New York and the Montreal Forum before they changed it there. Toronto, Detroit and Chicago always had the players' benches on the same side, so that was one thing I didn't have to worry about. I worked the other side and had a clear path.

A lot of officials didn't like to work in Boston because the crowd was so close it was right into the game. Because they'd had some great players and great teams, they seemed to think they should always win. They were upset any time the Bruins even got behind. But I liked that atmosphere. I liked fans who cared, even the night they broke down the doors because they couldn't get tickets to a playoff sellout. I also liked old buildings and the Garden dated from 1928. It was built above the Boston & Maine railway station off Causeway Street and part of its offbeat charm was that they'd have to go in there from time to time with rifles and shoot the pigeons and the rats after they multiplied.

I wish the Boston fans had felt the same way about me as they did about the Bruins. I had a metal bolt—a big piece of hardware—thrown at me one night. It just missed and scraped about two feet along the ice surface. It was odd that years later, when I was referee-in-chief of the National Lacrosse League, the Boston franchise was named the Bolts. Another time, I thought I'd been sent for. As I bent forward to make a call, something hit the back of my neck with a SMACK! I was sure it was a bullet, especially after I looked at the front of my sweater and it was dark red. I thought I was bleeding to death but I didn't feel any pain except for a dull ache in my neck. I realized when I saw the seeds it was a very ripe tomato that had hit me. Thrown from the the top deck of the Garden, it felt like a lot more.

Another night I was standing along the side boards at the Garden when suddenly one of the linesmen screamed at me, "Look out!" I ducked down by instinct and whirled around and there right behind me was a lasso dangling from the balcony. It looked exactly like a hangman's noose and had been just above my head and neck when I was warned. Some guy in the front row upstairs had been trying to snare me. I spent the rest of that game with my head up—and my eyes, too.

Chicago was the dirtiest, worst place I refereed. The Stadium was in a slum area and that was just the way you felt going in. The organist would always play "Three Blind Mice" when we skated out and then the crummiest crowd in the league would be on us for the rest of the night. Even with octopus fever in Detroit, Chicago was the worst for throwing things. Someone once tossed a bag of live mice onto the ice, and one man threw a denture at me, which I guess he thought was one way of putting teeth into an argument.

But those fans, I felt, could be worth two goals a game to the Blackhawks. They could whip the team to the kind of effort it would never show in someone else's rink. Yet no one will ever convince me that those same fans didn't cost the Hawks a chance to play Boston for the Stanley Cup in 1953. In the seventh and deciding game of the semi-finals against the Canadiens, the Hawks were ahead in the third period until the fans started throwing stuff to protest a call. There was a long delay and the break seemed to change everything around. The Canadiens came to life and Chicago lost the game and the series. The Canadiens, who had been on the ropes, went on to win the Cup.

I had one frightening personal experience in the Stadium. During a brawl between the Maple Leafs and Blackhawks, a guy threw an egg from way up in the seats. If an egg hits you at the right angle, it acts just like ground glass, and that was what happened to me. It hit me high up on the side of the face and literally took a strip of skin off, right down to my lips. Everybody quit fighting immediately. George Armstrong, the Leafs' captain, went to his bench and came back with a towel, telling me: "You look terrible, Red. Wipe your face." I finally got the bleeding stopped, and we were ready to resume the game when someone asked me, "What are the penalties from the fight?" I had no idea by then who had done what. I looked around and said: "I'm the only one that got hurt. No penalties. Let's get this game going again." They all thought it was funny when I said I was the only one hurt, and I had no more trouble in a game that had looked like it was going to blow up. I couldn't shave that side of my face for a week.

One of the things the league told its officials in my day— and still does—was to be very careful about the kind of people they associated with, particularly on the road. There were some fellows in Chicago who used to drive me to the train station after games. They were quiet and well-behaved and never gave anyone any trouble that I could see. One spring, they phoned me in Detroit and asked me to get them playoff tickets there, and I fixed it. We arranged to meet at the Bagley Bar for a sandwich and a beer after the game. I arrived and the place was jammed, hockey fans everywhere. I saw the guys from Chicago at the other end of the bar. Since I'd had a tough night, I thought I'd have a beer before I tried to get down there.

I ordered it and the guy sitting on the next stool turned around and said: "We had to put up with you at the Olympia all night. Is there any reason we have to put up with you here?" I said I'd worked hard and was just trying to relax with a few beers. This big clown, who was half-sloshed, just got more abusive. He turned back to get his drink and suddenly his neck turned dead white. I figured he might be having a heart attack, so I went around to look. I saw one of my friends, just a little guy, had stuck a gun in his belly and was telling him, "If we were in Chicago, I'd blow your guts out for talking that way to my friend Red." I was scared stiff and got right out of there. I had the little guy traced and it turned out he was the leader of the mob that controlled a big section of Chicago. I checked him off my list of friends and acquaintances.

New York's old Madison Square Garden on 8th Avenue at 50th Street was a very special place. It was busy almost every night of the year, which was fine if you didn't follow the circus or the dog show in. It was a brick building with two balconies, served by three subway lines, and it could hold about 19,000 fans. They all had two things in common: strong voices and not a lot of knowledge of hockey. But they knew a lot about enjoying themselves and they enjoyed the game. Despite the fact that they chanted constantly, "Storey is a bum, Storey is a bum," I liked the New York crowd. They yelled at me, but they amused me, too. During a stoppage in play one night, a loudmouth hollered: "Hey, Storey. The dog show opens next week. Are you entered?" I almost laughed out loud. Another time, a guy yelled out: "Storey, is this your last year? Or was that last year?" And still another Rangers' fan shouted, "Hey, pinhead, how can you sleep out there with all the lights on?"

Once after a game, a well-dressed elderly gentleman with a

beautifully wrapped package stopped me in the hall and said, "Mr. Storey, this is just a little something to show some of us fans here in New York appreciate your work." Startled, I mumbled something in appreciation and opened the parcel. Inside I found a cork from a thermos bottle, with a note that read, "For the hole in your head."

Some New Yorkers weren't as polite. One night there was a crowd of about 50 people waiting outside the Garden. I walked through them and when I started to cross the street, a snowball hit me from behind on the head, jolted me a little and knocked my hat off. I turned around to face them, and asked if the guy who had thrown it had enough guts to come out and meet me in the street. Nobody moved. I repeated the challenge, and still nobody moved. I called them all yellow, dusted off my hat, picked up my bag and walked on with no trouble at all. It's a funny thing. In my lifetime, nobody has ever touched me from in front. Nobody ever tried to touch me as long as I was looking at them. Referees generally eat in a restaurant with their backs to the wall. John McCauley didn't take that precaution one time in New York. Someone sucker punched him and he lost an eye.

When I was the referee-in-chief of the National Lacrosse League, we went into Quebec City late in the season for the team's big awards night. They honored guys for most goals, most assists, most penalties, most gentlemanly, most everything. There was a fan in Quebec City who was the most obnoxious fan of any sport I've ever seen anywhere. He was absolutely terrible. He sat above and to the left of the visiting team and hollered non-stop abuse and personal insults. Well, the final award was for fan of the year. A name was called, and this yahoo came out right through the gate at the visitors' bench. He collected a beautiful trophy but when he came waltzing back towards the bench to get off the floor, he couldn't resist throwing some taunts at the Long Island players while waving his silverware around. Morley Kells was coaching Long Island, a good coach but a little crazy in the head, a sort of crackpot who could cause more trouble in a game than a herd of cattle. He got so mad he walked out and flattened the fan of the year, knocked him absolutely cold. It was the only time all season that I agreed with Morley.

For many years, Scotty Alexander was the trainer for the Hershey Bears of the American Hockey League. He also was one of the many trainers who served as backup goaltenders in the old days, and one night he had to go into the nets in Buffalo when the regular was injured. There were two women sitting behind the net and they were giving him a going-over that was out of this world. Scotty figured out how to handle it. He pointed right at them during a lull in the play and shouted: "Hey, I thought I recognized your voices. You're the two babes I met in Mary's whorehouse last night." There wasn't another word out of them for the rest of the game.

I think the best line I ever had directed at me by a fan, at any time and at any level, was during an old-timers' game in Lethbridge, Alberta, a few years ago. We had a terrific match-up, the Detroit alumni with Ted Lindsay and Red Kelly and all those guys against the Western all-stars, who included the Bentleys—Max and Doug—and Bill Mosienko and people like that. We had a full house, which meant a lot of money for charity, and we had a great game. It was tied as we came out for the third period. There was a hush before I dropped the puck and this huge voice came down from the top corner of the building. "Hey, Storey," the guy yelled. "You must be pregnant. You've already missed two periods."

15

A Travellin' Man

You'd have had to paraphrase Charles Dickens to describe travel in the old NHL—A Tale of Six Cities—by saying it was the best of times, it was the worst of times. The companions were great, the schedule wasn't. For nine years, I was home in Montreal no more than four nights per month during the seven-month hockey season. I'd have travelled about 50,000 miles, most of them while dead tired, before I'd get home for good in the spring.

A referee skates longer and harder than anyone on the ice during a hockey game. I'd be out there for the full 60 minutes and I had to cover both ends of the rink as well as the neutral zone in the middle. After the game, I'd usually have to sprint for a train and then I'd spend two or three hours trying to relax enough to go to sleep—if I was lucky, by three o'clock in the morning. Then at 6:30, a conductor would be shaking me awake for the next stop and the next game. Sleeping on trains and in hotel rooms night after night became a physical and mental strain.

It was a lonely life on trains and in hotels, too, because there was an unwritten league rule against fraternization between the officials on the one hand and the players and coaches on the other. They didn't want you staying in the same places, or even eating in the same restaurants. There would be times, I must admit, when the exceptions to that regulation became the rule. But I've sat on trains for hours knowing there was a good card game going on a few cars back. I couldn't join in, unless I knew and trusted the officials who were travelling with me, all the guys in the game, and all the players on that team. I had to be sure they'd keep it quiet.

Even getting a meal on a train could be a problem for us. Often there would be two teams travelling on the same train, along with an officiating crew, and there was only one dining car. One team would go in first and have a drink and eat and chat over coffee. They were in no hurry to leave because they knew the other team was waiting. The second team would finally get into the diner and after they were through, if there was time—and any food—to spare, we'd get to eat. If the two teams had played that night, which was often the case because the league scheduled a lot of home-and-home weekend series, often with the same officiating crew, there probably had been a rhubarb or two. Because of the potential for trouble, I didn't want to be anywhere near any of the guys who might have been giving me a problem. A lot of the time the officials never got to eat at all.

In a six-team league with only three top referees, the scheduling could become a little ridiculous. I can remember leaving home in Montreal and doing 10 games before I got back. I worked in Toronto, Detroit, Boston and New York in the NHL, and St. Louis and Cleveland in the minors on that trip. Another time, I worked games in Omaha, Nebraska, New York and Montreal on successive nights, logging more than 2,000 miles. "What's the matter?" one of the Canadiens asked me before the opening faceoff of the last of those games. "You look tired." I was too exhausted to think of a comeback.

The worst single trip was for the second part of a double-header between the Canadiens and Blackhawks. Saturday night was always hockey night in Montreal, and we'd always have to rush out after the game to catch a train to somewhere, but the Chicago trip was the most gruelling. As soon as the game was over, both teams and the officials would dash to get the Montreal-Toronto night train at Westmount, a couple of miles west of the Forum and closer than Windsor Station downtown. Each team would have a private car of its own. When the train reached Toronto, they'd just shuttle those cars and hook them up to the next train. The players were able to sleep right through it. We were in regular sleepers and we had to get up and get off and find the next train ourselves. We'd finally reach Chicago at about six o'clock Sunday night for a 7:30 game. The teams would get police escorts from the station to the arena, but we had to find a taxi and make it on our own. It was always tough on the nerves because it was cut so fine.

Getting home was even worse. On a train leaving Chicago at midnight, I'd arrive in Detroit about seven o'clock in the morning. I'd have time to go across the street for breakfast and then I'd get on an 8:30 train for Toronto. I'd be there by 3:30 that afternoon, catch the four o'clock train for Montreal, and reach home around 10 or 11 p.m. I'd have been almost 24 hours getting home on three different trains. The whole round trip took about 48 hours and you'd really only be off the trains to go to the game in Chicago. I always said that when I left the NHL I'd never get on a train in my life again, and I don't think I have, except in the direst emergencies.

People asked me why we didn't fly. We did once in a while, but, strangely enough, only when we had lots of time. Airline schedules still aren't written in concrete, but then they were even more uncertain. Weather also was more of a problem for flying than it seems to be now, and we were always travelling in the winter in Canada and the northern United States. We were working in cities that really weren't that far apart, unlike today, when the NHL is spread from coast to coast and into the Deep South and everyone has to fly. Another argument against our flying was that we could be fined if we missed a game. No excuses were allowed—not weather, not mechanical problems, not missed connections, nothing.

The league preferred to have one officiating team do the home-and-home games because you'd know what had gone on the night before and what to watch for. I always looked at a home-and-home series this way: when I'd leave Montreal, say, for Chicago, I'd feel I was only halfway through the game. Over the years, there were some incidents on trains between players on rival teams, but not many because it was carefully planned that they wouldn't bump into each other. One team's Pullman, for example, would be in front of the dining car, and the other team's would be behind it. There was no excuse or reason for anyone to walk through the other guys' car.

The one thing the NHL didn't want you doing was refereeing back-to-back games in the same building. They'd try to keep away from having you do two games on Saturday and Sunday in the Forum, for example. Even if the home team was playing two different teams, they'd keep you out of the second game. They figured it was too much pressure to do two games in a row before the same fans, and they had a point. Let's say that Saturday night I had a so-so game in Montreal and there were a lot of beefs and hollering and throwing stuff. The league wouldn't want me coming back into that atmosphere right away. Even if the guy who was coming in to referee the Sunday game had had his worst night of the season at the Forum a month earlier, the crowd would be tickled to death to see him because they thought I'd been so bad on Saturday.

I'm not saying all of our travel wasn't fun, and or that all of it was routine. Some of the times I remember best came from pre-season games, which often were played in out-of-the-way places to give fans in the smaller cities a chance to see NHLers in action—and, incidentally, to make an easy buck or two for the teams involved. They'd assign you exhibition games near your home and one time I had assignments on successive nights in Quebec City and Three Rivers with Curly Davies, a linesman who lived around the corner from me in Montreal.

After the game in Quebec, we checked into a local motel for the night. In those days, it was up to each official to take care of his own equipment and our habit was to put our wet working clothes on the radiator in the room to dry. We did that this night and went to bed. I woke up coughing sometime during the night. The place was full of smoke. We got out of the room, and were standing outside wearing only underwear shorts on a frosty October night when the fire trucks arrived, sirens going and lights flashing. They got the flames doused in short order. Our clothes had caught fire from contact with the coils in the radiator, which we hadn't realized was electric. The chief said that in another 30 seconds we both could have been dead. We had to replace our damaged clothes ourselves, since the league provided no help in that department, which meant we ended up working those two exhibition games for nothing. Even so, we were happier and more relaxed than the guys who popped out of several of the motel rooms when they heard the sirens and made a fast exit while buttoning up their clothes.

Another time I was doing a pre-season series between two NHL teams and after they played in Quebec City, I went over to this club I knew for a few beers. I was sitting out of the way in the rear and I noticed the coach of one of the teams up front at a ringside table. There was a singer on stage, a great looker, and in between acts she would come down and light cigarettes for the customers and all that. The coach was hot for her, she seemed to like him, they were doing some nuzzling and I thought he was going to get lucky. Right at the end of the last show, however, it was revealed that the singer was a female impersonator. You could have fooled me. The coach left in a hurry.

The next night we were in Chicoutimi and at one point the coach sent out his captain to find out about a call I had made, as in, "What the hell were you doing?" I said to the captain:

"Look, you're not going to have any idea what I'm talking about. But I want you to go back and you tell him this: 'Red says when you can tell the difference between a broad and a guy, he'll explain the rules of hockey to you.'" The captain said, "What the hell?" but I told him, "Just say exactly that." I watched the captain go back to the bench and pass on the message. The coach just turned and ran up the hall and out. I never saw him again the whole night. I guess he'd thought no one he knew had seen him.

The scariest trip I can remember was for the first game I ever refereed in the American Hockey League, in Hershey, Pennsylvania. The NHL had an agreement with the AHL to supply officials for a certain number of games. One Friday evening Clarence Campbell, the NHL president, called me and said there was an emergency. I'd have to replace another referee, who was sick, for an Indianapolis-Hershey game the next night. That was worth $50 to me, so I said okay and phoned for airline reservations—a flight to New York and a flight to Harrisburg, followed by a 22-mile taxi ride to Hershey, arriving in plenty of time for the Saturday night game. Sounds simple, doesn't it?

It would have been except that a bad winter storm blew in the next morning, there were long delays, and by the time I reached New York, my connecting flight had left. I tried every airline, but no one had a flight to Harrisburg. I tried the railways and the bus companies; same thing. I called Lloyd Blinco, the general manager of the Hershey team, and told him what was happening. He said the game was an important one between two bitter rivals, they needed me badly and I'd better get there even if I had to rent a plane. I made those arrangements and went to meet the pilot, who turned out to be a guy in a leather jacket with a couple of days' worth of beard and a big cigar.

We went out the gate and right in front of me was a big four-engine job. I was thinking, "Wait till I tell the guys about this first-class deal." I headed for the plane, and the pilot said: "Not that one. Ours is on the other side." What a letdown. The plane I had rented and was going to fly in had wings that came up my waist and one small engine in front. We got in and the door on my side wouldn't close firmly. The pilot said there was something wrong with it, but not to worry because the air pressure would keep it closed once we got up. I leaned as far away from it as I could.

I really began to worry when we were ready to go and the pilot asked me to keep an eye out for other planes, which took off and landed at LaGuardia every 30 seconds or so. He said they didn't know we were there. When we reached the height he wanted to cruise at, he suddenly reached behind me and yanked my luggage over behind his seat. I asked him what was going on, and he said, "You're heavier than me and you're tilting the plane, so I had to even it up." We finally got over Harrisburg and he said, "I've never flown at night, so would you help me find the airport?" I spotted some blue lights and pointed them out to him. He had started to glide in for a landing when he suddenly gave it the juice and pulled out of there, snarling: "You stupid idiot. That's the gas works."

We somehow got down eventually. I was late and I told the cabbie to step on it. The next 22 miles were as scary as the plane ride, but we got there. I'd never been in the Hershey Arena and used the main entrance, which brought me inside halfway up the stands. They were just starting the second period and I asked an usher how it was going. He told me they'd already had to call the police to break up an awful riot. Obie O'Brien, a Hershey player out with a broken wrist, was refereeing and I guess with his inexperience and the players taking advantage of him, it was natural that all hell would break loose.

I found the dressing room and was ready for action five minutes later. O'Brien, who was one of the worst referee-baiters in the league, came over and said: "Am I ever glad to see you. Believe me, I'll never complain to an official again." I sort of doubted that. I realized I had to do something to straighten this mess out, once and for all. I blew the whistle as soon as I had dropped the puck for the faceoff to get the game going again, and penalized the player on each team nearest me. I did the same thing again, dropped the puck, blew the whistle and sent two guys off. Then I looked around and said, "Okay, now we've got some room out here so let's have a hockey game." We did, a terrific game the rest of the way.

One memorable trip came at a time when I needed it the most. It was just after I had resigned from the NHL when Campbell wouldn't support me in the playoffs in the spring of 1959. I'd agreed to do a post-season European tour with the Boston and New York teams. Campbell tried as hard as he could to stop me but the two general managers, the Patrick brothers, Lynn with the Bruins and Muzz with the Rangers, said: "We asked Red to go and Red's going. Our word is good." There was nothing like five weeks in Europe to take my mind off my troubles.

A couple of good friends, George Hayes and Bill Morrison, were the linesmen, and we were to do 23 games in 27 days, with a little R'n'R before and after. It was the toughest such tour ever in hockey and we went all over the place. The trip left everybody tired and some guys were hurt. One game in Berlin, we had 10 hockey players in the stands; nothing serious, mind you, just enough minor injuries to keep them out of the game. We felt good that the three officials were the only people who started and finished the entire schedule. Then I got strep throat the day the trip ended.

There were receptions everywhere we went, which was fun except when you had to get out on the ice the next day. In a game in Antwerp, there was a stoppage of play. The puck was at George's feet and he just kicked it across the ice to Bill. He looked at it, thought this was a good game, and kicked it back to George, who kicked it right back again. I went over to

George and said: "Geez, this is cute. What the hell is going on?" Bill kicked the puck back again and I said, "George, will you pick up the goddamn thing so we can get this game over with?" He said: "Red, if I bend over to pick up the puck, I'm not gettin' back up again. I've been into the vodka all day and I'm doin' very well just to be here." I told George, "Okay, I'll pick up all the pucks, don't you move too far, and we'll get through this."

By and large, the teams played hard. There were some games that were better than the Stanley Cup finals. That's pride. One thing about good athletes, they'll play anywhere. They'll go over to the sandlot and play as tough as they would in Madison Square Garden. One night in Geneva, the teams were playing a beautiful game, great skating and passing and stickhandling, and the fans weren't making any noise at all. The Patricks came into the officials' room after the second period, and Muzz asked: "What's wrong? This is the best game we've had over here and they're sitting on their hands." I told him that all I knew was it was a helluva hockey game.

Then Lynn said: "I think I know what's wrong. They've read all the time about how violent the NHL is and they're not interested in seeing nice hockey. They want to see a little rough stuff. I'm going back to my room and I'm going to tell my team to belt every Ranger sweater they see." Muzz said: "Oh, yeah? Well, I'm going into my room and tell them to kick the shit out of every Bruin they see." They were really getting mad at each other and as they were leaving the room, I stopped them. "Hold it just a minute. Are you going to tell them that I know this?" They said no, I was on my own. As soon as we got back on the ice, I called over the captains, Red Sullivan of the Rangers and Fernie Flaman of the Bruins, and told them: "Look, I know the rules. I know your instructions. I just want you to take a good look at me and George and Bill. These are white and black sweaters. Don't hit them. Apart from that, you're on your own for the third period."

They ran from here to Regina to hit each other. George and
Bill and I just stood around and marvelled at it. All we did
was stay out of the road. We could have called some boarding
and hooking, but mostly they were just great bodychecks. At
one point, there were only five guys standing up on the ice, the
two goalies and the three of us. The game finished and,
amazingly, nobody died and we didn't have to call an ambulance. The crowd gave them a 10-minute standing ovation and
some fans said it was the best show they'd ever seen in that
building. That was what Lynn and Muzz wanted, so we let
them play that way the rest of the tour.

Phil Watson was coaching the Rangers and he had some of
his guys nuts. Everyone else was over there to play hockey and
have some fun; Phil treated it like the Stanley Cup. Boston
took several injuries, so there was some animosity built up
and we had to work our asses off to keep it under control.
They even kept the teams in separate hotels. It could have
turned into a disaster, because there were guys on that tour
like Eddie Shack and Jimmy Bartlett. We taped over their
names on their sweaters once, and marked them "Nuts" and
"Bolts." They didn't care. Shack and Bartlett . . . The Good
Lord said brains and they thought he said trains, and they
both missed them anyway. We also had tough guys like Lou
Fontinato of the Rangers and Vic Stasiuk of the Bruins along,
so it meant something when Lynn, Muzz and Milt Schmidt,
the Bruins' coach, said the standard of officiating had been
very high. Watson was never happy about officials anytime.

There was time for some fun. One morning in Geneva just
as the tour was starting, a guy who's now in the Hockey Hall
of Fame came down to breakfast in the hotel and said he'd lost
all his teeth, or they'd been stolen. The Swiss Hockey Association found a great dentist and had him a new set of dentures
within 24 hours. We went off on the tour for four weeks and
came back at the end of it to Geneva, to fly home from there.
We were in the same hotel and this young lady arrived in the

lobby and presented this guy with a box. His teeth were inside it, and she said, calling him by his first name, "You left these under my pillow that night." Let me add that he was a single man at the time.

In another hotel, I came out of my room and directly across from me a door was open. A player I won't name saw me and said, "Red, what the hell is this?" He was gesturing at a bidet. My wheels started turning. "It's for tourists. When you go sightseeing or shopping and you come back, you're tired and dirty. You shower and change and feel great, but your feet are still hot from all the walking. This little basin is to wash your feet in nice cool water." He said: "No kidding? What a great idea. What the hell will they think of next?" A couple of hours later, we had a reception to go to, so I knocked on the door and his roommate, Eric Nesterenko, opened up. I could see the other guy washing his feet in the bidet, and he said: "This is the greatest invention I've ever seen. We should have these in Canada." I never had the heart to tell him the truth. He's also in the Hockey Hall of Fame.

No trip would be complete without a George Hayes story. We were in Vienna. I was a little tired after the game and decided to go back to the hotel early. I was rooming with George, who decided to stay out a little longer. I fell asleep and woke up to a racket outside. I looked out the window and there were squad cars blocking off the street and a lot of people yelling and milling around. I looked again and I saw that George was right in the middle of it, shouting and waving his arms. Traffic was piled up in every direction and I could see most of the Boston players, who were in the same hotel, hanging out the windows. They finally got it settled, broke up the crowd and George came in. I was back in bed, pretending I was asleep. He sat down and I heard him take off one shoe and throw it against the wall, and then the other, and he was yelling, "That no good sonofabitch" and so on. I didn't let him know I was awake.

The next morning, we went downstairs together. I let George finish his breakfast before I said: "Now, what the hell was all that about down here in the middle of the night? You had the Boston team up, you had me up, you had all the guests in the hotel up, you had the cops out from all over the city." George said, "No sonofabitch is gonna cheat me out of my money and get away with it." I asked him how he'd been cheated and he told me it was on the cab fare home, when he didn't get enough change. "I work too hard for my money and nobody is gonna steal it." We were dealing with foreign currency here so I grabbed a napkin, got the figures from him and worked it out. "George, you got this whole town in an uproar. Everybody lost a half night's sleep. The cops all had to make out reports, and do you know what it was all over?" He said not exactly, and I told him: "In Canadian money, 28 cents." He made a face, and said: "Are you kiddin'? I thought he was beatin' me for 28 bucks."

One man who really got something from the tour was Bobby Hull. He and Nesterenko and a couple of other Blackhawks had been added to the Rangers' squad to replace players who were injured too badly to make the trip. I was standing at the airport waiting to get on the plane for home, and Bobby came along. We started chatting, and I was bitching. "I can't wait to get out of here. This is the last time they'll ever get me on a trip like this. It's just too much work for one referee."

Bobby said: "You're right, Red, but I'll tell you something. Because of all the games and the parties and the pressure and all that, I've learned to pace myself over here. I know that's why Gordie Howe has had so many great years. He paces himself. He never wastes an effort. I'm going to lead the league in scoring next year because of what I learned on this trip." He did, too.

I was always tired after a hockey season. This time I was exhausted. Including the NHL, AHL, playoffs and European trip, I had worked in a total of 137 games during the 1958-59 season. But no more. I had resigned from the NHL in April and wouldn't be going back. During the previous nine winters, I hadn't seen my family as often as the man who came to read the gas meter. It was a terrible burden to put on Helen, who had had to hold everything together while I was away so much. I remember arriving back in Montreal and finding Helen and my young sons, Bob and Doug, waiting for me at the airport. "I'm home for good now," I told them.

And I was—except for refereeing at least 2,500 charity games and giving about 3,000 speeches over the next 35 years from one coast of Canada to the other.

16

The Real World

When I resigned from the NHL during the playoffs in 1959, I was leaving the greatest job in the world, doing something I liked that enabled me to give my family the things I hadn't had when I was a kid. I was making a guaranteed $6,000 per year from the NHL, and extra for extra work. At the same time, I had always wanted to have something as a backup. After Canada Car and Foundry cut back in the years following the Second World War, the job I'd come to Montreal for in the first place no longer existed. I added to the income I was making from my officiating work in various sports by selling auto parts for a while. Then, in the 1950s, I sold automobiles for three different dealers, moving around like all car salesmen do, but I didn't like that business too well. You had to stretch the truth and I wasn't built to do that. My conscience wouldn't let me.

In September, 1958, I had a chance to join the Adams Division of Seagram's, the distiller, working for $50 per week when I wasn't refereeing. That certainly wasn't enough money to support a family on after I left the NHL, but I took the gamble and they made it permanent. Everything worked out and I ended up staying with Seagram's for almost 25 years. I worked as a salesman and public relations man. Some of my buddies said I was also a test pilot for the company, but I never drank hard liquor. I disliked the taste. I did love my beer, though, especially after a hockey game, when I'd drop up to 10 pounds in fluids. Beer was better for me than having a bottle of pop or a gallon of water. There's more food value in beer than in those other things and it doesn't matter how much beer you drink: within 24 hours it's all gone from your system.

I used to tell people that Samuel Bronfman, the founder of Seagram's and probably the richest man in Canada, had offered me a partnership. They'd look amazed and I'd say, "Yeah, he keeps asking me when I'm going to take an interest in his business." His son, Charles, who later brought the Expos to Montreal, was very honest, but he could blow his top in a hurry. We had a sports dinner in Montreal one time with Rocky Marciano as the headliner, and I was handling the hospitality suite. Afterward, there had to be 200 people in the room and Charles and I got into a bitter argument about sports. We were screaming at each other and everybody stopped talking, thinking I was going to blow my job. Finally, he said, "I'll bet you $25 you're wrong." I said, "Charles, you don't pay me enough to bet 25 bucks." He started to laugh and said, "You're right," and walked away. I used to step on a few toes from time to time to get the job done and I know that in the last few years I was with Seagram's, some members of middle management—my immediate bosses—were writing Charles regularly, dropping hints to get rid of me. They were jealous of my freedom, travel and exposure. He ignored them. He'd always stand by you if you did your share.

I was totally away from sports for a while after leaving the NHL, and I really missed it. I got back into it, at least indirectly, through CKGM Radio in Montreal (the GM stood for "golden modulation," which certainly wasn't me). They were selling a package to Paré Lanes, a big bowling complex in Montreal, and offered me a sports talk show as part of it. I jumped at the chance, even though I had never done even one minute of radio and had no idea what to expect. I stumbled through the first three or four calls, but then got a really intelligent guy and it was okay after that. I also learned that whatever happens, keep going. If you pause, people figure you don't know what you're talking about.

That led me to doing sports for CKGM's morning man, Doug Burroughs. I'd go in and we'd just shoot the breeze, give some scores, have some fun. He went on to another radio job at CHSJ in Saint John, New Brunswick, and called me a while later. In the meantime, I'd given up my CKGM job because I was just too busy with other things—Seagram's, the banquet circuit, old-timers' hockey and so on. Doug called me and asked me to do a show with him for one month by phone until he could find someone full-time. That temporary arrangement lasted for 14 years. I did that show from wherever I was across the country, even from telephone booths beside the highway.

One time I got sick and the doctor said I had to take a rest. I knew that meant I'd have to get out of Montreal, so I planned on going down to Florida. I called Doug and asked him if he wanted to get somebody to replace me or cancel the show for a couple of weeks. He said I could do it by phoning in 10 minutes earlier than usual and getting the previous night's scores from him. It was terrific. I'd be out at the edge of the pool and we'd be chatting and I sounded like I'd been at every game played anywhere. We didn't tell the people I was in Florida. We didn't want them to think I was goofing off. But one morning about 500 goddamn seagulls flew over— squawk! squawk! squawk! Doug, trying to cover, asked: "What's going on? We must have a bad connection." But there was no way we could fool Maritimers about seagulls. They knew I wouldn't be out by the shore in Montreal in the middle of winter.

I also did several series of shows on location from bars and restaurants in Montreal for CKGM, with guests and an audience, and 10 years after I left the NHL I finally got onto

Hockey Night In Canada. Clarence Campbell, the NHL president, had managed to keep me off the league's telecasts for that long. It was silly, but I can understand what he was thinking. Red Storey was known as a bit of a rebel and they were afraid I might go out there and tear the league apart. But they didn't know me very well. I had a terrific love for the game, always did, and my beefs were never with sports, but with people. I think Campbell finally realized that I was running around the country making hundreds of speeches and speaking well of the league, never hurting it. Or maybe he just got tired.

In any event, I worked for about 10 years with the Montreal crew, Danny Gallivan and Dick Irvin. Danny's predecessor as the voice of the Canadiens, Doug Smith, was a good friend of mine and the only broadcaster I ever heard who would drop his voice down when a goal was scored. He'd just growl and it was really effective. Doug had one bad habit on the air; he was always running down the officials' decisions. He was working for Dow Brewery and they called him in one day and told him: "Either broadcast or referee. Make up your mind which job you want." That was the end of his knocking. The easiest thing for anyone is to sit there and rip an official. I always said that a referee was like a businessman who in two weeks has 10 days' work, some good, some bad, some so-so. Give a referee 10 games and he'll have seven great ones, two that are iffy and one that is, pardon the expression, horseshit. That's normal.

No one has five good days every work week. If you're only bad 10 percent of the time, you'll be okay. It was the same thing with players. They're human, too. I always thought it was better to say John Doe made a terrific shift on that defenceman and beat him than to say the defenceman made a lousy play. I've never liked second-guessing. I was always trying to sell the game. I've been doing that all my life.

Danny and Dick were the best broadcasting team hockey has ever had and they were as fair as any I've ever heard. They never knocked anybody. Working with them was a breeze. All you had to do was make sure you were prepared properly so you could anticipate what each team had to offer. Danny and Dick were so easy and professional that the first night with them, I thought I'd been there all my life. There was one curious thing about Danny. Ten seconds after the game was over, you didn't know where he was. He'd just drop the microphone and be gone. He was a very private person but as long as there's hockey, he'll be remembered as the No. 1 announcer of them all.

I guess the comment I made that drew the most reaction during those 10 years came at a time when the Canadiens were in a rare slump early in the 1970s and everybody was wandering around Montreal asking each other what was wrong. During one game I was doing, the Canadiens had a power play with Yvan Cournoyer and Jacques Lemaire on the points. The puck bounced out to centre ice and a player on the other team picked it up and took off. Cournoyer and Lemaire were two of the Canadiens' fastest players, they were going full out and the other guy was pulling away from them. He went in and scored and after everybody had settled down again, I told the TV audience: "There's the reason for the slump. It's no secret. I'm going to show you the play again. Here are the Canadiens' two fastest players and they can't catch this guy because the team is not in shape."

The next morning the phone rang at home, and it was one of my friends. "You're still alive after what you said last night?" I told him all I'd done was tell the truth and show it on TV. He said, "You're not supposed to do that in Montreal." It got back to the Canadiens' management and for the next two weeks they went through hell in practice until they got into shape. The problem was that they'd won the Cup the year before and the toughest thing to do in sports is to win again. You don't think you have to work as hard and everybody wants to knock off the champion.

Everywhere I go now, I'm asked about Don Cherry. He was after my time in Barrie, where he played junior hockey, and I never saw him in the American Hockey League. My brother George, who worked as an assistant for Hap Emms with the Barrie juniors, knows him well and has told me Don wasn't a goon, not the rough, tough hockey player you might expect from the way he talks today. He was a pretty good play-making, skating type of defenceman who was on a Memorial Cup winner for Emms in 1953. We never worked together on *Hockey Night In Canada* but I've been on his show on TSN, *Don Cherry's Grapevine*, several times. Don's a friend of mine, but I'd like to see him not preach so much violence and fighting. Kids see those shows and it has to have an effect on them. I wish he could get his great love of the game across in another way.

At one time or another, I've also done color on CKO Radio in Toronto for Maple Leafs' games and radio analysis for the games of the late, lamented Montreal Alouettes of the Cana-dian Football League. I wrote a general sports column for the weekly *Le Petit Journal* in Montreal for 14 years. (No, I didn't write it in French; I gave it to them in English and they translated it.) In my busiest year for Seagram's, I made 240 appearances on their behalf. I did 32 radio shows each week for a while at CKGM. I was giving about 50 after-dinner or luncheon speeches and refereeing in some 60 charity hockey and softball games each year, as I still do. In short, if leaving the NHL did anything for me, it was to make me busier than I'd ever been in my life.

I did do some serious officiating through the years. I always wanted to get as close to sports as I could, participating rather than observing. I got a chance in 1975 when Gerry Patterson, the former players' representative who had just become president of the National Lacrosse League, offered me the job of referee-in-chief. Gerry had taken over after the NLL had a disappointing first year. Toronto, Rochester and

Syracuse had been dropped, but there was a lot of optimism about the new Boston, Quebec and Long Island franchises. The holdovers, all strong, were Montreal, Washington and Philadelphia. I couldn't wait to take the job. I've always thought lacrosse was an amazing game. You have to be a better athlete to play it than any other sport I know. You have to be part football player, part hockey player, part basketball player, part boxer, even part jai alai player, and have the co-ordination of a ballet dancer. Lacrosse is fast. There are no offsides or icings, and it's rough. Even when it's played within the rules, it's a violent game. That means you must have high-quality refereeing.

I dealt with my officials the way I'd always hoped my bosses would deal with me, but never did. I told them not to worry about mistakes because if they learned from them, they'd become better officials as they went along. I never went into the dressing room until 10 minutes after a game, until they'd had a chance to shower and cool down. Then I'd just ask them if anyone had made any mistakes. I had a hard time getting answers for a while, but I kept at it and finally one guy said, "Yeah, I'm not too sure about this call." I looked at my notes, and said: "You were wrong. But don't worry about it. Just remember you were wrong and don't make that call for the rest of the year." They liked that.

There was an argument among the officials before the season about who would get which numbers, and I settled that by deciding we'd use names on the back of the shirts. We were the first league to do that and I thought it was an incentive for them to do a better job. The shirts, incidentally, were also a first—red and white diagonal stripes. They looked terrific but they clashed with some of the team uniforms, so we had to change them.

I also let the press into the officials' room 10 minutes after a game. The more we got the game known, the better. Any man who had the ability to run a game certainly was capable of answering questions about the game. I wanted my referees speaking to the media and getting some exposure for the league. It worked out well.

We did great in some places. We had 14,000 for opening night in Quebec City, the largest crowd in the Colisée since Jean Beliveau had played hockey there for the Aces some 20 years before, and we kept filling the place. We had good crowds in Montreal until a TV union dispute that had nothing to do with us. One group was unhappy with another and wanted to disrupt our telecast games to get some publicity and show its strength. Several times, what I called "soap bombs" were tossed on the floor. These were bags filled with powdered soap that would burst on impact. It was really slippery stuff and any players who stepped into it would fall down. It was very dangerous. We had to have the riot squad there one night to stop guys throwing things. The fans just began staying away. It made no sense, but that's the way it was.

I think the league might have been ahead of its time. One major problem was that we played our schedule in the summer and not all the buildings were air-conditioned. That had cost the league the Toronto franchise the year before and it hurt us in cities like Boston. The NLL folded after that season for a number of reasons, one of which was that too many people—not including me—were being overpaid. For example, Jim Bishop, the coach in Montreal, was making more money than Scotty Bowman of the Canadiens. It was a blow that the league went under, but I was happy when veteran lacrosse men told me the officiating staff had become the best they'd ever seen in the sport. Of course, I didn't have a tough act to follow. They thought they'd done a terrific job the season before because there were only three games when the officials didn't show up at all.

I still think pro lacrosse could have a future. It's a great spectacle, continuous action, and it's the cheapest game to operate now. You don't need thousands of dollars' worth of equipment to put a team on the floor. There's been a six-team pro league operating recently in the northeastern U.S. It's drawn full houses in arenas in Buffalo and Philadelphia, and done well in Baltimore, Boston, Detroit and New York. It also has a game-of-the-week package on ESPN-2, a U.S. sports channel. I'm not surprised because it's still the best game to watch.

I've done some hockey officiating other than charity games since I left the NHL, including the Quebec International Pee Wee Tournament for 17 years. I was part of the broadcast crew for the Air Canada Cup for midgets several times and for the Memorial Cup final the first year a team from outside Canada won the national junior championship. That was the Portland Winter Hawks in 1983, and they had great crowds that season because of good hockey and some terrific promotions.

One time they put 10,000 silver dollars on the ice, called people out of the crowd and told them they could keep all the coins they could pick up in two minutes and carry away. They'd advertised it and this woman, who had figured she might be chosen, had worn an extra large brassiere to put the coins in. She was picked and when the gun went off, she got down on her hands and knees and started stuffing the silver dollars down her front. In a minute, she had that full so she started putting them inside her pantyhose. When the gun went off to end the contest, she had $900 worth of silver dollars on her body and could barely struggle off. What they hadn't told her was that they'd had to freeze the coins to keep them from sticking to the ice. The woman froze herself in a couple of places and they had to call an ambulance to take her to the hospital.

Whenever I tell that story at a banquet, I finish by saying, "If any of you guys are ever in Portland on a sales mission or something and you run into this girl and she invites you up to the house for a cold one, be careful."

17

Have Speech, Will Travel

I don't think I've ever been as nervous as the day I spoke in public for the first time, in the late 1950s. My brother George asked me to give a talk to the Rotary Club in Barrie and bugged me until I finally agreed to do it as a favor to him. Despite the fact that I was colorful and outgoing once I put my referee's jersey on, I was very, very shy underneath. When I was a kid, I would cross over to the other side of the street if guys I didn't know really well were coming toward me. Red Storey as a referee was like a character I created, a role I played on the ice.

I didn't try to be funny during that first speech, I didn't even think of it. I just told them about the life of a referee in the NHL and I can't even remember how it went over. I was sort of in a daze. When I had finished, I told George: "Take me back to the house. I've got to change my clothes. I'm soaking wet." Then I added, "Oh, and by the way, you just heard my first and last speech ever." He laughed and said, "C'mon, Red, you'll make 100 of them before you're through." He was a little bit off. I'm at about 3,000 now, and counting—all across Canada, throughout the U.S., and in Europe, Bermuda and Jamaica.

That speech in Barrie was the only one I gave before I quit refereeing. People began to call me then because they wanted to hear my side of that story, local groups like the B'nai B'rith,

Kiwanis, Knights of Pythias, Optimists and different service clubs. I was very serious about everything I was saying in those days because I didn't know any other way to be in public and my situation with the NHL was not very amusing anyway.

One night, however, I'd used up all my usual stuff and had some time left to fill so I told a true story about some incident in the NHL. I can't even remember which one it was, but it was a funny story. The whole place exploded and a little light went off in my brain. "If that's what they want to hear," I thought, "that's what I'll give them." You've never heard anything too serious out of my lips ever since. I was still doing the hockey theme in the humor, but the humor was the basic thing. The whole world wants to laugh, so I've tried to keep them laughing. Word of mouth was my best advertising, and soon I was busier and busier. When I became involved in old-timers' hockey and started to travel with the teams, there was always a luncheon or a reception where they'd want someone to speak. Seagram's saw that I was becoming popular doing this, and soon had me making more and more appearances at their sales meetings and other functions where I might help them.

At the peak of my speaking career, I was on the road more than two-thirds of the time. These days I give about 50 or so talks per year, but I've never changed the philosophy I developed in the early 1960s. I don't like people to be serious when they're listening to me. I feel that life is too serious for most people anyway. When I stand up to speak, if I make people laugh, I figure I've accomplished as much as maybe a doctor has that day. By making people laugh, I've taken away some of the pressures they always face.

I've done a lot of big gigs in my lifetime—the Grey Cup Week dinner twice and luncheons during that week, the Dunlop Awards Dinner in Buffalo, major community events in Canadian cities from coast to coast, top corporate meetings and seminars, and even the Barrie Winter Carnival, where I was honorary chairman in 1964 and shared the spotlight with my mother in my old hometown, which was a terrific experience. The travelling has had its moments, too. I've gotten to and from speaking dates in small planes, snowmobiles, ancient buses and rickety cars, and by shank's mare. I've even ridden in a dogsled.

One of the worst trips came in the Canadian West in the dead of winter. I was speaking in Golden, B.C., and had to get to Calgary by early the next morning to make connections for Grande Prairie, Alberta. The guys running the banquet in Golden said that would be no problem, they'd drive me over, about three hours. The party didn't break up until about midnight. There'd been a lot of drinking and they decided it wouldn't be wise to drive. Instead we'd fly, leaving about five o'clock in the morning. They picked me up on time but when we got to the airport, it was closed. There were no lights on, no nothing. We drove up and down and around the field until we found the little plane.

We got in and the pilot had one light on, a flashlight up on the top. It was totally dark and he was taxiing up and down. I asked him what he was doing, and he said he was checking where the holes were in the runway so we'd have a clear run at taking off. He must have located them because we got off all right. Next we started going around and around in little circles and I asked him again what he was doing. He told me Golden was in a deep valley with mountains all around and he had to get high enough to get over them. It was still pitch black out and I was wondering how he'd see the mountains to get over them. Then he added that the plane wouldn't be able to get over the really tall ones, "so keep a sharp eye out for an opening. You'll be able to see it by the lighter color of the sky." We slipped through somehow and then the ride became even crazier. We'd go over the top of a mountain so close I could have reached my foot out and kicked the snow. Then an updraft would hit the plane and up we'd go like a roller coaster. I was sure it was my last ride.

But we landed safely in Calgary, don't ask me how, and I was never happier to be booked on a scheduled Air Canada flight for the 350-mile trip to Grande Prairie in northern Alberta. The dinner was a great success, but then the next day was a wild one, a blizzard with high winds, and the Air Canada plane we were supposed to take couldn't get in. The organizer said he had a fellow with a private plane and we could go in that to Edmonton. Hank Aaron, the old ball-player, had been featured at the dinner with me. He had an appointment in Edmonton and I was supposed to change flights there, so we took the little plane.

A few weeks later, I saw Hank at the Dapper Dan Dinner in Pittsburgh, the biggest sports banquet of the year in the United States. He was at the head table, too, and when I started to speak, I told them about our flight from Grande Prairie to Edmonton, and finished up by saying: "When we got on the plane there was one black dude and one white honky. We were so scared that when we landed in Edmonton, two white guys got off." Hank stood up. "Right on, brother. Right on."

I'd been a little nervous going into that dinner, because I was the first Canadian ever invited to be their main speaker. I was seated at the head table between two of Pittsburgh's greatest sports stars. They were Mean Joe Greene of the Super Bowl champion Steelers and Willie Stargell of the World Series champion Pirates, very large black guys who were also larger than life. I told the audience, "Tonight I found out what the middle of an Oreo cookie feels like." Then I stopped and put my hand up beside my mouth without looking around, gestured with my other thumb back at Greene and Stargell, and made a stage whisper into the mike, "Are they laughing?" They were, and everything turned out okay.

I've always gotten a reaction from my audiences, but some

of it hasn't been exactly what I had in mind. I was speaking at the Lakehead, at either Fort William or Port Arthur before they became Thunder Bay, at a doctors' convention. Right at the end of the pre-seminar reception, the organizer came to me: "Red, can people upset you? Do things the audience might do affect you?" I told him that after what I'd been through in my life, nothing bothered me. He said, "Well, I wanted to make sure because these doctors only get together once a year and they let their hair down a little bit." We went in and there were 400 of them in the conference room. The guy gave me a beautiful introduction, I got up to speak and I had to start ducking immediately. I didn't know that they'd given each doctor coming into the hall a little hard roll. When I stood up, they stood up too, in unison, and here came those rolls. It was like facing a machine gun and I went under the table.

I was a member of the old Caledonia Curling Club in Montreal, and was always one of the speakers at its sports dinners, which were generally the best in the city. One year they had a fellow named Joe Dolomont introduce me. He did a marvellous job but the moment he finished, everybody got up and walked out—including the rest of the head table and even the waiters. I was left standing there with a microphone and an empty hall. I said to myself, "My God, what am I going to do now?" But all of a sudden, I saw faces peeking out from behind pillars and posts and around corners, and they all trooped back in.

One of the audiences I worried about the most was in Edmonton. I'd been sent out by Seagram's and hadn't paid any attention to what the group was. I got there and it turned out to be a priests' conference. I had no idea what to do, because I wasn't sure if my usual material was at all suitable for them. When the introductions were made before the session, I learned they had the bishop there and I thought that if I could get him moving first, maybe they'd all follow and we could have some fun. That's all I ever tried to do, have some fun. I started off this way: "Well, first of all, I want you to know I have a lot of courage to come here and speak to you people because I'm a black Protestant and you're all Catholics. Right away, you can see that I'm on the hot seat. It was Seagram's that sent me out here and basically we're in the same business as you are. If you look at it, we're both involved with spirits." They were all watching the old bishop and he went, "Ho, ho, ho," and then everybody was chuckling and I had them.

I often have a question period after my talks, especially if it's a young audience. There have been three or four themes over the years in addition to the usual "Who was the best?" type of thing. I'm often asked about instant replay in hockey, which of course I never had when I was refereeing. I'd have liked it to help me on the toughest call of all, whether to allow or disallow a goal—you want every legitimate goal to count, but none of the other ones—but only if I requested it. If you're going to let a coach ask for it, there should be a bench penalty involved if the decision isn't overturned.

That's the case now when they ask for a stick measurement. Jacques Demers of the Canadiens may have won the Stanley Cup in 1993 when he asked the officials to check Marty McSorley's stick. The Los Angeles Kings were ahead 1-0 in the final series and leading by a goal with a minute or so left in Game 2, but the Canadiens got a power play on the stick violation, tied it up, won in overtime and didn't lose another game. But Demers was taking a chance. If McSorley's stick had been okay, the Canadiens would have been penalized, almost surely lost the game and gone into L.A. down 0-2. You should have an element of risk involved for coaches making those kinds of requests.

I'm often asked about how youngsters can get into refereeing, which has turned into a pretty good profession at the top, with much better pay and benefits than I ever had. My advice is to get started in any league you can, the lower the better, and work your way up. The qualities required include being able to skate as well as, if not better than, the players. You have to know the rules and, most important, you have to be able to enforce them. You have to have good eyesight and hearing, of course. You have to be intelligent and have the ability to learn. You have to be able to keep control of yourself under pressure. You also have to be prepared for a lonely life. No one cheers officials, no one asks for their autographs, no one cares if they have pretty wives or cute children and the only fan mail they get is either abusive or obscene.

Another thing people have wanted to know about is whether it's more difficult to be an official in hockey or football. I can tell you that running one hockey game is tougher than handling any five football games I've ever seen. In football, there are 24 players and five officials. In hockey, there are 12 players and only one official who calls fouls. The linesmen rule on offsides and break up fights. In football, officials start out standing in one place and concentrating on their own area of the field. In hockey, the referee has to make his calls on the fly while keeping up with the play and avoiding collisions.

In football, the captains always address the officials as "Mister." They are all very polite. The players know they'll be bounced for fighting or unnecessary roughness, and they usually behave accordingly. In hockey, you'd better leave your hearing aid at home and be ready for anything. Finally, I'll bet not one-tenth of the fans at a football game know or remember the name of the referee. But in hockey you're never just another guy in a striped shirt. You're always a marked man.

I've been asked about shootouts ever since Team Canada lost to Sweden in the Gold Medal game at the 1994 Olympics. People are surprised when I tell them that I was the first person ever to put the shootout into a hockey league. That was many years ago when I was the commissioner of the

Original Six, an old-timers' series taped for television. We had time limits because of TV and decided on the shootout to settle ties. We played the games in Markham, north of Toronto, and the first time we had a shootout, I went out on the ice to make sure everybody understood the rules and did it right. I looked around and saw that the guys who were playing in the next game had heard what was going on, and had come out in their underwear tops to watch it. They were all former NHL stars and they were just hanging over the boards. I said to myself, "Hey, we've really got something here."

I think the Canada-Sweden game proved that. So did Canada's later victory over Finland in a shootout for the 1994 world championship. By the time they were over, the emotions of the people watching them with me on TV seemed to be as high as they had been for the first series in which the NHL played the Russians in 1972. I'd be all for the shootout in the NHL, with a couple of riders. First, the winning team would get the usual two points for the victory, but the losers would still receive one point for having tied the game through regulation and the five-minute overtime. Second, I wouldn't have the shootout in the playoffs at all. Hockey is a team game, and important games and championships should be decided by teams. The shootout in that situation would put too much pressure on individuals.

I think, however, it would be just great during the regular season. Look what would happen when you have a really stinking game, and there are a lot of those now, say a so-so club against an expansion team that concentrates on defence only. It winds up in a 1-1 tie and it's been so boring that the people have been having trouble keeping their eyes open. Now you get to the shootout and everybody would be on the edge of their seats. That's also the last thing they'd see and the first thing they'd remember. The impression they'd take away from a dull, dull game would be one of excitement. That's what the NHL wants, isn't it?

The shootout, of course, is based on the penalty shot, which the NHL has had as long as anyone can remember, or at least since 1934. For many years there weren't a lot of them called, but there are more now. The game is different today. Defencemen stayed at home more then and didn't have to drag guys on breakaways down from behind nearly as often. Most of those plays in my time were borderline calls anyway, and in any borderline call, we always gave the benefit of the doubt to the guy committing the foul.

Goaltenders on average stop considerably more than half of all penalty shot attempts, and they should. In that Olympics shootout, Canada lost by one goal because our players scored on only two of seven tries. In the world championships shootout, the losing Finns got only two goals in their six chances against Bill Ranford. Goalies know the shooters, they study them all the time and they know the angles to play. For example, if a guy decides to try to deke on a penalty shot, nine times out of 10 he'll go to his backhand. Goalies know stuff like that.

I only called one penalty shot in my entire nine-year career in the NHL. The Rangers were playing in Detroit. I can't remember what the infraction was, or who committed it, but Gump Worsley was in goal for New York and the Red Wings chose Gordie Howe to take the shot. He skated in to about 15 feet from the net, there was a little flick of the stick and the puck was buried. There was no way Gump could stop it. If a good scorer puts the puck where he wants it from anywhere up to 25 feet, it's going to be a goal. Gump was disgusted and came over to me. "Why the hell did you waste time making the big guy shoot it?" he asked. "Why didn't you just put the goal up on the board and get on with the game?"

18

Legends Of The Game

Allen Abel, who used to do a sports column for *The Globe and Mail*, once wrote after watching our old-timers in action: "What a shock to tune in a hockey game and see players actually enjoying themselves. It almost looks like it's a *game* they're playing. It was a game devoid of all the horrible, phony grimness of hockey from peewee to pro, a game full of the free spirit that died when the sport came in from the ponds where kids played without their parents watching. It was a marvellous game. Funny, as the players grow older, how we grow younger watching them."

A lot of other people have come to feel the same way about going back to the roots of the sport. There are more old-timers registered in hockey in Canada today, more than 700,000 of them, than there are players in youth and minor leagues. I think it's added years to the lives of many, many adults in this country. Instead of sitting at home, watching TV and drinking beer, they're out getting some exercise, helping their hearts and bodies and, most important of all, having some fun.

Old-timers' hockey has been around for a long time, of course, although the guys playing it didn't like calling it that. Back then, it might be known as a beer league. It began to get really popular when big-name ex-pros got involved. The first time I heard of this was in the early 1960s in Lachine, a suburb of Montreal, when some former Canadiens like Petey Morin, Buddy O'Connor, Kenny Reardon, Glen Harmon and a few others decided to have a little practice session once a week, scrimmaging against the local guys in the same age group. They invited me out to referee and pretty soon we were playing against teams in various cities and towns around the area.

After a while, someone suggested: "If we're going to play hockey and we're going to have actual games, why don't we do it for charity? We could charge the local team something for our expenses, then they can sell tickets and do whatever they want with the proceeds." There was a big argument, with a couple of guys saying it wouldn't work, that people wouldn't pay to see washed-up pros more than once every five years. We decided to try it, and it went pretty well. We made sure the charity always got at least $500. No money ever went to the players.

The idea really went over the top in 1966, when we were able to arrange for the Detroit old-timers to play us at the Forum in Montreal. People remembered the great rivalry between the two teams in the 1950s and so did the clubs. The Red Wings gave Gordie Howe, who was still active, permission to play in the game and that reunited the old Production Line, Gordie with Ted Lindsay and Sid Abel. Rocket Richard lined up with the old Canadiens, so there was a lot of interest. The Forum was filled to capacity, within three people of the all-time record for the building, and CFCF-TV in Montreal taped it to show later; that was the first time Dick Irvin ever did play-by-play. I refereed with the Mundey brothers, Ernie and Sibby, as the linesmen, and it was a fabulous game. We had some fun, but when it got serious it was fitting, I guess, that the Rocket scored the winning goal with about a minute to play. The place went absolutely crazy and the Montreal morning newspapers, both French and English, ran front-page photos of the Rocket putting it home.

Meanwhile, one cloud appeared on the horizon, but no one

noticed at the time. There was an incident right at the start of
that game. I'd told all the players the rules: no slapshots, no
bodychecking allowed. I dropped the puck, the Rocket got it,
and Leo Reise knocked him on his ass with the best check any
Red Wing, past or present, threw that season. I said to Leo:
"I just told you there was no bodychecking. What the hell do
you think you're doing?" Leo said: "Red, that was the
Rocket. He was just sitting there and I couldn't resist." Try as
we might, we couldn't keep that stuff totally under control.
The guys were just so competitive, even if these were supposed to be friendly games. Reardon and Lindsay, in particular, began to take it far too seriously so we called off that series
after four years. Then we started to tour anywhere they'd have
us and we've raised several million dollars since.

We opened the new arena in Vancouver with a record crowd
for that city. In fact, we had huge crowds everywhere. In
Regina one night, they had the biggest attendance in something like 13 years and the Rocket scored on one of his trademark backhand shots. It was so hard that it lifted the net a
little bit when it hit up under the crossbar. Instead of cheering
right away, the crowd seemed stunned at what they'd seen.
After a few seconds, it sunk in that this was something really
special, a piece of hockey history come to life, and they gave
the Rocket a standing ovation. I'll bet some of those folks are
still telling their kids and grandkids about it.

We were developing a format and routines to entertain the
fans. A game in Toronto on a Sunday afternoon in March,
1986, was a pretty good example. The old Maple Leafs beat the
former Canadiens 8-7, and there were some pretty plays and
standout goals for the purists among the 16,000-plus on hand.
But I think we're like the Harlem Globetrotters. They're a great
basketball team, but if they played it totally straight, a lot
fewer people would go to see them. I had the Rocket and Bill
Friday, the former NHL official, with me for this one and we
called some very unusual penalties, to say the least.

Jacques Lemaire got a 30-second penalty for half a slapshot. Howie Meeker, by then a TV screamer, was given 15 seconds for his trademark "Gee whiz" and another 15 for "Holy cow." Gilles Marotte, who was little overweight, was sent off for "deliberately injuring the ice." Ivan Irwin was flagged for holding "back in 1957." I sprinkled some tonic on Carl Brewer's bald head because "the shine is distracting the television cameras," and then gave him a penalty for not using the hair formula that the Rocket was advertising in TV commercials at the time. No one escaped, not even the officials. Larry Carriere and Irwin got me to go over to the Leafs' bench to look at a hole in the ice and Punch Imlach, who was coaching, dumped a bucket of water over my head.

But make no mistake. Most of these guys can still play hockey. Sometimes I turn around and watch the crowd to see what the reactions are, and what you hear the most gasps about is the passing. I can have my back to the ice and I can hear the puck hitting the sticks as it goes from one guy to another—CRACK! CRACK! CRACK! With good pros you hear the puck hit the stick, with the others you don't. It's a matter of pace.

That's one of the reasons for the success of our old-timers, the fact that the level of ability has remained pretty high. Andy Bathgate, who retired in 1971, was asked a while ago if he thought he still could play in the NHL. "If they had slow motion," he said, "we'd be all right." The old-timers still can do almost everything they ever could, it just takes a little longer now.

They're popular, too, because they're known in the communities where they grew up or played. Today's old-timer was an ordinary guy and didn't make so much money that he wouldn't go into a tavern and have a beer with the boys. He made a decent living, maybe a couple of bucks more than his neighbor. Everybody in town knew him and he was always available to lend a hand to a good cause. Today's superstars make so much money that, with only a couple of exceptions, they don't associate with the public; hell, they don't even associate with their own teammates off the ice. If a charity calls, they're likely to say, "Phone my agent."

Another factor is that people know what the old-timers look like. They didn't wear helmets, so the fans still recognize them. We've got guys who haven't played in the NHL for 30 or 35 years, and the public still knows who they are. Today's stars, after they've been out of the game for five years, could walk through the middle of town and no one will have any idea whether they're athletes or accountants. That has to be the best argument ever against having players wear helmets.

With the old-timers not wearing them when they played— and most of them still don't—the fans could see their faces and their expressions, and realize how much they enjoyed playing the game. The more I'm around them, the more I understand how much they really love hockey. I still get a thrill when I see Guy Lafleur, his long hair flowing out behind him, flying down the wing in one of our games, and so do the fans. Why would anyone want to put a helmet over that show? Kids come out to watch the old-timers and they see that you can play this game without a helmet and not get killed if you go by the rulebook. As I've said, NHL players now have more equipment on than a guy going to war, and he's got to stop bullets.

Recently, I've been involved in another way with the old-timers—only they're calling them "Legends of Hockey" now, which is accurate but may be a little highfalutin. I'm the rules commissioner of the Danny Gallivan Cup, a league which has teams representing the six NHL franchises before expansion, a regular schedule and playoffs. We play it in the summer in Sydney, on Cape Breton Island in Nova Scotia, Danny's birthplace. People say they've been surprised at the speed of the games when they've seen them later on TSN. The main reason for that is we got rid of the centre-ice red line. Players can now pass from their own end to the other team's blue line. It really opened the game up and made our players look much faster than they really are. I wish they'd do it in the NHL. Spreading people out is one way to get rid of a lot of the interference. Can you imagine the plays that the fastest skaters in the world could make? It gives the talented players some room to work in.

Those games have a great flow, too, because we're very strict on when player changes can be made. You have to change on the fly, the only exception being after a goal. You can't even put a new lineup out for the start of a penalty. So there are very short delays for faceoffs. Compare that to the average Saturday night game at the Forum or Maple Leaf Gardens when there are 18 stoppages of play just for television commercials. Then there are coaches jockeying with line changes, guys delaying the game to get new sticks or have equipment adjusted, and so on.

Hockey games don't have to take forever. I remember that one night when Detroit was playing the Rangers in Madison Square Garden there was a fight on television that everybody wanted to see. It was the rematch between Yvon Durelle, the fisherman from New Brunswick, and Archie Moore, the light-heavyweight champion. The first time they fought, Durelle had knocked old Archie down three times in the first round but couldn't put him away. Archie came back and knocked Durelle out later, so everyone was talking about the second fight.

We had an 8 p.m. opening faceoff and the big fight was probably going to start shortly after 10 o'clock. I went to each of the captains during the pre-game warmup and asked them if they wanted to see the fight as much as I did. They both said, "Damn right, the whole gang does," and that they were sorry they were going to miss it because we'd never be able to get out in time. I said: "Not necessarily. Just listen to me for a minute. If you go along with this, we'll all get to see it." I told them I wasn't going to call any more penalties than I absolutely had to and that anyone who got one had better be in the penalty box before I got over there. I said I'd delay all offsides, so no one should stop skating until they heard the whistle. I'd call only the most flagrant icings and I didn't want any arguments about anything. If we can do all that, I said, we'll make it.

The fight started right on the dot of 10 and the officials and players from both teams were in the same bar, around the corner from the Garden, watching it on TV. We were through in less than an hour and 45 minutes, everybody dressed and gone. There was a hardly a whistle and I'm sure the coaches spent a lot of time trying to find out what happened in that game. From my point of view, it was hardly worth the effort. It was a one-sided fight, Moore dominating completely until he knocked Durelle out.

The old-timers still have a lot of pride in what they do. Eddie Shack once said: "You know what this team is, the old-timers? It's the university of hockey, the highest you can go for the smarts. These old guys, they got all the brains." Eddie also told Ivan Irwin, "You're so old you were retired before I started." They went out to practice and Shack wound up for one of his famous end-to-end rushes—skating, as Scott Young once wrote, like "a patented imitation of a buffalo stampede." Eddie got to the other team's blue line and suddenly found himself on the seat of his pants. WHAM! Irwin had hit him with a hip check, so quick it could hardly be seen. He skated over and looked down at Eddie. "Shackie," he said, "I haven't retired yet."

The Lady Byng Trophy is one of the major annual awards given out by the NHL but since it's for gentlemanly conduct as well as good play, some players think it's a little wimpish. Gilbert Perreault won it with the Buffalo Sabres in 1973. When he was introduced before the first game he played with the old-timers, the announcer mentioned it. Gil came right over to me: "Red, don't let them say that any more. I don't want to hear that."

One time the team went to Sudbury by train the day before for a Sunday afternoon game. Jacques Plante and I had to stay in Montreal because we were both doing color work on the Saturday night NHL telecasts, so we had arranged to fly up by private plane, leaving at five o'clock in the morning. Halfway through the night, Plante phoned whoever was in charge of the arrangements and said he couldn't go, without even giving a reason. He was a strange duck.

However, he had been used in all our publicity in Sudbury; he was a hot item, having just come out of retirement to line up with the Junior Canadiens and stone the Russians. I got up there and the team found out Plante wasn't coming and we didn't know what to do. Finally, we went looking around town and found some guy who had played goal for somebody, sometime. We took him because we had to have someone, anyone, in the nets.

The people in the arena booed when they learned Plante wasn't there. It was building into a bad scene, when the Rocket got onto the P.A. system and said something like: "I don't think it's right that we apologize for Jacques Plante not being here. We have no control over that. Instead of booing us for him not appearing, why don't you give the boys a hand who did come to put on a show, and we'll give you the best show we can." It turned out to be a helluva game. We won 6-5, or something. The Rocket got five goals, so you can imagine that the people soon forgot all about Plante. I remember that day for another reason, too. A circus had been in the building, I think the bears used the referees' dressing room and I don't think they were housebroken.

One of the things I've suspected for a long time is that hockey players don't know the rules of the game in any depth and often shouldn't be arguing. But they're proud there, too. Yvan Cournoyer, the former Canadiens' captain, proved that to me during a practice game one night. Someone on the other team got turned around and went across the blue line backwards but in full control of the puck. I didn't call it offside, they scored on the play and Cournoyer started yelling at me. I told him that as long as a man had control of the puck, he could go anywhere he wanted. His stick was considered to be part of his body. Cournoyer kept insisting it wasn't right, saying he knew because he'd been in hockey for 25 years and had been captain of his team. I kept telling him it was legal and that all he had to do was look in the rule book. He wouldn't have any of it, so finally we bet $50. I brought the rule book to the next game a week later, with the key part all underlined. Incidentally, Yvan, if you're reading this, you still owe me that 50 bucks.

The old-timers have great pride as a team, as well. They play some pretty good clubs around the country and, like the Globetrotters, they never lose. The ideal situation is if the opposition is good, but not quite as good as we are. That gives us the leeway to run our show, the comedy part of it, which the people enjoy. If we run into a team that's just as good or really wants to beat us, then we have to pretty well eliminate the comedy because these guys are pros and even now they can't stand losing. They say, "Hey, you want to play hockey, we'll play hockey, and you're not going to beat us." So the other team might as well say, "Okay, let's enjoy the show."

In 1969, we went on an overseas tour to play teams from the Canadian armed forces. The night before our first game in Lahr, the army base in Germany, we were in the sergeants' mess and this sergeant named Bourgeois said to me, "I hope your team are good sports." Our guys were lined up all along the bar, and I said: "Yeah, we're getting in good shape for tomorrow. Why would you say a thing like that?" He did some boasting. "Well, this team we have, we drafted them from bases all over Canada and all over Europe. They've been together for quite a while now and they've won 27 out of their

last 28 games. They're a great hockey team and we don't want
your team to be embarrassed or get mad."

I told him they shouldn't have gone to all that trouble. He
asked me what I meant. "Because you're not going to win."
He wanted to know why not. "Because I'm refereeing." They
were a pretty good team, but Bill Mosienko saved us. He got a
couple of goals in the last minute and we won by one. In fact,
we had a great trip, a fabulous one, but we worked too hard.
We had five games in twelve days, and won them all. That was
the easy part. What was tough was that we also had 32
receptions and 11,000 miles of travel.

As always when I've been in Europe, that trip made me
realize how much we have in Canada. It seemed that everything we saw was old and smelled bad. If everybody in Canada was forced to make one trip to Europe, they'd realize that
what we've got here is the best anywhere and we should be
working as hard as we can to keep it. I found out one night
that a lot of people still can show off their pride. We were in
Sarnia early in 1994 and they didn't have a record of the
national anthem to play before the game. So we said, "That's
okay, we'll sing it on the ice." We started and the next thing we
knew, everybody in the building was singing. I hadn't seen
such Canadian pride, such an impromptu display of feeling
for this country, in a long, long time. I thought it should
happen that way at every game. It's too bad it doesn't.

19

The Americans And Our Football

When the Toronto Argonauts won the 1938 Grey Cup game over Winnipeg, 30-7, we beat a team that relied much more heavily on American imports and style than we did. We won with the Argo end run, an extension play that involved options from which I scored two of my three touchdowns in the decisive fourth quarter. Writing in *The Ottawa Journal*, Ross Trimble, the coach of the Rough Riders, explained the Blue Bombers' loss: "Winnipeg could not adjust . . . They play in the American tradition. U.S. football is machine football. The man is sacrificed to the mechanism. He must not think for himself. He must do what he is told; nothing more . . . Thank heaven our Canadian game is still a man's game. It permits of, it demands, that players think for themselves." That is no longer true, unfortunately. It hasn't been for quite a while.

Angelo Mosca, the huge lineman who came from American college ranks to a great career in Canada, once told a dinner I was at: "The U.S. has the best four-down game in the world. Canada has the best three-down game in the world. And Canada has the best game in the world, period." That may still be true, because the National Football League has become so flat and bland. But the Canadian game today is far less exciting than it once was. The American influence, as passed on through general managers and coaches from the U.S., has not helped us in Canada, to say the least. We seem to take whatever they think we should have, despite the fact that we're not exactly Johnny-come-latelys to this sport. After all, there was a Grey Cup game as early as 1909—58 years before there was a Super Bowl.

When I was playing, we looked on Americans coming in as a challenge. Lew Hayman, who ran the Argos, used them to motivate us. Every year he'd say he had a guy in camp who was going to take my job. It would make you think, "Am I as good as them?" because you'd heard and read so much about U.S. football. I never saw an American I couldn't beat and the guys Hayman held up before me never lasted through to the end of training camp. I didn't need that to spur me on, not when I already had the best motivation possible in the middle of the Great Depression. I had to make the team to keep eating.

Hayman was from Syracuse University, but he learned the Canadian game as well as anybody ever did. He designed offences that took advantage of our wider field and other distinctive rules, and won consistently. Most of the Americans who have come here since haven't been nearly as smart. They've ruined our game. It's been getting worse and worse and now there's not a doubt in my mind that they've destroyed it completely. Of course, there's been an element of suicide in all this. That's our national inferiority complex in relation to the U.S., the belief that if something's American, it must be better.

The Canadian game was made up at the start, going back to the old days, of running and kicking, which was fine. Then it became running, kicking and passing, which was fine, too. Coaches from the U.S. like Peahead Walker and Pop Ivy continued to take advantage of what made our game different, and won doing it. In his later years, Frank Clair from Ohio did the same in Ottawa with outstanding Canadian players like Russ Jackson at quarterback, Ron Stewart running and Whit Tucker catching. But earlier with the Argos, starting in the late 1940s, Clair didn't want Canadians around if he could help it. My brother George could have played with any team in the country on ability alone, but he was one of those Canadians Clair never gave a chance, didn't even take a look at. Clair learned, however, and his Ottawa club with Jackson in the late 1960s was the last great Canadian-style team. They came at you in so many different ways.

In the meantime, a new generation of American coaches had been coming in and they said, "Our drop back passers have to have equal distance on each side of the field to throw the ball." They wanted to bend our game to fit their ideas and their knowledge, which was about U.S. football. The people who ran the league listened and moved the hash marks, where the ball is put into play, closer into the middle of the field. That removed the great advantage its wider field gave Canadian football and it changed the running game completely. One man now carried the ball, period. They took all the imagination out of our football, making it more and more like the U.S. game. How bad has it become? In the last few seasons, by far the most exciting players in the CFL have been on special teams—return men Henry (Gizmo) Williams of Edmonton and Mike (Pinball) Clemons of Toronto. They're the only real game-breakers and—this is no coincidence—the only guys in the league with terrific nicknames. Doug Flutie is a marvellous quarterback and there are others who can really play. But they don't give you that one moment you'll never forget.

I spoke at the 75th anniversary Grey Cup dinner in Vancouver a few years ago and I had a private meeting with the coaches and assistants, who were all from the U.S. I guess they weren't too happy with things like the lower attendance and shaky finances of some of the clubs, because they asked: "You've been around for a long time. What can we do to improve Canadian football?" I told them they might not like what I had to say, but they wanted to hear it anyway. I spoke for 10 or 15 minutes and I got a lot off my chest.

"First of all, Lew Hayman won more Grey Cups than most people will ever dream of. One man. He ran the team, he coached the team. He had one of the senior players help with the drills, but that was it. Why do we need nine coaches in the Canadian game? You need guys to take one another to the toilet or something? Your overhead is killing you, but it could be cut in half. I'd limit the coaching staffs in the CFL to three people. One of them would have to be a Canadian because, quite frankly, you Americans don't know anything about our game, our field or our rules. So you have to have a Canadian in there as part of your organization to show you how to get the most benefit from it." I was just warming up.

"A Canadian would know enough to put running back into the game, the greatest asset you could have in Canada. Believe me when I tell you you've never seen anything so beautiful as the Argo end run in the old days, with its options and laterals. But you had to have a wide side of the field to run it toward, and that doesn't exist any more. The other thing moving the hash marks closer together did was to make it easier to kick field goals. The kickers are so good that it's become boring because they're almost straight on all the time. Move those hash marks back out again and with a little wind blowing and the angle they'll be on, there's no more sure three points. So you might have to gamble a little. You'd hate that but the fans would love it. Since you guys came up here, you've taken our game away from us and all the thrills out of it. Now you're asking me what the hell's wrong with it?"

There was a moment or two of silence, and then one of them said, "Red, you're 100 percent right." I said: "Yeah, you know it. But you'll never change what you're doing because to do it, six of you on each team would be out of work. So you're going to keep on ruining our game and then, when you're fired or quit, you're going to go back to the States and you're going to say that Canadians really don't like football. Canadians loved football when we had the best game in the world."

Let me admit right now that I have very personal reasons for feeling as strongly as I do about the way Canadians are treated in the CFL. It was in Canadian football that I first made my name but if I had to do it all over again, I'd take some other direction. I could have gone into one of three or four other sports. Football in Canada is a dead end. A kid should run a million miles to get away. As a Canadian, they treat you like a slave. You can't make any money, you've got no security and as soon as they can't get anything more from you, they throw you away. It'll do one of two things to a Canadian. It will break your heart or your body. That's what happened to me. I wouldn't have been through at the age of 23 if I'd gone into something else.

Twenty-five years later it was déjà vu with another Storey, my son Bob. He'd been a good enough football player to earn a scholarship at Tulsa University in Oklahoma, and joined the Hamilton Tiger-Cats after graduation. They used him as a punt returner and backup defensive back and he played on their Grey Cup champions of 1967. He moved on to the Alouettes in 1969, but was confined to the return units, even though some of the Als' players told me he had the best hands on the team. But the one guy who didn't like him, or Canadians in general, happened to be his position coach, an American. Bob had an unfortunate bobble on a punt early in the 1970 Grey Cup game and was benched. The Als went on to beat Calgary and that made me and Bob the only father-and-son combination ever to be on two Grey Cup winners apiece. I'm as proud of that as of anything in my life. Bob got out of football at that point, realizing that for him it was a one-way street going nowhere and he might as well get on with the rest of his life.

I helped Bob make that decision. I told him he'd be treated like a piece of meat over and over. He already knew he wouldn't play while less talented Americans did. He already knew he'd never make a big living in the CFL; they'd give the real money to players from the U.S. I also reminded him of what the Argos had done to me. I'd been lucky with injuries, nothing too serious, until a game against Hamilton in 1940. I was carrying the ball and was sandwiched by Abe Zvonkin and Lefty Jordan. My knee took most of the impact, I went up in the air and I knew it was really bad before I even hit the ground.

It didn't get much better during the week and the next Saturday morning, I was in the Wellesley Hospital in Toronto. The club doctor, whom none of the guys on the club would let touch them, walked into the room. He had some goons with him, big husky guys. He took a look at my knee, which was still blown up like a balloon. He took out this huge syringe, which looked like he was going to siphon an elephant. Suddenly he said, "Hold him down," and the goons grabbed me and he drained all the stuff out of my knee, no anaesthetic at all. It was really killing me, but they froze it and taped it up, took me to the stadium and I played that afternoon against Ottawa. That led to the complete destruction of my knee and, within a couple of years, to the end of my careers in football, hockey and lacrosse.

I told the coaches in Vancouver that they were ignorant if they didn't think Canadians could play the game. There are a lot of Canadian kids with the same kind of ability as anyone else. Nobody has to teach them how to run and catch; those talents come naturally. But the automatic attitude seems to be that because they're Canadians, they can't be as good as Americans. They're never given a chance to show what they can do. Instead, the teams prefer to bring in guys who come with pedigrees from U.S. colleges. These are guys they've never seen and who've never even seen a Canadian football game. Hell, they couldn't even find Canada on a map.

Did everyone notice that in the 1994 Super Bowl, the place-kickers for both Dallas and Buffalo were Canadians? Eddie

Murray, born in Halifax, kicked for the Cowboys and Steve
Christie, from the Toronto area, for the Bills. Both were
perfect, too. I got a kick out of it, if you'll pardon a bad pun.
They must have 100,000 kids kicking field goals in the States
and they got our two Canadians beating them out. It's being
proved more and more in other sports that it doesn't matter
where you come from—the U.S., Canada, Russia, China,
wherever—if you have athletic ability and are given the
opportunity, you're going to go to the top. We've had ski jump
champions from Japan, figure skating medallists from
China, winning tour golfers from Fiji and Zimbabwe, pro
basketball stars from Nigeria and the Sudan. Why not top
football players from Canada? Not in Canada, apparently.

It's a dreadful situation and it doesn't look like it's going to
improve. One U.S. franchise—Sacramento—started play
during the 1993 season without either artistic or financial
success. Despite that, three other U.S. teams were accepted
into the league for 1994, in Las Vegas, Baltimore and Shreveport, Louisiana. Shreveport was given to the Glieberman
family of Detroit, who earned it by almost wiping out one of
the great Canadian franchises, the Ottawa Rough Riders. The
four teams in the U.S. aren't bound by the same Canadian
player content rules as the eight Canadian clubs. How long
can those rules last at all if they put the Canadian teams at a
disadvantage? It seems inevitable that there'll be still fewer
jobs for Canadian players, even the not very important jobs.

The CFL has talked of even further expansion into the
U.S., amid reports that there's already pressure from the
American partners to change the name of the league. It seems
inevitable, too, that there'll be rule changes to draw our game
closer to the U.S. version. It'll be easier to do that than to try
to educate the American audience. I also have to wonder how
long it will be before the last great sports tradition that is ours
alone, the Grey Cup game, moves to the Nevada desert or the
Maryland shore. They've already taken something away from

it by defying geography in moving Winnipeg to the East, which the Blue Bombers represented in the national final four times in six years. Does anyone worry about what Canadians will think when the Grey Cup is won by the Las Vegas Posse, or the Shreveport Pirates, or whomever?

I realize that's a lot of heavy criticism and you're probably asking, "Okay, smart guy, what would you do?" I like Larry Smith, the commissioner of the CFL who has spearheaded the move into the U.S. I admire him for trying hard to save the league, even if he's been looking in the wrong direction. What he should have done, I think, was sit down and say to his board of governors, "What were we doing when we were successful that we're not doing now?" More accurately, perhaps the question should have been, "What are we doing now that we were not doing when we were successful?" The answer to that is everything I've been complaining about.

Part of the pressure to do anything necessary to keep the CFL alive comes from a fear of the National Football League coming to Canada and our league fading away to nothing but a collection of farm clubs. I think the CFL is inviting just that by moving into the U.S., where one main objective of the new owners is to prove that their cities (and they) are good candidates for future NFL expansion. But that's beside the point. The NFL people know they have a lot of things to do before they think of any further expansion, starting with the fact that their game has become dull. They admitted that in 1994 by adopting the two-point conversion and trying to cut down on field goals by making misses a little more costly.

The NFL also has weak sisters and, with two new expansion teams already on the way, has to do something to improve parity. Putting any new team into Canada would just make that situation worse. A lot of Canadians got excited at the '94 Super Bowl when Paul Tagliabue, the NFL commissioner, for the first time mentioned Toronto, Vancouver and Montreal by name among the league's possible future expansion sites. My feeling is that the NFL simply didn't want to turn off people in Canada who have made overtures to the league, although they may indeed be serious about Toronto down the road. There's a lot of money there in a huge regional market, so it would be a pretty good place to take the first step towards a worldwide league, which seems to be what they want to do. But much of the rest of Canada has been living on lotteries and unemployment insurance, and there's no money for fun. Football is great fun, but it's also very, very expensive.

I get plain mad when I hear that someone wants to put an NFL team in Montreal, where the CFL let the franchise just go down the drain. If that club had been properly operated and promoted, it never would have happened. Whenever they had competitive teams, the Alouettes filled every place they played during their 41-year history—Delorimier Downs, McGill Stadium, the Autostade and Olympic Stadium. Then the carpetbaggers from out of town—Nelson Skalbania at the beginning and Norm Kimball at the end—got hold of the franchise, and it all went down the tubes in less than eight years, despite a temporary mid-term rebirth as the Concordes under Charles Bronfman and his partners. Larry Smith, who played on two Grey Cup winners in nine seasons as a halfback with the Als, hasn't been able to revive football in Montreal.

If you live in any of the eight current CFL cities in Canada, there will have been a period when you worried whether the same thing might happen to your team. You know about good times and huge crowds, followed by poorer teams and declining attendance. There've been bailouts—loans and advances—by the league needed by several teams, including Ottawa, Hamilton, Saskatchewan and B.C. In recent years, those clubs and the other four—Toronto, Winnipeg, Calgary and Edmonton—have had direct or indirect government help, including funds from provincial lotteries, amounting in some cases to millions of dollars. Yet there have been threats to fold up in some of these cities, followed by demands for even more assistance from various levels of government.

Meanwhile, the NFL should be happy with the CFL expanding into the U.S. It probably provides just enough competition to keep the NFL out of anti-trust trouble, without a salary war and without battles over markets or TV contracts. There's also little chance, as long as the CFL is there, that anyone would try to start a new league that could give the NFL real problems in the U.S. But I don't really care what happens to the NFL. What I care about is Canadian football. I feel I have a stake in that since I played it for six years and officiated in it for another 11. I still love our game despite what it did to the Storeys; it's the people who have run the show over the years who have betrayed us.

20

The Europeans And Our Hockey

In 1972, before the National Hockey League played the Soviet Union for the first time, the only guy I knew who got it right was Maurice Richard. The Rocket had spent a lot of time in Europe as a special guest at world hockey championships and so on; he was as big a hero in Czechoslovakia as he was in Quebec. I interviewed him on radio for CKGM in Montreal. "I've seen their games, Red. I've seen how they play. Our guys may think they're going to run them right out of the rink with the body, but they're not. The Russians are as tough or tougher than we are and I've never seen hockey players in better shape. They have a very good chance of surprising everybody in Canada."

I'd only seen the Soviets on TV from time to time, and I began to doubt the Rocket's sanity after I went out the morning of the opening game of the series in Montreal, September 2, to watch them practice. The NHL all-stars had finished their skate earlier and they were all sitting in the stands to get a look at the opposition. The Russians came out looking like a bunch of guys who had been dressed by the Salvation Army Reject Company. They had sweaters with holes in them, pants that didn't fit, mismatched stockings and battered old skates. They were missing passes and tripping over the blue line and stuff like that. The Canadian players were laughing their heads off. I can remember thinking, "We're going to kick the crap out of these guys tonight." The Soviets had been beating up on our amateurs for years, but now they were in against the big boys.

Eight hours later, I was back in the Forum. The Soviets came out in brand new uniforms and equipment, they really motored in their drills and I thought, "Oh, oh." Team Canada scored two goals in the first six minutes or so and everybody was celebrating, but I turned to my wife, Helen. "We're going to get clobbered. We haven't even played 10 minutes and our guys are bent over resting on their sticks." The Soviets, meanwhile, had been flying. They won 7-3 and the cakewalk developed into a great series that Canada finally won 4-3-1 with the three "miracles in Moscow"—three late winning goals in a row by Paul Henderson.

That series changed the way we played our hockey in several ways. Fans loved the September Showdown and the slower, more violent NHL game suffered in contrast. On the positive side, we were forced to change how we conditioned our athletes, how we practiced, how we passed the puck, how we set up our five-man units and so on. It shouldn't have had to take an embarrassment to get us to do those things; we already had someone who knew this stuff. The Soviets copied Eddie Shore and the training and conditioning methods he used with his Springfield club almost to a "T" (as in totally), including special skating and game-situation drills. We said he was crazy and they imitated him. Eddie's knowledge of hockey set him apart. I wish when I'd left Barrie I'd gone to him and had him teach me how to play the game. I guarantee you I'd have been in the NHL in two years. It's too bad that Eddie's reputation as a tightwad and an eccentric overshadowed his knowledge and teaching skills.

Eddie was a Hall of Fame defenceman during his career with Boston and I really admire some of the Soviets who play that position. They had to be great skaters and puckhandlers on those big ice surfaces. You can't bodycheck on those rinks either, they're so large, so they learned to cut off avenues and passing lanes. That's why you couldn't be successful shooting the puck into the Soviet team's end and chasing it. When I was a TV analyst, I kept track of that play for several seasons. Even in the NHL, teams got the puck back only three out of every ten times they shot it in, making it the stupidest play in hockey. You know, "I don't want it, you can have it, it's too flat for me." They're still doing it, and it's even dumber now because all the defencemen in the league, European and North American, are more mobile than ever.

The old Soviets, on the other hand, were successful in their great years because they never stood still and they didn't give up the puck. They'd just keep skating and working it around until they got a shot on net. If they couldn't get a play going, they didn't panic and fire away wildly. They'd just throw it back to the blue line and start all over again. I wouldn't have wanted to play goalie against them. You might go long stretches without getting any work, which makes it tough to keep your concentration. You might get only 15 shots during a game, but almost every one would be a clear chance from the slot. That's why even when they gave up four or five goals in a game in the 1972 series, Ken Dryden and Tony Esposito were playing great.

On the negative side, the Soviet series triggered the stick fouls that have become the worst cross the NHL has to bear. There was no fighting, no escape valve, in European hockey and not nearly as much bodychecking. The Russians made up for their frustrations with their stick work, and many Team Canada players told me later they were the sneakiest, dirtiest guys they'd ever played against. In addition to copying their style and grace, our pros also began to copy their cross-checking, butt-ending, slashing, hooking and spearing. This was a tremendous change for our game. In the old days, when

I was refereeing, there was self-policing on stick work. Your own coach, even your teammates, would tell you to keep your stick below the waist. Refereeing, I'd allow a player one little touch or one little tug with the stick, but any more and he was gone.

Stick fouls spoil the game. Along with holding, they bring truly skilled players down a notch from what they could be if they had the freedom to show off all their talents. They prevent many small players, who can be the most skilled, most exciting and most popular, from having the kind of success they should. They can even interrupt careers, as with the chronic back problems Wayne Gretzky and Mario Lemieux have had as the result of constant illegal cross-checking in front of the net. It's ironic, in a way, that it's the new superstars from Europe like Pavel Bure, Teemu Selanne, Alexander Mogilny and Sergei Fedorov who have become the prime targets of the stickmen. Someone up there should realize, once and for all, that it's superstars playing at their best who put people in the seats.

The European invaders have not been greeted as heroes by everybody. Don Cherry runs them down at every opportunity —and Grapes has a lot of those—but they are the players who are selling the game today. The young players coming into the league now who can snap a crowd to attention are mostly Europeans. Their game is speed and they can score. The only Canadian impact player to come into the league in the last couple of years has been Eric Lindros. He can score, but his game is muscle. Grapes also was quick to point out that the Canadiens won the Stanley Cup in 1993 without a European on the roster. That's true, although they did have a couple of Americans in key roles in Mathieu Schneider and John LeClair, who scored two overtime game-winning goals in the final against Los Angeles.

Perhaps more of a prototype for future Stanley Cup champions were the Pittsburgh teams that won in 1991 and 1992.

They had Canadians, Americans, Swedes, Czechs and even a Canadian-trained native of South Korea (Jim Paek) in leading roles. I don't think you can win with all one nationality. I think the best teams from now on are going to be a happy mixture of Canadians and others. Everybody at this level has some talent for skating, passing, stickhandling and so on, the Europeans perhaps more of that. But Canadians have something else. Ludi Bukach, who coached the Czechs, told me once he could plan strategy against any team except Canada. He said that Canadian teams played with emotion, an emotion to win, that Europeans didn't have and couldn't imagine.

If I was drafting from today's NHL rosters for an expansion franchise, I'd take a mix of players. The only rule would be that I wouldn't pick anyone over 26 years old, as of January 1, 1994. In addition to being more than just competitive immediately, I'd want to build for the future. That would also save me some money in salaries, not a bad idea since I'd probably have paid $100 million or so for the franchise.

Goaltenders (3): Felix Potvin of Toronto seems a likely eventual successor to Patrick Roy as the best in the game. Arturs Irbe was the main reason San Jose had the best year-to-year improvement in NHL history and became a playoff team in 1994. Martin Brodeur, the New Jersey youngster, is a franchise player for the future.

Defencemen (6): Brian Leetch and Sergei Zubov of the Rangers provide great offence. So does Sandis Ozolinsh of the Sharks. Glen Wesley of Boston, Mathieu Schneider of the Canadiens and Niklas Lidstrom of Detroit can play it either way. I could mix and match with these guys.

Centres (4): Sergei Fedorov of Detroit may be the best all-around player in the world today. His teammates, the huge Keith Primeau and the nifty Vyacheslav Koslov, are just coming into their own. Robert Reichel of Calgary showed he can do everything when injuries hit the Flames in 1993-94.

Wings (8): I'm not specifying left wing or right, because so many players today can play on either side. Vancouver's Pavel Bure is the NHL's purest skater and stickhandler, with Pittsburgh's Jaromir Jagr just a step and a shift behind. I'd play Alexander Mogilny of Buffalo with Fedorov and Bure on an all-Russian line. The under-rated Brendan Shanahan of St. Louis and Adam Graves of the Rangers may be the league's next megastars. Keith Tkachuk of Winnipeg is both tough and good both ways and his fellow Jet, Teemu Selanne, has a great scoring touch. So does Mark Recchi of Philadelphia.

Power Play: I'd have Jeremy Roenick of Chicago, a natural scorer, and Jason Arnott, who made such an impact with Edmonton in his first season, playing up front with Bure. On the point would be Leetch and Zubov, the Rangers' pair.

Penalty Killers: I'd add the pesky Theoren Fleury of Calgary and the bruising Eric Lindros of the Flyers as forecheckers, and start with Wesley and Schneider on defence. Playing Fedorov and Bure as forwards while a man short would give the opposition something to worry about.

I'd end up with a team of 25 players including 10 Canadians and 15 others—five from the former Soviet Union, four Americans, two Czechs, two Latvians, one Finn and one Swede. These guys would need a gate-opener more than a coach but, if you must have one, I'd take Scotty Bowman. He'd steal one game in a playoff series all by himself.

The natural extension of what we've been seeing would be a true world league of hockey. They're playing the game all over now. I was in Battle Creek, Michigan, with the old-timers a while ago and the game on in the arena when I checked it out was between youngsters from China and the U.S. I was amazed at the talents of the Chinese kids, who had never even seen top-calibre hockey, including one defenceman who reminded me of Doug Harvey. Art Skov, the former NHL referee, saw the same things I did. "We're going to have a problem with these guys in a few years," he said.

The NHL is going to take its game to other countries, just

like the National Baskeball Asssociation and the National
Football League have. It's already started, in fact, with pre-
season exhibitions in Europe the last few years. I just hope
they keep in mind that it's our game and we should protect it. I
hope they look past the old malarkey about having to have
violence to sell hockey. They've been saying that about the
U.S. public for years and I think I can prove it's not true. The
NBA is the one I took a cue from. Their players at one time
were mostly in the 6′5″ and 6′6″ range, weighing 220 pounds
or so. All of a sudden, they had guys seven feet tall, 250
pounds of muscle. The NBA said, "Okay, you guys are bigger
and stronger, so we're going to be tougher on the rules to
control you." And they did. If you breathe wrong, it's a foul.
If you throw a punch, you're gone. The result was that Magic
Johnson, Larry Bird and Michael Jordan became household
names and the NBA became a money machine. Basketball
today is the biggest drawing game in the world.

The NBA also solved another problem similar to one that's
been a large part of the less-attractive hockey we see today.
That goes back to the discovery that a large forward parked
right in front of the net could cause a lot of problems for the
goaltender. The Canadiens might have done it first with Yvon
Lambert, who was just fabulous in the job. He'd stand there
and you couldn't move him. So everybody started doing it,
and players began jamming in there and it's become a mess.
The NBA has a rule that says guys can stand in the lane under
the basket for only three seconds at a time, and they enforce it.
That opens up some room for the smaller players. The NHL
should do something to hold down the number of people in
the crease area.

Americans live on heroes, and the U.S. is the market where
television contracts will determine whether hockey can keep
up with the other pro leagues. The NHL thus needs heroes,
not plumbers. The only way to get them is to tighten up on the
officials' calls. Elmer Lach, the former Canadiens' star, once

told me, "There's gotta be something wrong with a league where you hire the greatest athletes in the game to put on a performance for the paying fans and then you hire mediocre players to stop them from putting on the show."

Opening up the game also would let the stars stand out as colorful individuals, rather than almost everyone being out of the same cookie-cutter mold. That was the key with super-stars like Gordie Howe, the Rocket and Bobby Orr; they had their own styles. They'd be cheered at home and booed on the road but people always came out to see them play and went away satisfied, even if they'd been part of a trouncing for the local team. That's not true today. Who could hate Wayne or Mario or Patrick Roy? The one player I see today with the old-time kind of star appeal is Lindros. He's not the most popular guy God ever created. He causes problems every now and then but people want to see him on the ice whether they love him or hate him.

I've heard many hockey fans say it should be simple to fix what's wrong. If the referees just called everything by the book, the problems would go away. The rules are there, they say, just enforce them. That's true, but it's not quite that easy. The referees take their orders from above, so the way the game is called is the way the people running the league want it called. If a change were decided on, it should be done by going back to the rule book at the start of an exhibition season. Call everything. In the first game, there might be 70 penalties. In the next, it would come down to about 40. In the third game, it'd be about 20. After that, it would round out to about 15 a game, which should become about average.

I guarantee you that by the first league game, every player in the NHL would know how to play and you would see a lot of talent from people you're watching today who don't show it now. Everybody in the league would become a better player, because they'd have to. There are probably 30 guys on second and third lines who were great on offence as juniors and are not allowed to play that way now. What they are allowed to do is hook and hold because the coach says, "You're a checker, do your job." As time went on, I think you'd see 26 teams that could sell entertainment, and not some of them going into a defensive shell for 60 minutes because the other team is better, and ruining the whole night out for the paying customers.

I'm firmly convinced it could be done. The league would have to stick to its guns and close its ears to the complaints for as long as it took. As soon as one team lost three or four games in a row by big scores, its owners and fans would be crying. They might have to ride through a rough spell, even make some trades and spend some money. But they would be bringing their team up to the level around them, rather than taking the game down to its lowest level for the sake of parity.

As in the NBA, there would have to be full support for the officials from the league administrators. Pardon me for not holding my breath. This is a concept which the NHL has never grasped. In fact, it's the administrators who worry me the most in this situation. Most of the people running hockey today never played the game and it's very difficult for someone in that position to know what should happen or not happen on the ice. The NHL dropped its finest administrator, Brian O'Neill, when the disastrous and power-hungry Gil Stein began his short stay as president. He changed some things that didn't need it and didn't change some things that did. Brian was a Canadian who'd played college hockey in Montreal, knew the game and had some common sense. He'd never have moved even one game of great geographical rivalries like Montreal-Quebec and New York Rangers-New Jersey to neutral sites like Phoenix and Halifax, respectively. That's what happened during the 1993-94 season.

I'm sorry to see that almost all of the league offices, and the decision-making powers, have taken off across the border to New York from Montreal and Toronto. It may be a good move from a marketing point of view since the NHL's great growth potential is in the U.S. But that raises another depressing thought. What's going to happen to the smaller-market Canadian franchises in the future? I firmly believe that in years to come, as things now stand, there will be only three teams in Canada—in Toronto, Vancouver and Montreal. They are the only cities with population bases large enough to be viable in the coming era of new buildings and higher prices. The other teams seem doomed unless they are helped by governments, which would be a stupid mistake since that almost always is a case of throwing good money after bad, with the problems still unsolved after it's all been spent. There have been unhappy noises in recent times from Edmonton, Quebec City, Winnipeg, Ottawa and Calgary demanding rental and leasing relief or new-arena construction assistance. I see no commitment by the league to keep teams in Canada. In fact, when Peter Pocklington was threatening to move the Oilers to Minnesota, NHL commissioner Gary Bettman was standing beside him as he tried to blackmail the city of Edmonton and the province of Alberta.

My own dream is for a separate Canadian division in the NHL. That would be one way to ensure some degree of security for our teams. It could also lead to super rivalries if there were a separate European division formed as well. The playoff system could be arranged so that either a Canadian team or a European team played one from the U.S. in the Stanley Cup final. The Americans would love it as another opportunity to wave the flag. It probably makes too much sense ever to happen, though.

One thing is for sure. Hockey eventually is going to be played a lot more like it was in the 1950s. It has to happen because, while the players have become bigger, stronger and quicker, with better shots and in better condition, the game isn't as good or as entertaining. The Europeans are here to stay and, thank God, we're never going to turn them into fighters or grinders. It's inevitable that the NHL game is going to be faster and cleaner because it's a better spectator sport that way. Think of recent all-star games, in which there was no interference or holding or stick work, just great offensive hockey. Add legal bodychecking to that and you'd have the greatest game in the world. The purists (mostly media types who get in free) would hate it, but what's wrong with a 9-8 score? The fans (who pay) would love it. And they're the ones who matter.

I'm certain Commissioner Bettman understands that. He came from the No. 3 job in the NBA, where the same exercise, the transformation of a league, was carried out with spectacular success. And he has learned a lot about hockey since he joined the NHL in 1993. That day, Pat Williams, the general manager of the Orlando Magic of the NBA, was asked how he thought Bettman would do in the world of hockey. "Well," Williams said, "I gave Gary a puck and he spent the whole afternoon trying to figure out how to open it."

21

It All Starts With The Kids

One year at the Quebec International Pee Wee Hockey Tournament, I was invited to speak to a special luncheon they put on for 500 out-of-town parents. I started off with a question: "How many of you fathers and mothers here today love your boys?" Every adult hand in the room went up. "How many of you would like to do your boys a favor?" Every hand went up again. "In that case, when I'm through speaking, go back to your hotel rooms, pack your bags and get out of town. This week you're the worst friends they've got. You're the only people who can ruin the week for them. So go on home."

There was complete silence for a few seconds, and then some clapping started and then they stood up en masse and applauded. The parents realized what I was telling them: that if anything went wrong, if the kids didn't have the kind of fun they expected, it was almost certain they'd be the ones responsible. Parents, and the pressure they bring with them, whether they know it's there or not, are one main reason so many kids quit playing organized sports before age 16 today. They're just not enjoying it. They're over-dressed, over-coached, over-supervised and they're not having any fun, so they quit. Even the ones who stay with it don't have the love of the game you used to see.

So I told the parents: "Supply the equipment, supply everything, and drive your kid to the arena. But then go home and leave him be." If I was running minor hockey, no parent would ever be allowed in the rink. I'd let them in for only the final game of the year, and that would be it. We don't allow parents to go into a school and disrupt the class where their child is trying to learn. Why should they be allowed to disrupt an arena where their child is trying to learn how to play hockey?

I have to admit it was partly a case of "do as I say, not as I do" when it came to my son Bob. I never tried to coach him or his brother Doug or interfere with their coaches, and I never forced them into anything. Quite the opposite, in fact. I was proud they were playing sports, but I knew there were more important things. Doug came to me when he was 13 and asked, "Dad, do I have to play sports?" It turned out that he hadn't really liked it but he thought he had to play because I'd been an athlete, his aunts and uncle had been and his older brother was. I told him: "No, you don't have to do a darn thing in this world you don't want. Just try to be the best at what you do. If you want to be a garbage collector, be the best. If you want to be a teacher, be the best. But you don't have to be an athlete." He said, "Thanks, Dad," and he never played another thing.

Bob was a good athlete. He played both football and hockey for West Hill High School in our neighborhood. I was away refereeing most of the time but I wanted to see how he was doing, so I went over to the school one afternoon when I was in town. I was standing along the sideline with the rest of the fans when he got the football and was heading right toward me. I scanned the field quickly and realized that if he moved it up a notch he could go all the way. I ran out onto the field and I was yelling, "Go! Go!" He scored the touchdown, but when he came home, he said: "Dad, will you do me a favor? Never come to watch me play again." I asked him why. "It's not because of what happened today. It's just that when you're there in the crowd, everyone starts trying to compare me with you. It's not fair. I'm never going to be you. I can't. I don't feel the same when you're there. It's not as much fun." I said, "That's fine, Bob," and I meant it.

But a while later, during the hockey season, I couldn't resist. I went to the rink. Here I was, dark glasses on, wearing a fedora, scarf up around my chin and coat over my ears, hiding behind a post that I was peeking around. West Hill won the game and Bob scored a goal or two, but at home he came storming in the front door, and said, "Dad, I told you I didn't want you at any of my games." I tried to lie and said, "I wasn't at your game." He said, "Everybody in the arena knew you were at the game." I said, "Okay, okay," and the next time I saw him play anything was close to 10 years later in the 1970 Grey Cup when he was with the Alouettes and they beat Calgary.

So I know it's tough for parents to stay away, and when they're there they want to see their kids, even the tiny ones, play in an actual game, which is not the best way to learn to play hockey. If I ran a team and I had 30 kids trying out, I'd put 15 on a side, drop the puck and go into the dressing room to read the paper. You don't learn to skate, stickhandle or shoot under instructions. Kids learn more by being on the ice and doing it. In my day, every backyard had a little rink, the lakes and ponds froze over, and if there was nowhere else you could pretend the snow-covered street was Maple Leaf Gardens or the Forum. You wore skates and regular woollen mitts, which taught you how much a slash could hurt, and old rolled-up magazines instead of shin pads. And perhaps the greatest thing was that everybody got to play, not just the best kids. It was the same with pick-up football too; there might be 20 guys on a team. That's how you learned a stickhandler's and running back's moves. If you gave up the puck or the ball, you might not get it again until next week.

In both sports now they've got so much stuff on they look like little aliens and they can hardly move. I saw a bunch of eight-year-olds on the ice a while ago and instead of skating and stickhandling, they were practicing slapshots. What a waste of time! The puck didn't even reach the end of the rink. Rocket Richard once said that players learn to play when they're young and that's the way they play all their lives. "There are a lot of skills this generation doesn't have," he added. Start with skating. I'm 76 years old and nobody has ever shown me the right way to skate. That's wrong. No boy should be on skates without someone showing him things like what the blades are for, about using the arms for perfect balance and the knees as shock absorbers.

Any time you see a little kid who's a great skater, you're looking at pure natural ability. But you can be taught to skate; they even do it with guys after they reach the National Hockey League, like Doug Riseborough, whom the Canadiens sent to a power skating teacher after his rookie year. I think it's fine to give a youngster hockey skates when he's four or five years old, but he should start out in a figure skating school to learn the basic techniques. The first year, maybe even the second, should be just skating, perhaps with a stick in his hands, but no organized games. Shinny games, yes, but no more. But these days they're being taught skills before they're taught tools, which is ridiculous. And a few kids, the best players, get all the ice time.

In Europe, on the other hand, they pay much more attention to the fundamentals. I think the reason the players from the former Soviet Union who have come into the NHL recently have done better than most people expected is that they're more talented. It's as simple as that. And most of it has to do with the way they were taught to play the game. They spent a lot of time in their early years on power skating and other drills, including dry land training. Instead of trying to win a game, they were trying to learn a game. They didn't play hockey itself for a long time. The Soviets used to take a promising kid as young as seven and, in effect, turn him pro. From then on, he was a hockey player. We can't do that, obviously, but there has to be a happy medium because the equation is the same. It's like education. You go to public school and high school to learn the basics so you can go to college. In hockey, if you want to be great at 19 or 20, you'd better learn much earlier.

Let's take it a step further. If a youngster arrives at the front door of a college but can't read or write, is that the fault of the college or of the schools he came from? There's no point in blaming the NHL for the fact that Canadian players come into the league able to skate hard and with a great slapshot, but nothing else. They can hook and hold and cross-check because they learned that in junior, which is much more violent than the NHL. The Europeans, on the other hand, have the skills that allow them to be more than grinders. The response of many Canadians is to blame the Europeans for taking our jobs. Wrong target. The Canadian Amateur Hockey Association (CAHA) runs minor hockey in this country and a change in its outlook is the only way to improve the situation.

I remember a few years ago, there was a fellow out in the Western junior league. He was trying to take a backhand shot near the net, and was cross-checked from behind into the end boards. He broke his neck and wound up paralyzed for life. There was no penalty on the play, which horrified a lot of people. The president of the league said, "That was a legal check in our league." The youngster almost died, he was finished for life and they condoned it. The CAHA didn't take any action, either. Unless they pick up the tempo at the CAHA and get some things straightened out, Canadians might some day be in the minority in pro hockey. There is that large a talent pool to tap in the U.S. and Europe. We shouldn't be crying about foreigners because they're better than we are. We should be trying to get better than they are. We're blaming the wrong people.

The NHL, however, is not without its share of responsibility. It is stuck with what comes out of CAHA ranks each year, true, and that product isn't as skilled in general as it once was. But kids imitate the pros, and what they learn to do from NHL telecasts sometimes is not exactly what the doctor ordered. I'd see examples of that at the big Quebec pee wee tournament, where I refereed for 17 years in a row until the separatist Parti Québécois won power in the province in 1976, and the organizers told me they were sorry but they couldn't have me back because I was English. But that's another story.

There were some great kids in that tournament over the years—Guy Lafleur, the best 10- or 11-year-old hockey player I ever saw; Brad Park, Dick Redmond and Syl Apps Jr., among others, come to mind. Then there were Mark and Marty Howe. The first game I saw them play I wasn't working, so I was sitting up on the catwalk with a great view. After a couple of minutes, I said to the guy beside me: "It's amazing. I'm looking at a miniature Gordie Howe." That was Mark and he skated like Gordie, held the stick like Gordie and made plays like Gordie. He also was so cool and calculating for a kid that age. You could tell even then there was no way he wasn't going to make the NHL.

Marty was something different. He didn't have the natural ability of Mark, but he was strong and tough. They played in one of the finals and after it was over, the two teams lined up to shake hands. Marty reached one kid and, instead of shaking with him, he decked him. These are 11-year-old kids and there was a big uproar, of course. Gordie and Colleen were up in the stands and Colleen said: "That's terrible. Gordie, you'd better go down and talk to Marty. We can't have him doing that." Gordie went down to the dressing room and asked Marty what it was all about. Marty pulled up his sweater and showed Gordie a long, nasty red mark. "He got me with his stick. I told him I'd get him for it before it was over. So I got him for it." Gordie said, "Okay," and went back to his seat. Colleen asked him, "Did you straighten the boy out?" And Gordie said, "I think we should give him a bloody medal."

22

They're All Taking It Too Seriously

When Neil Armstrong was about to break George Hayes's record of total games worked by an NHL linesman, George told an interviewer: "You can say one thing: I worked all my 1,544 games in a major league, but since 1967 Armstrong has been working in a minor league." I wouldn't go quite that far, but I will say that the overall quality of play has never been anything like it was before the six-team league expanded. I know the game isn't nearly as colorful as it was then. I know that nobody is having any fun at all now, never mind as much as we did. All of those things have happened because that's the way the league wants it.

One thing that hasn't changed, however, is the quality of the NHL's officials. They're the best in the world, in the toughest game to run. They are in great shape, because they have to fly up and down the ice all night long. In baseball and football, you can be 65 years old and 80 pounds overweight but as long as you manage to get your boots laced up, you can keep working. The NHL officials arrive well qualified after working in junior and minor league hockey, which is far dirtier and has far more outbursts like bench-clearing brawls. Proportionately, there aren't as many really top-flight officials because of expansion, however, so they are lasting longer in the league, 20 years and more. In my day, you wouldn't have been allowed to go on that long because of the physical demands of the job. There is some difficulty in finding good new ones today, as was shown during the regular officials' strike in the fall of 1993, when replacements had to be used and weren't entirely satisfactory.

I parted company with the members of the lodge over that, just as I did when a crew refused to work a playoff game a few years ago. That was after New Jersey coach Jim Schoenfeld had gone nearly berserk, insulted referee Don Koharski ("Go have another doughnut, you fat pig!"), been suspended for his actions and then won a court injunction allowing him to continue behind the bench. The regular officials assigned to work the game decided to sit out in protest. Some local guys were called in and even looked silly on the ice, besides being incompetent.

My idea was always that I was hired to referee a game. My job was to go out and make sure there were six men on the ice from each team, drop the puck to start the game and then keep it moving along. I had no jurisdiction over who coached, who managed, who was the president. I didn't give a damn about any of that. The only people who meant any-thing to me in sport were the people playing the game. On the ice, on a football field, on a lacrosse floor, the only people who counted were the players.

Incidentally, I like the current setup of one referee and two linesmen just fine. I'm not in favor of the two-referee system many people have suggested to enforce the rules more tightly. I worked that way years ago in the Quebec senior league, and with a great partner like Kenny Mullins, it was fine. But I also worked with other referees who were weak, so I'd have to take over control of the game anyway. If you have one referee and he's having a bad night, it's the same for everybody. But with two referees and one being bad, you have two games going on and the players don't know how they're supposed to play. One referee can see the whole ice surface, or enough of it that he isn't going to miss anything. I've demonstrated that to guys over and over, taking them out on the ice with me to prove it. I show them I can see the 11 players involved in anything that might be going on, all except the goalie at the other end. Another thing to remember is that it's not because they're not seen that fouls aren't being called; they're not being called because that's the way the league wants it.

There are a couple of other things I see that I don't like. One of them hasn't changed at all since my time. The officials continue to be over-supervised by the league. That's wrong in principle; it's even worse when some of the supervisors were linesmen who weren't good enough to be referees. The result is that there are referees in the NHL who were better when they came into the league than they are now. They get worn down by the constant criticism and second-guessing.

I don't like to see officials wearing helmets, because I think they're unnecessary from a safety viewpoint and they take away from the quality of their work. I never would have worn one, and still don't. You simply can't see as well, obviously; your peripheral vision is particularly impeded. Perhaps as important, you can't hear as well. Elmer Lach told me one time that he could tell by the sound the skates made whether a man behind him was on his team or the opposition, because the blades didn't sound the same if the fellow was moving into position for a pass or chasing him hard. Players today can't hear as well, either. How many times have you seen a team with a three-on-one break and a pass was never made? They might have been screaming their lungs out, but the guy with the puck couldn't hear them.

The helmets have taken away a lot of the color of the game, in terms of fan identification and so on. As for the referees, how can you really hate someone if you can't see what he looks like? Hating the ref is an integral part of hockey and I have to admit we used to encourage it a little by being flam-

boyant in our calls. There's none of that today, no fun at all.
It's just so obviously a business. The officials are straight and
stiff, and they've become confrontational in many arguments
with the players. We weren't afraid of admitting we were
wrong, and we didn't mind the players poking fun at us. Hell,
we'd even poke fun at ourselves. Today's officials will never
have memories like these . . .

When Phil Watson was coaching the Rangers, he started
screaming one night just before the opening faceoff. "Red,"
he yelled, "you're nothing but a blind so-and-so. You're a
redheaded no-talent bleep-bleeper. You shouldn't be here,
Red, because you're a bleeping such-and-such." It went on
and on, and finally I skated over to the Rangers' bench.
Before I could open my mouth, Phil pointed out to centre ice
and said, "I was talking to him." I turned around to look and
the Ranger waiting there was Red Sullivan. Phil had me dead
to rights. Grin and bear it.

In the 1950s, in addition to my refereeing, I was working as
a salesman for Blue Bonnets Automobiles in Montreal. Traders Finance used to store cars that had been stolen in Toronto
and recovered in Montreal there. One day they asked me if
sometime when I was going to Toronto, I'd like to drive one up
and collect a fee. Later that week, on the day before a game I
was on my way in a brand new Lincoln. I got into Kingston on
the old No. 2 highway and stopped to have the gas tank filled.
The service station guy was walking around the car inspecting
it and said, "Hey, you got no licence plates." I realized I also
had no registration papers, but I was halfway to Toronto so I
thought I'd take a chance and keep on going.

I only had about 40 miles to go when I came up behind a
police car which was driving well below the speed limit. I
didn't want to pass him going that slowly. He'd get too good a
look at the car, so I figured I'd drop back a hundred yards or
so, put the pedal to the metal and still be below the limit when
I whistled past him. It was dusk and I thought I'd be by him

so quickly he wouldn't notice I had no licence plates. Within a half a mile he had me over on the shoulder. He was so huge he made me look like a midget, but he wasn't as bright as he was big. He didn't really know what to do with me, and took me to the station in Bowmanville, where I told the sergeant: "Look, I'm Red Storey and I'm refereeing an NHL game in Toronto tomorrow night. Traders asked me to deliver this car and that's all I'm doing." He wanted to check on my story, but it was after five o'clock by now and the Traders' office in Montreal was closed. When the sergeant said he'd phone Maple Leaf Gardens, I thought my troubles were over.

I was right beside him listening in and suddenly I heard Conn Smythe's voice. He was quiet as the sergeant told him he had Red Storey in Bowmanville with a car with no licence plates or registration and so on, and didn't know what to do. Smythe said, "Keep the big bugger in there all weekend. We don't want to see him." Bang! He hung up. The sergeant said, "Well, you're true. You're Storey and you're supposed to referee there tomorrow. So I'll tell you what we're gonna do. I'm gonna give you my name and phone number on a piece of paper. You get out of here and if anyone stops you, you tell them to call me immediately, before they do anything." I got into Toronto all right and even drove around there with no trouble. I enjoyed the surprised look on Smythe's face when I came out before the game. I didn't enjoy the papers getting hold of the story and running headlines like STOREY CAUGHT WITH STOLEN CAR. I heard about that from fans all over the league for a while.

I was doing a game in Chicago one time, and I had my hand in the air for a delayed penalty to the Hawks. The guy on the other team with the puck roared in on goal, was turned away and everybody chased him all the way back into his own end. I was behind him skating like hell, with my hand still up in the air. He rounded his own net and started another rink-long dash, still with the puck. I was still chasing him, my hand still up. He got turned away again at the other team's blue line and made another big circle, with me still chasing and waving. Finally, he lost the puck at centre ice. I dropped my hand; in fact I almost fell down I was so tired. But I couldn't for the life of me remember who was supposed to get the penalty. I looked around and the Hawks' Larry Zeidel, a bit of a bad guy, was standing there. "Okay, Zeidel, you're out of here." Little Bill Mosienko came over and protested, "You got the wrong guy, Red, you got the wrong guy." I looked down at him. "Never mind that, Bill. Did I get the right team?"

Once in Toronto I was going up the runway to the dressing room after a hectic Maple Leafs' loss and several angry fans were trying to get at me. The ushers were doing their best to ward them off, but some were getting close. There were a few cops standing around doing nothing. My brother, George, who was waiting for me, turned to one of them he knew. "You've got a uniform on, why don't you do your duty?" I really felt good about George jumping in like that. But then the cop looked at him and said, "Your brother had a uniform on, too. Why didn't he do his duty?" We were both speechless.

I played Santa Claus on *Hockey Night In Canada* for 14 years, and it was fun. I got dressed around 5:30 in the afternoon because they pretaped some stuff. I stayed in the costume all night because I was on during every intermission and, by the time the game was over, I'd be pretty beat. One time, Ralph Mellanby, who ran the *HNIC* telecasts, asked me to drop in on a post-game show for a half an hour or so and wish everyone a Merry Christmas. I hesitated, so he said, "There's an extra $100 in it." I told him, "Just point me in the direction you want me to go."

The show had the format of three guys quizzing someone in the hot seat, and I asked who the victim was. They said it was Harold Ballard. It turned out that Dick Beddoes, the writer, was one of the panelists. He was as eccentric in his own way as

Ballard, so I could see we'd have some fun. I was walking around behind the set and I heard Ballard saying, "Beddoes, you don't know your ass from a hole in the ground." I thought: "Boy, we're lucky we're not on. What would the kids think of Santa Claus being involved in something like that?" Then I looked at a monitor and they were on live. I wondered: "What the hell do I do now? Maybe they'll run out of time before they get me on." No such luck. With about five minutes left, Mellanby gave me a pat on the bum and a little push.

I grabbed my bells and I came out shaking them. "Ho, ho, ho. I just dropped in, Mr. Ballard, to wish you all a very Merry Christmas." He looked up and said, "Hello, Santa, ya old fart ya!" Now I was getting mad and when Beddoes asked me what I was going to give Ballard, I said, "You know what they give the man who has everything, don't you?" Beddoes didn't, and I told him, "Penicillin, that's what." Beddoes made it worse. "Yeah, and with some of the broads he goes out with, he needs penicillin." Dave Hodge came running in from another studio, grabbed a mike and apologized to everybody across Canada, saying the real Santa Claus wasn't involved in any of this stuff, and so on. When it was finally over, Beddoes made the truest statement of the night, "I'll guarantee nobody turned their dial."

I was still mad and told them that was the last time they'd ever catch me involved in anything like that. But there came another time when I was Santa again. Hodge was running the show this night and we had two or three practice runs of the introduction and entrance to make sure it was done right and there'd be no embarrassments. They told me they were set to tape, let 'er roll, and I went through the door going "Ho, ho, ho." Everybody was in on the gag but me, and I almost fainted when Hodge said, "Here comes the drunken old sonofabitch now."

Eddie Shack of the Maple Leafs and Henri Richard of the Canadiens got into a fight in a game in the early 1960s. Eddie butted Henri with his head and opened up a pretty good cut, putting the Canadiens' fans in a rage. They never forgot it or forgave him. I had a radio sports talk show on CKGM in Montreal, from the Kiltie Lounge in the old Laurentien Hotel. The next summer I heard Eddie was coming to town for the Canadian Open golf tournament at Pinegrove, across the river. I called him and he agreed to come on. I usually just let the people sitting in the bar on the air, but for this one time we decided to have phone lines set up so that listeners at home could talk to Eddie.

The first call was a great one, from a gentleman who really knew his sports. He asked Eddie some good questions, and Eddie answered them like a pro. I let him take more time than usual but finally jumped in to explain there were a lot of other fans on the line waiting to talk to Mr. Shack. The caller asked if he could say one more thing. I agreed. We weren't on delay so I couldn't do a damn thing when he said to Eddie, "I think you're a big prick." There was a stunned silence. I panicked and shut off everything, then realized I couldn't do that and switched it back on. Eddie had recovered by then. "Red," he said into the open mike, "I think he meant you."

I was refereeing a game between the Red Wings and Rangers in Madison Square Garden, when New York's Nick Mickoski was tripped by Black Jack Stewart right in front of me. Mickoski's skate came up and caught me right where the sun don't shine. I went down on the ice wondering where to send the application for the Vienna Boys' Choir. They dragged me into the doctor's office, he did a little search and a little massage, and found the only things really ripped were my pants. They sewed them up and about 25 minutes later I was back out there, but still not feeling all that great.

The Rangers had a right wing named Wally Hergesheimer, just a little guy but he led every team he was ever on in scoring. He was a great hockey player and a great guy so I wasn't surprised when he skated over to me before we started play again. I thought he wanted to give me some sympathy or say something nice. At this point, I'd better remind you that a referee was not allowed to laugh during a game; he was not supposed to do that under any circumstances. I laughed that night, however, because Wally said: "Red, I have something for you. I found these on the ice and I thought you might have lost 'em." I looked down and he had two purple jelly beans in his hand.

Postscript

A Summing Up

Several years ago, the composing room of *The Montreal Star* had processed a story by Red Fisher, the sports editor. When later developments meant it had to be done over, a young fellow was dispatched to tell the typographers. He ran to the foreman, breathless, and gasped, "Red's story's dead." Someone overheard that as "Red Storey's dead," and immediately called his wife. She phoned a friend, and eventually it got to someone who called a radio station that offered $5 for news tips from listeners. The phone began to ring off the hook at home, and I kept repeating Mark Twain's line about the reports being exaggerated. The Old Redhead is pleased that's still true, although there have been a couple of close calls along the way.

In 1972, rheumatoid arthritis and a touch of diabetes left me with only about 10 percent use of my right hand, arm and shoulder for a while. I noticed it first when I couldn't bend over to pick up the puck at an old-timers' game in Detroit. I thought it was just an old injury flaring up, but in 24 hours I could hardly move. The whole body just quit. I lost 25 pounds and, Lord, I was scared. I had to sleep in a chair because it hurt too much to lie down. I made up my mind I wasn't going to be a couch potato and good doctors, a lot of medication, a lot of time and a lot of support from family and friends got me up and around and back to normal again.

A while later I was in the hospital for a minor operation and the doctor came in to see me afterward. He didn't recognize my name and he asked me, "What do you do for a living anyway?" I said I had spent my life in sports and he asked if I was ever hurt. "Try every day," I told him, adding, "Why do you ask?" He said, "Well, all your organs are in the wrong place. They've been pushed over by the injuries. Didn't you ever tell anybody you were hurt?" I told him I hadn't because if I had, I'd lose my job and I wouldn't eat. He said my body wouldn't take what I was doing to it any longer, and I'd have to give up beer. "Not one beer?" I asked. "Could you drink just one beer?" No. "Then you can't have any the rest of your life." I never have. I stopped cold turkey, which wasn't new for me. In 1959, I came back from a long European hockey trip with strep throat and the doctor gave me two years to live unless I quit smoking. I was a three-packs-a-day guy but never had another cigarette. The doctor said I smoked too heavily to quit too fast, but I've always had a lot of willpower. It was rough for about three months until I got my body straightened out.

In 1986, I had surgery for cancer of the colon at the Jewish General Hospital in Montreal and again, with a lot of help, I was able to resume my life and the same schedule of speaking and charity refereeing. I was taught by my mother from the time I can remember that when you fell on your ass, you always had to get up and try a little harder the next time. I just deal with each day as it comes along. If you don't quit, you'll find the world treats you pretty well. There also is some longevity in our family. Ma was 96 when she died in 1983, and I had two aunts who each lived to 98.

With everything that's happened to me, I've often wondered if lives are somehow predetermined. I was a successful athlete, got injured and couldn't play any longer, and sort of fell into becoming a successful referee. After I couldn't do that for a living any more, I sort of fell into becoming a successful after-dinner speaker. It just seems that one thing led into another. I've been lucky all my life.

That particularly applies to the family I've been fortunate enough to have. My mother was a rock in a childhood that could have seen me head in the wrong direction. My older sister Irene was my inspiration. She was a great athlete who married and became a swimming instructor in San Francisco after being unable to swim a stroke until she was 30. She died before her time at 69 from a mysterious virus. My younger sister Helen now has her own business in Toronto as a trouble-shooting consultant to foreign governments. She graduated as a teacher, and students at West Hill High School in Montreal and Havergal College in Toronto will remember her as Mrs. Lahti. My brother George owns and operates Delta Pipelines Supplies in Toronto after being a newspaper writer and an assistant coach to Hap Emms with the Barrie junior hockey team. He could have been a fine coach in the NHL, but chose another career.

Helen, my first wife, died in 1981, after we had been married for 37 years. Neither she nor Bunny, my second wife, knew anything about sports, which was not necessarily a handicap. Helen gave me two sons. Bob is the top executive in Canada for Tropicana, the fruit juice company that is part of the Seagram's empire. Doug is a senior official with the world-wide Transcendental Meditation organization, working out of Ottawa. Bob has two children. Bob Jr. is a highly success-ful engineer with a conglomerate in Philadelphia. Michael has been studying at the University of New Brunswick in Fredericton and has a great interest in the environment.

I met Bunny a few years after Helen's death. She was a neighbor in the Notre Dame de Grâce district of Montreal but I didn't know her. Driving to work one morning during a blizzard, I saw her standing at the bus stop at the corner and asked her if she'd like a lift downtown. We were married in December, 1989.

I've been lucky to have been able to continue to live in Montreal, the one city in my life that really made me feel I was wanted. Looking back, I think I was always a little bit depressed in the other places I've lived for any length of time. The people in my hometown of Barrie, the ones who had money, accepted me only as an athlete. I wasn't wanted for myself, but because I was good. It was the same thing during the six seasons I played with the Argonauts in Toronto. I would see only a few of my teammates—the Stukus brothers, Art West and a couple more—away from the field. The others belonged to a different social world than the poor kid from Barrie and I never really fit in. I always felt like an outsider.

Montreal changed all that. I'd been there with the Argos and absolutely loved it from the first time I saw it. It seemed mysterious and wonderful to a young man. I thought that the people of Montreal really lived; in Ontario, we only existed. There was a sort of freedom of spirit about the place. I always hated to leave. When I arrived in Montreal early in 1942 to work and play hockey, I thought I was going to spend a year or so there, and then go back home to Ontario. But I soon realized that with all the travelling I'd done, I'd never been to a better place or been treated better. After 52 years, that statement still stands. Despite the fact that I can't speak French, I'm made welcome in cities and small towns all across the province. I've never regretted the decision to make Montreal my home and to stay.

In fact, I have only two regrets. First, I wish I'd been 5'10" or so, instead of 6'3". Being tall, my legs were very vulnerable. If I'd been shorter, I think I'd have avoided most of the injuries I had and been able to play longer than I did. Second, when I quit the NHL in 1959, I wish I'd taken a shot at umpiring in baseball. I'd been a good player with a feel for the game, I knew the rules and I was colorful. It was the sport paying its officials the most and I think I could have been in the major leagues within two years.

I'm sort of sad that the selectors have never seen fit to elect me to the Canadian Football Hall of Fame. I think I've been kept out because I left the Argos before the playoffs in 1941 to play hockey. The Argos weren't going to pay me anything at all for the extra games, and even when they changed their minds, I wouldn't play. It was a matter of principle, not an act of rebellion. But I have been named to both the Hockey Hall of Fame and Canada's Sports Hall of Fame, and I was given the Order of Canada in 1992. Those honors are probably enough for one guy. I was shocked each time they told me and thought someone must have made a mistake. Nothing good is supposed to happen to officials to start with.

In all, I'm the luckiest man in the world because I've been able to follow one of Casey Stengel's rules: "The trick is growing up without growing old." I keep myself young by staying active. I'm in my eighth decade on skates. People tell me the heavy schedule of games I do for charity is an awful lot of work for a fellow my age, but I don't think of it as work. To me, it's a kind of reward because I started out poor and did well, and this is a chance to give something back. I'm happy to have reached this stage of my life and still have the ability and strength to go out and help other people. I stopped counting a few years ago when the total of funds I'd helped to raise passed $20 million.

There's no better world than the world of sports that I've been part of almost since I can remember. Fred Shero, the hockey coach, once said, "Life is just a place where we spend time between games." It's been a great ride, and more than that.

For me, sports has literally been the salvation of my life.

Appendix A

A Satisfactory Referee

I think that I shall never see
    A satisfactory referee;
One who calls them as they are
    And not as I wish by far;
About whose head a halo shines
    And one who rates reporters' lines!
A gent who leans not every way
    But lets the players decide the play.
Poems are made by fools like me
    But only God can referee.

—Anonymous

Appendix B

Red's Rules

When we were growing up in Barrie, Ontario, my mother gave us four rules to control our lives. I've lived by them ever since.

- It doesn't cost anything to be neat and clean.

- It doesn't cost anything to have good manners.

- It doesn't cost anything to be honest.

- If you don't own it, don't touch it.

Appendix C

Red's Lists

NOTE: These lists are purely personal. They mix different eras, which may be unfair because of the different styles of play and conditions. But they do represent the best I've seen over the last 60 years. The names are listed in alphabetical order in each category.

HOCKEY

BEST SKATERS
Pavel Bure
Paul Coffey
Frank Mahovlich
Henri Richard
Bobby Sheehan

BEST STICKHANDLERS
Jean Beliveau
Max Bentley
Jaromir Jagr
Mario Lemieux
Stan Mikita

HARDEST SHOT
Tony Demers
Bernie Geoffrion
Bobby Hull
Al Iafrate
Al MacInnis

HARDEST WORKERS
Bobby Clarke
Doug Gilmour
Teeter Kennedy
Kirk Muller
Henri Richard

BEST FIGHTERS
John Ferguson
Gordie Howe
Ivan Irwin
Orland Kurtenbach
Bob Probert

BEST GOALIES
Johnny Bower
Bill Durnan
Glenn Hall
Jacques Plante
Terry Sawchuk

BEST DEFENCEMEN
Doug Harvey
Bobby Orr
Denis Potvin
Larry Robinson
Eddie Shore

BEST FORWARD LINES
Kid Line — Joe Primeau, Charlie Conacher, Busher Jackson
Kraut Line — Milt Schmidt, Woody Dumart, Bobby Bauer
Pony Line — Max and Doug Bentley, Bill Mosienko
Production Line — Sid Abel, Ted Lindsay, Gordie Howe
Punch Line — Elmer Lach, Toe Blake, Maurice Richard

BEST PENALTY KILLERS
Guy Carbonneau   Donnie Marshall   Jerry Toppazzini
Doug Gilmour   Derek Sanderson

BEST ON POWER PLAY
Point Men
Max Bentley
Ray Bourque
Bernie Geoffrion
Bobby Orr

Centres
Jean Beliveau
Wayne Gretzky
Mario Lemieux

Scorers
Mike Bossy
Phil Esposito
Maurice Richard

Diggers
Wayne Cashman
Dickie Moore
Bert Olmstead

BEST FOR SHOOTOUT (OR PENALTY SHOTS)

Goaltenders	Shooters
Johnny Bower	Mike Bossy
Glenn Hall	Gordie Howe
Jacques Plante	Guy Lafleur
	Mario Lemieux
	Dickie Moore

BEST COACHES

Al Arbour	Scotty Bowman	Glen Sather
Toe Blake	Punch Imlach	

FOOTBALL

BEST PASSERS	BEST RUNNERS	BEST RECEIVERS
Sam Etcheverry	George Dixon	Hugh Campbell
Doug Flutie	Normie Kwong	Terry Evanshen
Indian Jack Jacobs	George Reed	Tony Gabriel
Ron Lancaster	Alec Webster	Garney Henley
Tobin Rote	Art West	Hal Patterson

BEST ON DEFENCE   BEST OFFENSIVE LINEMEN

John Barrow	**Centre**—Al Wilson
Tex Coulter	**Guards**—Herb Trawick, Kaye Vaughan
Wayne Harris	**Tackles**—Clyde Brock, Frank Rigney
John Helton	**Tight End**—Peter Dalla Riva
Angelo Mosca	

BEST ON SPECIALTY TEAMS
Dave Cutler, kicker
Fritz Hanson, returns
Ron Howell, returns
Bob Isbister, punter
Gizmo Williams, returns

ALL-PURPOSE PLAYERS
Johnny Ferraro
Cookie Gilchrist
Joe Krol
Jackie Parker
Bobby Simpson

COACHES
Frank Clair   Lew Hayman   Peahead Walker
Bud Grant   Teddy Morris

LACROSSE

BEST PLAYERS
Jack Bionda
John Davis
Bill Fitzgerald
Bill Isaacs
Bucko McDonald

ALL SPORTS

TOUGHEST GUYS
John Ferguson
Bruiser McLean
Jimmy Orlando
Eddie Shore
Jack Stewart

MOST COURAGEOUS
Bobby Baun
Bobby Clarke
Bob Gainey
Eagle Keys
Milt Schmidt

WORST BITCHERS
Anyone having a bad game

Index